Praise for

Coaching Teens well
A way of being with teens and their families

"This beautiful and heartfelt book is the wakeup call humankind needs now. Instead of viewing ourselves and others through a conditioned lens of pathology, Aila reminds us that our being, our essence is peaceful, loving, whole. And when we reconnect to that truth, living and loving flourish whether you're a parent, coach, teen . . . A MUST-read book for everyone and ALL relationships!"

~ **Melissa Ford,** Business/Life Coach and author of L*iving Service: The Journey of a Prosperous Coach*

"By being fully present, Listening deeply, and having the highest regard for young and wise Souls — Aila transforms lives. This has changed the trajectory for many - to remain alive when they wished they were not, to become engaged, and in a loud world, to find themselves and their own Inner Voice. The gift of Aila's coaching is priceless. Coaching teens is not for the faint of heart and she has become a master. If you are a Coach, parent, aunt or uncle, someone who spends time with these young human aliens, or merely a human yourself — give yourself the gift of *Coaching Teens Well.*"

~ **Renée Adams,** Professional Life Coach, author, and facilitator of Love YourSelf, Love Your Body, Love Your Life

"This book offers readers a highly unusual gift—a way to support anyone in your life. Aila has shared her wisdom, love and creativity she uses with each of her clients, and although her typical clients are teens, don't let that fool you. Through deeply personal and professional stories, she reminds us of our natural state of being, which is filled with possibility, and shares successful tools for change, communication and growth. At once, practical and spiritual, this book is a MUST READ."

~ **Tina Quinn,** author of Invisible Things, Life & Leadership Coach

"Aila writes the way she coaches—straight from the heart. This is her brilliance. She has a gift of inquiring and communicating in a direct, deeply loving manner, which has the consequence of illuminating one's own inner world and knowing, reminding us that guidance of the highest authority lies within. From this perspective, we see that no teen, and no one, is in need of fixing—only loving. As a parent of two teens, I highly recommend this book to any parent, coach, or human who desires more easeful, joyful, relationships and engagement with life. It is a goldmine!"

~ **Tracy L. W. Poff,** Ph.D. Candidate, M.A., M.B.A., Transpersonal Psychology Researcher

Coaching

Teens

Well

To Barb —

You are one of the most joyful, authentic, funny, kind + wise people I know. Thank you for sharing your insights + love with me. My life is better because of the time I've spent learning + discovering with you. Love + Appreciate you!!

♡ Aila

Coaching

Teens

Well

A Way of Being with Teens and Their Parents

Aila Coats, M.A.

Coaching Teens Well: A way of being with teens and their parents.

Copyright © 2023 by Aila Coats

Contact the author: www.ailacoats.com

Editing: Chris Nelson, www.prose-alchemy.com
Cover Design: Josephine Poff, www.josephinesahara.com

ISBN: 979-8-9870494-0-2

Library of Congress Control Number: 2023901800

Nevada City, California

Disclaimer: Names and identifying details of clients referenced in this book have been altered and in some cases are composites. Any resemblances to individuals alive or dead are coincidental and unintentional.

The author of this book is not dispensing medical, therapeutic or business advice or prescribing the use of any techniques or practices as treatment for physical, medical, psychological or business issues, or for any other type of issue. The intent of the author is only to offer information of a general nature to help you in personal and business development. In the event you use any of the information in this book, neither the author nor publisher nor other representatives will be liable for damages arising out of or in connection with the use of this book. This is a comprehensive limitation of liability that applies to all damages of any kind. The use of this book implies your acceptance of this disclaimer.

Dedications

To my mom for taking me to a Buddhist nun when I was 12. There were a lot of choices you could have made in how to support me and I am eternally grateful for where your wisdom guided you. I found myself and my path in life because of your unconditional love, encouragement and support.

To my dad for throwing me in the river before I could swim. I didn't drown. I discovered my strength and determination because of your belief in me that I can do hard things. Like, really hard things; like, insanely hard things, and survive to tell the tale.

To all the teens I have the honor and privilege to love and support. You inspire me to no end and bring my purpose to life.

Table of Contents

Table of Contents

Foreword

Can they actually be coached?

I often wondered if teenagers could actually be coached.

I had four children of my own, and when they were in their teenage years I questioned whether I could have any kind of positive influence on them. Their energy and emotions were intimidating to me and I once even caught myself praying that I would die before they got their driver's licenses.

Somehow we all made it through those teenage years and my grown children and I are able to look back and laugh at the misadventures that were created by their energies and emotions and my own tragicomic attempts to guide them into rational adulthood.

Later in life I had occasional coaching clients who wanted me to try my hand at coaching one of their teenage children. I tried one, and it went fairly okay, but I noticed how happy the girl was that it was over. I tried another, and I failed to create any kind of trust or rapport. We both gave up quickly.

My conclusion was? It can't be done.

Or maybe, it can, but it would have to be a very special coach, who had far more patience and courage than I ever had.

I never expected to find such a person.

Until I met Aila Coats.

When I observed how successful she was at coaching teenagers (and their parents!) I hoped that someday she would tell us all how she does it. Maybe she'd even put it into a book. And here it is . . . my wish come true.

Boy, do I wish I'd had this book back in the day when my kids were teens. But no time for regrets; it's so great that it's finally here.

Aila is one of those rare coaches whose loving humility and compassion just put people, even teenagers caught up in their emotional distress and insecurity, at ease. She has a way of connecting and relaxing her clients that transforms "coaching" into friendship and respect.

But as you read on through this insightful book you start to realize that it's not just compassion and rapport. There's a great level of skill and intelligence coming from Aila that's guiding the whole process.

Her wisdom shines from every page of this book, centered on her almost mysterious level of understanding of how (even teenage) minds work. Like when she says, "When we're not trying so hard, when we relax in our thinking, our minds settle down, and what is actually beneath all that thinking is a wellspring of wisdom. Wisdom that transcends our intellect and our problem-solving abilities."

She's talking about what she sees in her young clients who come to her with their life stories and crises that seem to feel so unmanageable. She sees the inner wisdom in people so clearly and so immediately that her clients can't help but see it too and feel new hope.

The stories and case histories she shares about the various young people she has coached are told in these pages with captivating clarity and wit. The writing makes these kids and their coach come alive. It's surprising to learn that this is her first book, because the way this book flows, you'd think she'd been writing books all her life.

And what I love even more than the secrets shared about how to coach teenagers well are the personal insights Aila shares along the way that have led her to this level of extraordinary coaching. Helping her clients relax into their innate well-being is obviously something she's learned for herself, calling to mind what psychologist Dr. Nathaniel Branden once said about counseling others: "We must become what we teach."

That's exactly what Aila Coats has done. In her words, "This is an ongoing practice for me—letting go of really serious, intense thinking, ruminating, problem-solving, and instead doing something that gives my mind an opportunity to actually help me. This is a process of surrendering what I think I know and dropping into the unknown."

Aila's love for working with teens shines through this book, and is the polar opposite of what most people feel about the subject. I've been guilty myself of heaving a big sigh and rolling my eyes whenever the subject of parenting, teaching or coaching teenagers comes up. It's a given for me that my exasperation will be met with commiseration and agreement. Seeing the teenage years as a problem is practically built into the culture.

This quip by comedian Joe Heenan is always good for a knowing laugh: "Having a teenage daughter is a lot like your house being haunted. Every now and again you'll see a figure in the corner of your eye, followed by a moaning sound, and then a door will slam shut."

Had I been in his audience, I would have laughed at that. I don't know of many people who wouldn't. It's how we all seem to see it.

Which is why it's safe to say there aren't any books out there quite like this one. A book that advocates beginning the conversation with love and appreciation. And then growing a trusting relationship from there.

This book actually tells you how she does that. And it's backed up by describing a track record of surprising and consistent success.

If I ruled the world, every parent, every coach, every counselor and every school teacher would be issued a copy of this book with mandatory testing on its contents. We'd all be living in a different world if that happened.

But maybe the distribution of this book won't have to be mandated by anyone. Maybe I don't have to rule the world. Maybe the wisdom and power in these pages might just be enough to do the job through a secret marketing tool called word of mouth. I know I'm going to be telling everyone I know about it.

Steve Chandler
Birmingham, Michigan
October, 2022

The winds must come from somewhere when they blow,
There must be reason why the leaves decay;
Time will say nothing but I told you so.

W.H. Auden

Setting the Tone

1

The piano rebel

"The way is not in the sky. The way is in the heart."

Buddha

I was on my way to my office a few weeks ago. Eight teens were waiting to meet me there on Zoom for a three-part series called Peace of Mind for Teens. On my way in, I was feeling antsy. I had a twenty-minute drive, and because I was feeling antsy I did what I always do: I pulled out the voice recorder on my phone and started talking. I thought about what I most wanted these teens to know and to remember over the course of our time together. I was feeling antsy because there were so many things that I wanted to share with them. Several of them were struggling in big ways. There was depression and suicidal ideation; there was social anxiety and self-harming, eating disorders and agoraphobia. So what was the heart of the message I wanted to share with them?

It wasn't coming clear, so I started talking. Once I start talking, I usually get clear, and below is what came out, and it felt worth sharing here with you, reader, as well, because it sums up what I most want you to know as you embark on the journey of reading this here book I wrote.

(I made some adjustments to it to make it relevant to you, but below is the essence of what I shared with the teens and what I would like to share with you.)

What if everything that we have ever been taught about how life works—how instruments work, how money works, how the school system works, how success works, how coaching works, how coaching TEENS works, how parenting works—was just a *suggestion*? Or at best, it was just somebody else's good luck or bright idea that was turned into a doctrine or "the" way?

My husband, Dhiraj, recently told me about musician Kenny Warner, who wrote a book called *Effortless Mastery*, in which he said something like, "If kids were allowed to simply explore musical instruments and let their creativity lead them, instead of one musical language we would have literally millions—there'd be millions of ways to create songs and symphonies."

What a concept! What a truth. What a gateway into a whole new world, brimming with possibilities and creativity and fun and expansiveness.

That idea is so freeing and inviting to me. In fact, in the days after he shared that with me I found myself at our piano, plucking away at the keys, and instead of the usual self-talk that went through my head— "Aila, it's okay to be bad. It's okay to have fun and do it your own way, I know I'm not doing it right, but I'm at least letting myself play. I know I won't be creating great songs but it's fun to make sounds!"—***instead*** of that it went something like, "This is my way, I'm doing it right, this is the way my body wants to touch the keys. I can create songs like this. It's fun to do it how I want to do it, and it's working. This is right for me."

It's a subtle shift, but, really, it's a big one for me. I've always felt like a rebel, at times, even in my coaching work, going against the grain, and the thing that shifted inside of me was this insight that perhaps there *is* no grain. There is no "right" way.

Like really, truly.

Not just as a nice-feeling idea, but as a FACT.

There's one person who had a bright idea or a positive experience, (like myself sharing the ins and outs of my work coaching teens), one person who stumbled upon some piano keys, created some sounds that they liked and called it a note or a key or a chord. Who then decided, "This is the way! This is what will be taught! This is what everybody shall do!"

Even as I say that, I hear a voice in my mind saying, "What a load of baloney."

There is no right way to do this life, or any given moment in our lives. There is only what feels right, to you, right now, in the moment.

So really, this book and the ideas in it aren't the right way, or an act of rebellion, although it has felt that way to me at times, but simply another creative path that one person has taken that has been helpful—for *one* person. *And* perhaps reading some of the ideas in the book will inspire you to find your own way of coaching, of mentoring, of parenting, of living. Knowing that all the ideas and concepts about how we *should* be and how we *should* do things are ALL made up.

All of them.

Every one.

They are ALL somebody else's idea that may be helpful at times, but which are certainly not the only path to take. They worked for that person, in their life, given their gifts, their abilities, their financial situation, their needs, their desires . . . They worked for them. And in fact if that path feels constricted or controlling or uninspired for YOU, what if that's an indication that it's truly not your path?

What if the truth is that it has *never* been for you, and that is not a problem? What if you can get what you want—a degree, a relationship, peace of mind, success financially and otherwise—by trusting in yourself? By following your own inclinations and inspiration? By knowing that your wisdom and the way you are naturally compelled to pluck keys, to move your body, to sing, to speak, to take classes or not, isn't taking you off track if you haven't seen it done before, or if you are not being supported by those around you, but just the opposite? It is guiding you toward a meaningful and fulfilling, aligned life. Your wisdom and natural knowing . . . your instinct. It has your back and it cares about you and what you want in your life. It knows YOU. It's not wrong. It's right. It gets you on a deep level that no one else ever could. It knows your heart like no one else. It knows your soul and your gifts, your natural whimsy and natural knowing. It KNOWS you and knows how to guide you—if you just listen. Listen to yourself and trust what you hear.

And know that if it feels like an act of rebellion, or that you are doing it "wrong," perhaps you have just found your own, "THE WAY".

2

There's no conspiracy here

In this book, I'm speaking directly to coaches.

However, within my coaching practice I am transparent with parents, and I will be completely open here as well. I have no secret agendas, scripts, or processes that I keep hidden.

The intention of my coaching practice is to be of service to teens, and this naturally includes being of service to their families as well. I don't engage in a conspiracy with the teen against the parents, or with the parents against the teen. It's an open system. Parents are directly involved and an important part of the process.

Although this book is essentially for coaches, if an interested parent were to pick it up and take something away from it, I would find that incredibly rewarding.

3

Teens are already well

Coaching teens well is not about helping teens *become* well. It's about helping teens see that they are *already* well.

There is a place of peace, wellness and wisdom within each and every one of us, including teenagers. Yes, it's even in teenagers. We often don't fully realize this. Sometimes both our inner and outer worlds feel like they're in complete chaos. This can be especially true during adolescence and young adulthood.

When I'm working with a teen, I'm always looking for the wisdom that lies behind any action, any emotion, and any thought or behavior. At first glance it may seem like there *isn't* any wisdom there—that the teen is just randomly reacting to the angst and confusion that most of us experience in our teenage years. In fact, this may be why a teen or their parent has reached out to me in the first place.

But when I slow down and look in the direction of the teen's well-being, I always find their natural wisdom. It's always there. And the real change takes place when they see it in themselves and begin to look to it and for it. This is the goal of coaching teens well.

Similarly, when I talk with parents about their teen, much of the

8

conversation often revolves around helping them see that their kids' problems are often not "problems" at all. Instead they're expressions of their teen doing the best they can to navigate their world, inner and outer. When a parent can begin to see and appreciate that their child's behavior is a simple reflection of their child's state of mind in the moment, it can become less scary and worrisome.

I recently had a session with Dicken Bettinger[1], a wonderful coach and mentor, who reminded me that it's much more helpful to myself and my kids when I am not fixating on their behavior. In fact, instead of parenting their behavior, it would be much more supportive for everyone if instead I parent or relate to the child, the being, the one who is having the thoughts that are hard, and then the emotions that are scary and then, expressing those emotions in upsetting behaviors. When I slow myself down and see that erratic, irrational behavior is NEVER the actual issue, but is instead a natural consequence of an overwhelmed or scared kiddo, I have more compassion and caring to bring to my child. I help them in more meaningful ways. I support them through their low mood.

This is much easier when I appreciate that my state of mind will be in play as well. When I am caught up in my own squirrely thoughts, gripped by some thought that feels worrisome, I have less capacity in the moment to bring compassion to my kid. And when this is the case, I do my best to do very *little* parenting. I do my best to acknowledge the fact that my level of consciousness is impacting the way I am seeing my child and their "problem." When my lens clears, when I begin to feel more free and light within myself, I know that this is the

---

[1] Please visit: http://3principlesmentoring.com/

best time to help my kid—and often, from that space, their "problems" don't look much like problems any more, but more like a natural expression of a human being, experiencing thought in the moment and responding to those thoughts in the best way they can.

Throughout this book I'll share how these ideas have woven themselves into my practice and how they can lead to improved communication and a greater sense of well-being and connection for teens, their parents, and everyone else in their lives.

4

Your way of being (matters)

"We don't see things as they are. We see them as we are."

Anais Nin

This book has been tricky for me to put together for several reasons. The main one is that the territory is so rich and complex, and it's continuously evolving. I learn more about coaching and being human every day, so to take a screenshot of where I'm at today, May 27th, 2022, put it down on paper and send it out to the world feels challenging. I love the living and organic nature of this work. As I grow within my own consciousness I see things differently. So some of the understandings I write about here will evolve for me in the years to come. At the same time, I hope that what I'm sharing is helpful right now, as it is. It has certainly been helpful for me and my clients, and if this book supports you in some small way in finding a new or deeper way of being with your clients, it will have served its purpose.

I say "way of being" because no matter how much I learn and grow, the way of being part of coaching stays the same. That is, no matter the coaching strategy or modality that may emerge organically in the moment—whether it looks like I'm focusing on spiritual psychology or the three principles or neurolinguistic programming or cognitive-behavioral therapy—my presence, my *way of being* with my clients, is at the heart of my coaching, and I believe it is THE factor that creates the biggest impact.

This way of being affects everything that happens between client and coach. From it flows the goodwill, the trust, the love, the care and the warmth—or lack thereof.

As a coach, part of my natural way of being with teenagers is to never tell them what to do. I don't put myself in a position of authority as some wise person who knows what's best for them—and I don't want to do that for you, my fellow coach, either. My way of interacting with teens when they are trying to learn something new or to discover something about themselves is one of inquiry. I sit across from them, eye-to-eye, present with what bubbles up within them as I ask questions that lead them deeper into themselves. It's very "in the moment," intuitive, and responsive, the opposite of a one-size-fits-all prescription for how to actually work with teenagers and their parents.

As you read this book, I want to invite you to do something similar—to listen within yourself and see what resonates and what doesn't. To drop it like it's hot if it's not feeling in alignment, and to experiment with the ideas that do "click" for you. Just like the teens you are coaching, you have a built-in guidance system that will meet you in the present moment each and every moment of your life. It's there for you and will guide you—naturally, gracefully, with great ease and commonsense—into how to do this work of supporting other human beings.

In terms of supporting teenagers, one of the best gifts we can offer them is the insight that who they are, as they are, is sufficient for them to navigate their lives. They are not inherently flawed or incomplete in some way. They are not missing some vital piece of information. They already have the answers and resources they need within themselves.

And so do you. Any learning or education you get from this book or elsewhere is icing on a cake that's already baked perfectly. It's a nice embellishment, but not required for living a happy and fulfilling life and creating a thriving coaching practice.

5

Wisdom has no age

When I was eighteen my mom helped me tune into my own wisdom about whether to go back to Whittier College or attend the University of Santa Monica—an unaccredited spiritual psychology program. I chose the latter and it profoundly changed my life. The answer to what to do in that moment came from inside of me—with some help from my mom in showing me how to draw it out. That was one of the first times I became aware of how to use the inner guidance system within me.

The program at USM lasted two years, although I participated in some way at USM for nearly thirteen years after I graduated, either as a student or as a volunteer. During my time there I spent hundreds of hours sitting across from people who—once they physically relaxed and let their minds slow down—began looking for the wisdom within themselves. And it was always there. The program was designed so that we first listened to a talk on a particular topic related to spiritual psychology. Then our class would break up into groups of three and have conversations about what was going on in our lives as it related to the topic discussed. Subsequently, going in a round, we would each alternate between the roles of facilitator (or coach), client, and neutral observer (someone who is simply present and who "holds" the space).

I sat with people who were trying to decide whether to end a thirty-year marriage or continue working on it. Others were trying to decide whether or not to continue aggressively treating their cancer or to move into end-of-life, comfort care. My fellow students were trying to find peace in challenging relationships, heal broken hearts, recover after the loss of a child or partner, and so on. These were not "light" situations. As classmates we were exploring some of the most intense experiences of our lives, day in and day out. In a way it was a trial by fire—though with plenty of love—for ourselves and for the idea that we have an inner wisdom that we can always rely on. And in the end we saw that no matter what we were working on, the answers always came to us. No matter how young or old or how much education or life experience, wisdom found us right where we were. Every. Single. Time.

When it was my turn to hold the space as a neutral observer, I so often saw the "client" in our trio get caught up in worry, fear and doubt and then, slowly but surely, access their inner wisdom to reach a greater sense of clarity and peace. I also found it fascinating that when it was their turn to step into the facilitator role, and time to take their attention off of themselves and their own personal concerns, it seemed to me that they had IMMEDIATE access to their inner knowing, their compassion, wisdom, patience, and unconditionally loving selves.

This was not an anomaly. It happened each and every time. Once again, things like age, gender, race, education and experience didn't matter. If they were a human being (and we all were, or at least I think we were!) a wisdom and love emerged from inside of them.

I could see that when I was less focused on myself, when I was less caught up in my busy mind, I was more tuned into a deeper space of wellness within. As a coach I think it's one of the gifts that comes from embodying that space—to be more easily put in touch with the essence of who we are, as we are in service to others.

I assisted in several workshops at an organization called Insight Seminars,[2]—still a place I refer people to—where teenagers engaged in a similar process with each other. Again, no matter their age, there was a peace and wisdom that emerged from them when they were given time to think clearly, whether they were in the "client" or "facilitator" role. They were also capable of neutrally holding a loving space for someone else. Their brilliance always emerged. And, of course, I've seen my own clients, teen and adult, connect with their own guidance. So I've come to accept without doubt that we truly do have wisdom within us, we have a healthy and balanced mind, and the most important gift we can give ourselves is to learn to connect with it.

These experiences aren't locked within the walls of USM or beyond closed workshop doors. They are available wherever and whenever we are open to them. People are people. We all have the same equipment inside ourselves, and the same ability to step back, tune in and truly know what our next step forward is.

---

[2] https://www.insightseminars.org

6

Being versus doing

I get asked a lot about what I actually DO in sessions with teens. What worksheets or exercises or healing techniques I use. And while I will share about some of the specific exercises and techniques I use in my coaching practice with teens, the emphasis of this book is on a way of being—because anything it might occur to me to DO in a session with a teen springs from that space within me, as it will with you.

So I might bring forward certain **exercises**, such as creating priorities, honing in on values, using a calendar, reaching out for help, clarifying communication with a friend or parent, ideal scenes, intention setting, or living visions (many of the tools I learned at USM). I might use **healing practices**, such as gestalt, EFT, self-forgiveness, gratitude, meditation or visualization. I might open up **discussions** around a soul's purpose, habit-stacking, goal-setting, and so on.

But I do all of that at the moment it occurs to me with a particular person. I do not have a prescribed set of exercises, healing modalities or discussion topics, as they are not all applicable to each person. All of it springs from my way of being, from my listening, from what I am seeing and sensing and tuning into in the moment with each particular person. I think it's great to have an arsenal of tools and techniques to draw on, however none of them hold any value without my first simply *being* with another human and having something organically emerge in the moment that is for them, springing from the vibrant and alive energy that is always available to us, that is always there to help us, when we slow down and deeply listen. There is a trust in this way of coaching, and it can be very exciting and rewarding.

7

Rapport

"Nobody cares how much you know until they know how much you care."

Theodore Roosevelt

If you only read one chapter in this book, read this one.

Truly, if I had to take away every single idea but one in this book, I would write about the value of **rapport**.

For me rapport is absolutely everything. It doesn't matter how much you know about liberating a human being from their suffering or masterfully coaching someone into a state of perfect peace and self-expression—if you don't create rapport with a teenager *first*, the door is closed before you even get started.

So how do we create rapport? You will see examples throughout this book, because it permeates every interaction we have with our clients. The foundation is set by bringing our human self, our soul, the undefined nature of who we are into the first and second sessions, and, of course, beyond. This means we don't show up first as our coach or consultant or counselor self. Or perhaps we do, but it's redefining what that even means. It's not about showing up and looking smart and fancy. For me, coaching is about being present, listening and genuinely caring about the person I am with. It's about deciding to access a place within myself, where I am calm and relaxed. This creates a helpful space and also a very sweet rapport. Especially with teenagers. When we can bring our completely imperfect, perfect selves to the table, the part of us that knows we are free—in spite of and because of all of the challenges in our lives. In spite of and because of our fearful thinking. The part that knows we are capable—in any moment—of choosing to redirect the entire course of our lives, no matter how bleak the future looks or how the past has unfolded. We get to decide in the moment to look toward our own health and well-being and capability, to look toward heartfelt visions and goals. We get to choose to buck the odds, to strip off the labels, to be new right here and right now, again, perfectly imperfect.

This is the space we get to invite our teenage clients into. From this space we look at them knowing that they're lacking nothing, that they're full to the brim with wisdom, regardless of what they're presenting to us in the moment.

Our state of mind *matters* when we meet our clients. In fact, it may be the most important thing at first, and always, for that matter. Our perception of ourselves as individuals and as human beings will convey itself loud and clear to teens.

When we can humbly and confidently appreciate our wonderfully flawed selves, knowing that nothing stands in the way of us creating a life that is truly filled with happiness, peace and joy, we don't need to be afraid of the flaws that we might be seeing in our client. When we know that no matter how scary a feeling or thought might be, when we know we get to decide what to do with those thoughts and feelings, we get to slow down and pause and reflect before taking action. At that point a sense of safety comes in.

When we understand that procrastination, acts of rebellion, fear of failure, fear of success, stage fright, performance anxiety, are all symptoms and not causes, we can, in a level-headed, calm way, connect with our clients. They may be going through any number of these things, and we can help them understand that there is nothing to fear.

From this it's clear that our own level of understanding about how human beings work can help us create rapport with our clients. If we are afraid of our own imperfections or struggles, it will be hard to embrace them in our clients. If we are afraid of our own low moods and scary feelings, it can be harder to see the natural health within those experiences for our clients. Every time we have an insight where we know that who we are as valuable, worthwhile human beings is independent of the temporary experiences that pass through deeply impacts the way we are able to show up for ourselves, our families and our clients.

8

Do you feel free?

Below, I'm sharing an exchange I had with a coach I work with who serves teenagers. She was having a hard time making an impact with the teens she was enrolling. She was getting to the first enrollment session but had a string of teens not wanting to go beyond that first one. In our session we slowed this down a bit and looked at what might be going on on a deeper level. This is a condensed snapshot of our session (I took out a lot of the dialogue to cut to the chase so to speak, but hopefully the message rings clear).

It felt relevant to include in this book simply because her seeing more deeply into this understanding for herself helped her bring it to the teens and the young adults that she was wanting to support. It made a difference. It opened up her practice. The more we see things like this for ourselves the more we have to offer our clients.

"Do you feel free?"
My client bursts into tears.
Clearly she doesn't.
I ask again, "Do you know that you're free?"

"I don't even know what you mean, but I know the answer is no."

"What I mean is this: Do you know that you can choose to do what you feel called to do today and tomorrow and the next day? You can listen to your intuition and your inner guidance, even if it doesn't look like you'll be supported by life or by people, or even if you can't see that the path is leading anywhere?

"Do you know that everything you thought you were meant to do, everything that you believed about yourself and what your life is supposed to be up until now, do you know that you can change your mind about ALL that and create something completely new?

"You can live in a way that is completely new to you.

"You can let go of old conditioning, old repetitive thinking and feeling and doing.

"You can tap into yourself in this moment with fresh eyes and listen to what is speaking to you.

"You are free to create from this moment anything that's in your heart. I know that there are bills to pay and there are people to feed, and I know that those concerns are on your mind as you are considering what to do next. But what if bills will get paid and people will be fed even quicker and with more ease if you follow the guidance that you receive within yourself? If you listen deeply and trust that the guidance you get from the deepest part of your wisdom will support you and those that you care for?

"What if you knew that?

"I wonder what you would do next?"

My client laughs out loud at this, tears streaming down her face and light beaming from her smile. She asks me to keep talking. So I do.

"And beyond that, what I mean is that you are free to sit in a moment in your life where there might be a challenging conversation or a situation that feels uncomfortable, and you have the capacity to sit inside a sphere of peace and contentment—you can sit within yourself, within your true self, and look for the peace of mind and the wellness, the aliveness, the optimism that dwells within, no matter what is going on on the outside.

"I know this isn't always possible, to remember this and to tune into it. I am in no way perfect at it.

"But it is the direction that I am looking in more often than not. I am looking to remember that my internal experience is coming from whatever thoughts or judgments I am attached to in the moment—no matter what is going on in the outer world (kids fighting, food burning on the stove, arriving late to a meeting)—and those thoughts and judgments are fleeting and flimsy and optional.

"When I wake up to that, I am free. Or rather, I am aware that I am free and always was.

"There isn't a circumstance that defines me. There isn't a life event or relationship that dictates how I **must** feel. Nothing has that kind of power over me. Nothing. Not my husband, my children, my clients, my fees, getting a yes, getting a no—nothing. I am free, and so are you. Sometimes we remember it in the moment, and sometimes we don't. But it doesn't change the fact that we FREE. And even when we don't remember we are free to feel peace of mind, no matter what, it's still a fact. That never changes. We can tap into and out of the awareness of it. We can feel stuck in our lives and in our thinking, and those moments of "stuck" get easier to endure when we remember that even though we feel stuck, we are not. We are free."

We sit in silence for a long while as she takes this in. And she does see something new for herself. Something takes hold. Something that will help her in her own life, but also as she continues to serve her teen clients.

She explains that everything we have been talking about is familiar to her, and it had always *seemed* like a good idea to her—in fact, so much so that she was trying to convince her clients of it—*but it hadn't yet landed in her.*

This is something I see in many of the coaches I work with, particularly those who work with teenagers—who seem to have a sixth sense for detecting inauthenticity. It repels them.

Somehow in the course of our conversation this coach realized the truth of what she was trying to teach teens for *herself.* And it made all the difference.

9

A quirky and compassionate human

None of this requires a spiritual perspective to lead the way, but I personally don't leave home without mine. My spiritual perspective forms the backbone of my life, my thoughts and my way of seeing myself and others. It permeates everything I do. The way that I relate to myself, my life, the people in my world and my clients has come from the essential nature of who I am as a quirky, compassionate, human, but also from the ongoing inner exploration I've been doing since about the age of twelve.

Just before my teenage years began, I learned a form of Buddhist meditation from a nun and began to absorb everything I could related to self-awakening and spiritual growth. I have attended countless seminars and trainings and devoured innumerable books and audio programs on various topics of personal and spiritual exploration. I've had dozens of daily practices over the years and have done what I can to be very intentional in my daily life.

I dedicated myself to a decade-plus of studying spiritual psychology at the University of Santa Monica. For the past six years or so I've immersed myself in the work of Sydney Banks. I have been enriched and reminded of who I am in very deep and profound ways.

The founders of the University of Santa Monica, Drs. Ron and Mary Hulnick, are my chosen godparents. They don't know this! But they loom so large in my heart because they've had such a profound impact on who I am and the growth that I have experienced. And— not only that—through their school, I met one of my best friends, and later was introduced to her brother, who has been my partner in love and life since 2009. He and I now have beautiful children, human and furry, and a lovely, sweet life together.

I have had the great benefit of working with incredible coaches and teachers, including Michelle Bauman, Carolyn Freyer-Jones, George and Linda Pransky, Aaron Turner, Dicken Bettinger, Rohini Ross, Barb Patterson, and more. I have also found HUGE, life-changing value and encouragement from the one-on-one work I have done with Steve Chandler for the past several years. If you have the privilege to know him, you know he is an amazing coach, author and, most importantly, human. He has been so helpful for me learning how to show up as myself in my work and serve people, including teens, in deep and meaningful ways. He demonstrates generosity of heart, humor, pure service and love in all he does. My work with all of these wonderful humans has enriched my life in countless ways.

One of my favorite teachings that Steve has continued to bring into our work together is the idea of showing up EMPTY with clients. The truth is, we are never EMPTY, never void of wisdom, compassion and presence. But the idea of showing up empty is an encouragement to set down our busy thinking, our ideas about what should happen, and to simply be in the moment with the person, to allow what needs to come forward to come forward, without attachment. Allowing this has been medicine to my coaching soul, and I know it is made much more doable by the hours I have spent in the quiet, listening within, slowing down, and tapping into that essential nature that is always there beneath the noise of the intellect. The spiritual nature that is always alive and well.

When I am working with a client, my heartfelt intention is to show up empty, with no agenda, no pre-planned prescribed path, nothing on my mind but an intention to serve. Showing up in this way means that what happens during the session is a mystery to both of us. We get to meet in the moment, in present time, receptive to what is being present here and now. We get to demonstrate a deep trust in our clients' awakening and healing process. To honor the wisdom, and the timing of their own soul. No pushing required—just gentle invitations to feel into readiness.

I draw on my own wisdom, which may guide me toward facilitating a meditation. Or it may compel me into the practice of compassionate self-forgiveness. I may talk a lot or very little. I don't have any idea what will spring forward, but I listen, both to my client and within myself. All of the areas of personal and spiritual work I have studied, and continue to study, have a common denominator in my experience. They are guiding me to see and honor and get more acquainted with my essential nature, beyond the physical form I see. Beyond my thoughts and emotions. They wake me up to the resiliency of the human spirit. They're about seeing through the illusion of form, the illusion that if I fail at something, or break some bones—or even my heart—in truth I'm unbreakable. I can get up with love and self-compassion, wipe my tears, brush myself off, and step into life with nothing lost—and perhaps with a lot gained. Trauma and mental illness don't define who we are in our essence. We don't have to wear them as labels. We can integrate them into our experience and move forward.

It is a beautiful thing to sit across from a sixteen-year-old holding in my mind that no matter what she has been through, she is whole and complete. She is not damaged by her past or limited by her thinking. She is free and has the potential to feel that truth for herself. In fact, I also love holding the idea that this person, this sixteen-year-old, might be centuries older than I am on the soul level. Who knows whether that's true or not? But it's a fun thought, and one that puts me into a much more humble state of mind. It reminds me to focus on the client's wisdom and to point them in the direction of discovering the truth for themselves—because this is what really matters.

The more I understand these things for myself, the better I am able to support my clients.

10

Do I share my personal experiences with my teen clients?

I don't always share my personal experiences with the teens I coach. Meaning, I don't make it a requirement or some rule of engagement, but I also don't hold back if I think it would serve. In fact, the more vulnerable I am, the more honest and open, the more rapport I tend to create with my clients, especially teens, and in doing so, I feel I do have a greater impact.

There are three experiences in my life that I tend to talk about – A LOT. They were defining for me. They went in deep. Even if I don't talk about them, they are moments that have impacted who I am and how I relate to myself and life. They are moments where I saw something profound for myself and was changed by it.

We've all had moments like this. Many, I am sure. I never hold back from sharing meaningful insights I have had and the life experiences that brought them about. Often in sharing my own insights, I create an opening for my clients to see something deeper for themselves. I am going to share those moments here. And whether or not there is something helpful for you in the details, I hope that my sharing serves as an invitation to you to share your own insights and moments of clarity with your clients. Know that these realizations might not only have been gifts for you, but that they might also be gifts given to you so you can give them to others.

1. My Grandpa

On September 28th, 2008, after sitting in the hospital with my grandpa on and off for a month while he slowly made his ascent into the spirit world, I heard a gentle clicking noise at 6:15 in the morning. I was lying on a cot next to his hospital bed. As I heard this clicking noise I quickly got up, cracked the curtains a bit so some light would creep in, and inched into the bed with him. I realized the noise was coming from him. I took a washcloth and I started to wipe his eyes, which had been shut for about five days. He had been taken off life support about two days prior. I heard the clicking noise again coming from his throat and I leaned in very close to his face looking at him eye to eye, although his eyes were closed. He opened his eyes— although one didn't open all the way, because of the goop I hadn't yet cleared out.

He smiled at me and I knew that he was about to leave.

I started talking to him, telling him how much I loved him, how much we all loved him and that it was okay for him to go.

I had been dreading this moment for about three years, ever since he first took a trip to the hospital, a trip I didn't know if he would come home from. In the three years since his hospital stay in 2005, I would frequently tear up in his presence simply imagining him not being on the earth, and he would comically and not so reassuringly say to me, "heaven forbid, you could go before me, so why waste these moments feeling sad about something that might not ever happen?" Yes it was dark, but it was true. It would snap me right out of it, and I'd keep pretending to enjoy the cheese enchiladas that he made "especially" for me, even though I am allergic to dairy.

I didn't have a very close relationship with him when I was a child—occasional holiday visits to see him, and for a brief period he lived near me, but even then I was too little to appreciate who he was.

When I was a teenager I had this out-of-the-blue feeling come over me which inspired me to connect with him. I had this deep knowing that I needed to be close to him and I didn't quite understand why. But I listened. I made trips to visit him in Mariposa, where he lived, and stayed very connected to him as I graduated high school and went into college. It was one of the first relationships that I intentionally created. I put time into it. I asked him questions to get to know him, I probed into his life in a way that I know was uncomfortable for him, but he also loved to tell some of his stories once he got going. I would listen to him talk for hours and hours, just riveted by the pure joy and love that beamed out of him. He was a comedian in his heart and one of the most generous and kind people I have met. He lived on a very limited budget at the end of his life— perhaps throughout his life—but he made sure to give extra money he had, every month, to feed children.

This was one of those sweet things that I noticed and deeply respected about him and his character.

He was one of my absolute favorite human beings. I loved every second of being around him. He was somebody that I would call frequently at 6:00 or 7:00 in the morning, knowing that he was awake. I often called him as I was walking my dog down the streets of Venice Beach, feeling slightly uncomfortable being alone. He never knew I called because of that, but I simply felt safer talking to him than if I weren't.

So there I sat in the hospital, looking into his eyes, telling him how much I loved him and how much we all loved him and would be okay if he left. As I said these words to him, bracing myself for his departure and what I imagine would be an onslaught of pain and tears, he smiled wider. And he looked directly into my eyes and he didn't inhale or exhale, he simply stopped breathing. I said his name a few times, but I knew he was gone.

And when it really hit me that he was gone, within a few seconds, I can't explain it, but I burst into laughter, I hugged his body and I felt compelled to get up and open all the windows in his room. As I was doing this his nurse came in and asked me what was going on. I shared with her that my grandpa had passed away and that he needed to get out of the room. That the room was too small for him, that he filled it and needed some support in exiting. She didn't laugh; she helped me by opening up the other window nearest her and then walked over to me, looking at me with incredible compassion.

She had watched me over the course of the month cry endlessly in the hallway after each difficult prognosis. She was there with me the night before he passed away, listening to me share with her about how afraid I was that once he passed away the ground would open up and I would simply drop into a hole and disappear forever.

So as she walked over to me, she looked at me with compassion and curiosity. I was absolutely jubilant. Filled with a joy and an expansiveness that I had not yet experienced in my life.

I literally felt my grandpa's spirit. He felt more alive than he did moments before. In the hours after he left his body, I couldn't cry. I couldn't even access the sadness that was there moments before he left. There wasn't any. It was sweetness. It was gratitude. That space within me was filled with love and an appreciation for him.

He wasn't the most physically affectionate human being. He would give sturdy handshakes to the men in his life and gentle hugs to the women, so when he did leave his body I took full advantage of hugging him, holding his hands, rubbing his feet, staring into his face, until it was time for him to go to the funeral home.

When I think back on those moments, what I really feel happened to me was that I had a lived experience of so many wonderful ideas that I HOPED were true. I hoped that we had souls, I hoped that death was another beginning, I hoped for all of those things—but they weren't facts inside of me, they weren't deep, gut knowings.

Getting to be with my grandpa, getting to be woken up by him so that I could witness and experience his transition, and know it in my bones, that he did not die, that he literally transitioned from one reality to another . . . It was the biggest gift that I could've asked for.

It has changed my life and how I view life and death. I can't say that I am looking forward to death; I'm not. In fact I don't like the idea of passing on and leaving my children, my husband and my family.

What that experience with my grandpa did for me is give me a deeper understanding of what the nature of reality is.

That it really is love. That we are love. That love is the fabric of reality, more profound and real than all other emotions and states of being, and that life truly is precious in the form that it is here, where we get to touch each other and smell the roses and eat delicious food. It is a very special and temporary experience. It is to be savored and appreciated in all its messy glory.

And most of all, it is temporary.

I so often hear myself encouraging my clients to make haste, not to live as if they're never going to die but to live as if death is imminent. Not to be morbid but to be honest.

So often young people don't think about their mortality, and rightfully so. But at the right time in the right way, especially with parents, it can create the most profound and helpful perspective in terms of making choices about next steps in their lives or how they want to be in relationship with themselves, their teens and their family members. Around risks they might want to take. To me, the awareness of the swift nature of life creates profound clarity, and I see the impact that it has for my clients when I am able to gently and lovingly bring it forward into a session.

2. Rowan

I wrote a book about this with my husband that you're free to find and peruse on your own, called *Love Rises, The Story of our Daughter, Rowan Bell Ashae*. And because we share our story with so much depth there, I'll only share briefly here.

In 2013, at 10:00 a.m., on July 22, I went into labor with our first baby, Rowan, two days before my due date. With a completely healthy pregnancy for both Rowan and myself, we had zero concerns about the labor.

We were in a state of joy and celebration throughout the day, knowing that Rowan was on her way. It was my mother-in-law's birthday, and she and my father-in-law were visiting; we were going to go out to lunch together. We called our midwife to come for a checkup, and when she arrived around 3:00 p.m., she couldn't find Rowan's heartbeat.

She told us to set up an immediate appointment with our OB, so we drove to the hospital. After a few hours of waiting for our OB to arrive and my contractions getting stronger and stronger, she did an ultrasound and confirmed that Rowan had zero brain activity or heartbeat and had indeed passed away.

Not knowing whether we would have a hospital birth or a homebirth, but planning for both, our OB gave us the option to stay in the hospital to deliver or to go home and do the homebirth that we had imagined and ultimately hoped for.

After a few moments of shock and deep, primal crying, somehow my husband supported us in finding our way back home. He knew that this was what I ultimately wanted, even though what I asked my doctor for was to be knocked out for the next week, have a c-section and to wake up once we had arrived in Hawaii, where we would then stay for the next six to twelve months. Somehow in the midst of trauma my sense of humor stayed intact.

My doctor said that this wasn't an option—at least not the best choice for my body at that point—so given that going unconscious to avoid the pain wasn't on the table and having a homebirth was still completely safe for me as a mother, Dhiraj made the decision that I couldn't: to go back home.

The reason I want to share this story is that it—like witnessing my grandpa's death—changed my life and the way I view everything. The way I view time, emotions, and human beings' capacity for feeling and surviving all feelings. It gave me a very real experience of the absolute, profound impact of love.

With the support of my husband, his mom, my mom and my sister-in-law, as well as our two midwives, I birthed Rowan into the world, and as much as I prayed throughout those thirty hours that she would breathe on the other end, she came out completely still. Even though it feels clinical at times, the term "still-birth" does feel appropriate, having lived through it. Still, peaceful, present. And she did feel present.

Her nature, the love of who she is, filled the room, our home. It filled and enveloped all of us. Again, I was dreading the moment that I would see her and that she wouldn't be breathing. I again felt that I would fall through the floor into the earth and be swallowed up forever. That the severe pain of it would be so overwhelming that I myself would die. Yet in the moment that she came out, into the water that I was sitting in, and I felt her tiny hand brush my leg, I open my eyes and looked down at her and felt a rush of love that completely overwhelmed me. I swooped her up, hugged her into my chest, and burst into tears—happy, grateful, joyful tears. Tears of gratitude and appreciation for her. It was pure love.

My family and I spent six hours holding her and rocking her and singing to her, and if you were an angel sitting on the ceiling looking down on us you would have believed 100 percent that a baby had just been born into the room alive and well, because she truly was, and we all could feel it.

It was a love that passed human understanding. A peace that passed human understanding.

The facts of what had just occurred didn't add up to the depth of love and gratitude that we all experienced.

There was true joy and laughter.

There was an appreciation for each other and the incredible range of emotions that we experienced within those thirty hours together.

There was an understanding that the love that lives within us trumps all things. That it's bigger and grander and more powerful than ALL things. That my mind can't even grasp the fullness and the enormity of the love that resides within.

It gave me this feeling of clarity that no matter the circumstance, no matter the pain and suffering that could arise from any given circumstance, love could also be there—and in fact, love *is* there.

It's always there. It's *always* here.

The year that followed her death was one of the hardest years of my life, and I know that it would've been immensely worse had I not been in touch with and looking for the love and happiness and peace that is my very nature and the nature of all of us.

Yes it gets clouded over, yes it gets lost in the fray, but it's always there.

It cannot be hurt, harmed or damaged. There is nothing in this life that can break us. We have the ability to tune into the truth of who we are, if we choose to.

It's there for us.

Waiting for us to look at it, to see it, to appreciate it, to tap into it. It's there now and always.

With my clients I'm often saying the words, "Nothing can break you, nothing can damage you, take the risk, kiss the boy, go for the job, write the book, fall in love; no matter what happens, you can come out standing, you can come out with a more open heart, even if it feels broken at first."

I'm pointing out to them moments where they feel peace,

contentment, a sense of okay-ness, even when circumstances say that they shouldn't. That is a great start.

For me I see that as pointing them in the direction of their true selves, their higher nature, their consistent selves. The part of them that doesn't change given a certain mood or scary moment of time.

That consistent, sourced self, sourced by love and wisdom that is the very foundation of who and what we are.

3. A Viewing Point vs a Point of view

In 2003 I began studying spiritual psychology at the University of Santa Monica. It changed my life. I felt at home. I was likely about twenty years younger than most of the people there, but they were my people. They were spiritual seekers and craved deeper, more intimate connections with themselves and others. I felt at home with each one of them.

Either during a USM weekend or while attending an Insight seminar through a sister organization within the same building, I had a profound moment of clarity come over me when the speaker was talking about the difference between a *point of view* and a *viewing point*.

They held up a big ball. To one side of the room the ball looked white. But all the people on the other side of the room saw the ball as black. When asked what color the ball was, half the people said it was white and half the people said it was black. Both were right—it was black on one side and white on the other, but each half of the room could only see one side of the ball. Both groups could argue their reasons for thinking what they thought. Both had their point of view and were correct in it.

However, being right about it and fighting for the others to see it their way—because, well, they were right—didn't create a very good feeling for everyone. It didn't create compassion and understanding for the other. It created against-ness and righteousness for those in the room who were fighting for their position. For the ones who understood there might be more to it than meets the eye, there was more calm, more curiosity, more wonder, and more peace of mind too.

The person facilitating went on to talk about the fact that the higher we go up within our consciousness and the higher we get in terms of our point of view, the more we can actually drop it and look at life from a "viewing point" where we can actually see that the ball is both black *and* white.

From this viewing point we can appreciate that those who think it's either black or white do so because of their perspective. And even if a person can't get to a viewing point and stays fixated on their point of view, from a higher perspective *within themselves* they will naturally have more compassion and more understanding for other humans and for themselves, even if they are still set on a point of view.

This conversation around a viewing point absolutely rocked my world. Up until then I really thought that I was essentially always right. I didn't take into consideration that there even was an "other side of the ball." And there is *always* an "other side of the ball," *with everything.*

Realizing this in a deep way created a lot of compassion for myself and others and the suffering that we put ourselves through when we hold steadfast to a fixed point of view.

I mean, what if every single thing—every event, every person, every thought and feeling—what if I'm only ever seeing one side, from my limited point of view, until I decide to drop it and ascend within my consciousness and get curious about the alternative realities that I could be overlooking? It means moving away from a way of "seeing" where everything is either right or wrong and instead, moving into a state that, at the University of Santa Monica, is referred to as a state of neutral observation. For me it's a way of letting my mind relax and simply take in reality without placing my opinions onto it.

In fact I have found that the more neutral I can become as I view myself, my opinions, my ideas about life and what happens in it, how other people are behaving, my feelings about it all . . . The more neutrally I can look at myself and other people, the freer I feel.

The happier I feel.

The kinder I am toward myself and others. The more open my mind is. The more receptive I am to new and different ideas and points of view.

I'm a better friend. I'm a better wife and mother, daughter, sister and coach.

I believe people when they tell me what they think, and I believe that they really do think what they think.

I don't think they are dumb or wrong, I believe that they are experiencing something real for themselves. When a teen tells me about something that they did that might at first glance look jarring or unwise, such as having sex on a whim, turning in assignments late or drinking to excess, I don't automatically jump to judgment that they did something wrong. I start and end with genuine neutrality and curiosity, and it makes such a huge difference in my work and my life. It allows me to be more helpful. To demonstrate to my clients a non-reactive way of relating to themselves. To lead with love and a pure intention to understand instead of punish, demean or judge.

I don't go into any conversation with a client, no matter how old they are, and think that I know better. I appreciate that there is so much more going on in every instance than meets the eye. I don't pretend to know what's right or wrong for another person but aim to truly trust their process and experience of life. I appreciate their point of view. I have compassion for them, especially if their point of view, their judgment, is hurting them or causing pain.

This concept is something that I bring up a lot in my coaching conversations, because it can be a stepping stone for significant liberation from suffering.

Becoming more neutral and accepting of what is, in a broader way, can create a very beautiful life. It takes the edge off of the constant emotional rollercoaster we could be on within, where we see things going well, and we feel good. Or we see things that we don't like, and we feel bad.

Being in judgment of oneself, and of others, creates a lot of suffering. On the other hand, being able to see through the judgments, to let them go knowing that they are only being generated from a very limited point of view, being humble enough to acknowledge that we don't know the full story, that our perceptions are likely very flawed most of the time, we can let them go more easily; we can be lighter about our inner and outer experiences.

We can gain more appreciation for other people's points of view

Do I share my personal experiences with clients?

and see that they are simply operating from their own standpoint. The ball really does look black to them—and it in fact *is*.

11

Compassionate self-forgiveness

"Real magic in relationships means an
absence of judgment of others."

Wayne Dyer

Compassionate self-forgiveness is a tool that I learned at USM, and it goes hand-in-hand with this process of becoming more neutral, being in a deeper state of humility about what is right and what is wrong and allowing for more grace and ease within our experiences. It's gently moving toward a more accepting attitude and perception of *everything and everyone,* including ourselves.

For me compassionate self-forgiveness is a process of deeply acknowledging that our *thinking about life,* when we take it as truth—*especially* the painful unhelpful beliefs and limited perspectives—IS what causes us pain and the experience of separation. It's not necessarily what happens in life; it is how we use our mind to judge events as wrong, to judge ourselves as wrong, to judge others as wrong, to position ourselves against others, to cling to our point of view, to make up stories about ourselves and others that are simply untrue and incomplete.

Self-forgiveness is a process of seeing through all this, having compassion for ourselves, moving to a higher perspective within our own consciousness and connecting to a much more accurate viewing point from within. It's not always easy, especially when people, for example, are behaving in dangerous, violent kinds of ways. It's **not** about condoning and agreeing with behavior that we see as inappropriate. It is more about simply accepting that *it is* what is occurring. *It is* what is happening and to entertain the possibility that bringing judgment to it, doesn't change it, but only adds to the sum total of judgment—and thus suffering—on the planet. Change can and does happen even within an accepting, neutral consciousness.

Neutral observation and compassionate self-forgiveness are both skills taught at the University of Santa Monica, and they have changed my life over and over and over again as I have integrated them into my way of being with myself and others.

I do not know who and what I would be without them as a working part of my psychology and spiritual growth.[3]

---

[3] If you want to learn more about USM you can visit their website at: www.universityofsantamonica.edu or purchase their amazing books, *Loyalty to Your Soul* and *Remembering the Light Within*.

12

Free the teens

"You aren't your work, your accomplishments, your possessions, your home, your family . . . your anything. You're a creation of your Source, dressed in a physical human body intended to experience and enjoy life on Earth."

Wayne Dyer

One of the reasons I think I am as effective as I am with teenagers is that I help them feel free.

I don't help them *be* free. I help them get in touch with the fact that they already *are* free. They are sovereign beings.

They're not here to be controlled. They are here to be ignited.

They are here to be encouraged and nurtured and supported in remembering who they are and all of the abilities that they came equipped with. They are intuitive and wise, and the knowledge and wisdom that runs through their veins hasn't been acquired through rote education, but is something that defies age and life experience.

These teenagers, like all of us, were once newborn babies who figured out how to navigate their environment without anyone giving daily lessons. They learned how to talk and walk and chew and drink through instinct and observation. They were discouragement-proof; they fell down a thousand times but kept getting up.

These teenagers have bodies that know how to heal. They get cut and their bodies automatically go into a full-blown healing experience without any conscious understanding or know-how.

These teenagers know on a deep level that the value of who they are does not lie in their grades, the college they attend, the jobs they hold, the clothes they wear, the moods they experience. They know that their worth and their lovability is independent of their performance, their emotions, their behaviors.

But many have forgotten this in their day-to-day lives.

And in the forgetting there is incredible pain and suffering. There can be the overwhelming experiences of depression, apathy, anxiety and a lack of drive or motivation.

There is a hiding under the covers and a disappearing into a screen. Until somebody pops in and reminds them of the truth about who they are. Somebody whom they can hear, whom they can trust, whom they can connect with.

So many of my teenage clients have parents who are continuously attempting to wake them up to this awareness. But at times a teenager's blinders go up and they develop a selective deafness to the words of those incredible parents and caregivers. They need someone else to slip in the back door and tap them on the shoulder and help them wake up to the truth that so many parents are trying to bring to their teens.

It's an honor to be a coach, to work alongside parents to awaken these incredible teenagers and young adults to the fundamental truth of who and what they are, and the truth about how experience comes to life within them.

This book is about being awake to that as a coach—to the truth of who you are—and about supporting teens in discovering the same thing about themselves. You're not good because you make a certain amount of money. You're not loved because of what you've built in your career. You're not worthy of respect because of how beautiful your home is.

You are good and worthy of love and respect and compassion simply because you exist. You are meant to be here. Your presence matters. The way that you walk through the world exactly as you are has a purpose. It makes a difference. You make a difference. And nothing about your external identity holds a flame to the truth of who you are underneath it all.

Your career can fall apart, your house can burn down, your spouse can leave you and, like a phoenix, you can rise again. Nothing external that you think defines you is real. It can all fall away again and again and again, and the truth of who you are will always remain.

You are resilient beyond measure; you are powerful beyond all comprehension. There is a force within you that commands the physical world to warp to your intention and your forward action. There is a creative intelligence that resides in your nature that can activate an entire new life to be birthed from your heart and imagination.

It doesn't matter how many times you have failed—you are not a failure.

It doesn't matter how many embarrassing moments you have endured—you are not an embarrassment.

You are a spark of divine intelligence in action. And, like nature, you are wild and free. You're not meant to live within the lines. You're meant to allow that aliveness to flow through you and into your life, into your cooking and your walking and your creating, your writing, your serving, your parenting and your coaching.

Break the rules. Not for the sake of breaking the rules—but break the ones that aren't meant for you. Be the maverick you were born to be. Let the world work for you and not the other way around. See through the systems that were designed for someone else's success. Break the systems that would try to break you, and find or create new ones that work for you.

Doing this for yourself—living in this way—will help you liberate the precious teenagers that will sit across from you day after day seeking your support and wisdom. You will have the ability to show up for them in a way that they are longing for. To show up for them and to be able to genuinely tell them,

"Yes, you are free! You are not defined by that C-. You are not an average person; you are infinite intelligence moving through life in a way that no one else can. You are creative and wise and resilient.

"You get to decide if you want to become a doctor or a surgeon or a lawyer or a gardener or a teacher or a cook, even if you have failed science classes and burned every dish you've cooked and squashed every seed you've planted.

"You get to decide if you keep going. YOU DECIDE. You are free and sovereign and do not need to conform to some other person's idea of who and how you should be and what your journey of getting where you want to be should look like. It can be riddled with detours and U-turns.

"Please go and fail at something you love, knowing that ultimately you're a success because you spent your precious life energy moving toward something you love. So many people are afraid to fail, so they stop trying. They build a life around something that feels mediocre so that failure and success don't matter. But ultimately this creates a less fulfilling life. So go and fail, and fail again, knowing that YOU are not a failure."

Sitting across from a teenager and giving them this gift of freedom is medicine to their souls. It doesn't turn them into apathetic, unmotivated, whimsical or ungrounded people. Instead, when they hear this message they tend to become very engaged in life, more than they may have thought they could be. They become very thoughtful and tuned into themselves. They let go of ways of doing things that were really to please their parents, friends or teachers. They start to live in ways that are raw and authentic, full of feeling and inspiration.

I care very little about them becoming productive members of society if society isn't healthy for them. I want them to learn how to tune into themselves so that they understand what they need to be healthy and thrive, to be successful by their own definition, according to their heart and soul.

I've talked about the internal guidance system we all come with. So many teenagers have forgotten that they come equipped with this, that they have something that will let them know if something is right or wrong for them in the moment.

From my own experience and what I see operating in our world, we're methodically taught to ignore this system. We're taught to stay awake when we're tired, to keep studying when our brains are screaming for a break, to look outside ourselves for guidance around our health instead of looking inside to the wisdom that resides there. We're taught to ask others for advice rather than seeking our own, to abdicate our power rather than claim our free will and wisdom.

There is a time and place for seeking support. My work is about showing up for teens in those moments and being a source of support and encouragement. But if I'm doing anything right as a coach, I am encouraging my clients to begin to trust themselves. To look within for the answers. To wake up more fully to who and what we are as humans. To realize that our guidance system is always active and simply needs to be nurtured and given some attention. It's there for us right now.

If I do nothing else as a coach but help my clients—including teens, parents, and other coaches—wake up to this awareness and start using it for themselves, then I have done my job.

And I do believe that this is what teenagers are hungry for. They are dying to be acknowledged for the incredibly wise, deeply intuitive and creative beings that they are.

I am not coaching them into wellness.

I am helping them see that they are already well, and that the health within them cannot be touched or tainted or destroyed by anything in this world.

Coaching Teens Well

"Love is the ultimate coach. Do what you love, let love guide you, and let love inspire you."

Robert Holden

13

Why do you work with teenagers?

One of the reasons I love working with teenagers is that I remember what it was like to be one—and it wasn't all that easy!

This despite the fact that I have always been interested in the inner dimensions of what it means to be a human. As I shared earlier, I started a meditation practice when I was twelve years old, right on the cusp of the teenage years. When I started feeling out of sorts and a bit lost within myself, my mom took me to a Buddhist nun and I was taught a meditation practice and given a mantra, which I was told had been chanted by monks for thousands of years, and which I was never to repeat out loud. It is so sacred that saying it out loud would diminish its value.

My mantra is—

Just kidding, I'm not going to share it. It is something I still hold very sacred.

But when I was a teenager I felt very much alone in my inner seeking. I had a brother I was very close with, who was two years older than me, a totally amazing person and to this day one of my all-time favorite people, but he had no interest in the topics in the books that filled my bookshelves. I was a full-on teenager: rebellious and self-absorbed. I wanted to be the best at everything. I wanted to be in the spotlight. I wanted to be popular and liked by everyone, even the outsiders. I wanted the starring role in every play and always felt the pain of rejection when I never got it.

At the same time, I didn't want to be seen by anyone. In fact, I was terrified of being seen. Don't ask me to explain it! I was a teenager!

I thought that I sucked, but I was simultaneously aware that at times we *all* suck and at times we're *all* great—or at least this is how we perceive things. I could sense that in reality there is a divinity, a preciousness inherent in who I am and who we all are. I've had this awareness from about the age of thirteen.

Eckart Tolle and Wayne Dyer were my favorite teachers. Their words resonated with me way beyond those of any of the people who taught me the standard high school subjects. (Though I have nothing but respect for all of my teachers and, in fact, for anyone who's a teacher of any kind.) During those years I took respite in the company of people who were talking about consciousness and spirituality. That was where I found a sense of peace.

I got my license when I turned sixteen and immediately bought myself a car. I'd been saving money since I was about eight years old, so by the time I was ready to drive I had about 90 percent of the purchase price in hand. The remaining 10 percent came from my mom's boyfriend, Bobby, whom I think of to this day, as a father figure. (My parents divorced when I was around three. I'll share a bit more about that later on.)

I bought a bright red 1996 Eagle Summit. It broke down on the way home from the dealership and turned out to be nothing but a hot mess until, with the help of Bobby, I traded it in a few years later for a 1996 black Dodge Neon (which had a salvage title because it had been stolen).

Since I had my own car and chose to drive, I'd often find myself with a car full of my friends. I had a cassette player on the backseat because the car stereo didn't work, and the price of admission for my friends was that at times they'd have to listen to whatever tape series I was into at the moment. *The Power of Now* by Eckhart Tolle was one of my favorites. So we'd often ride the twelve miles from our town to the school listening to personal growth tapes.

As a teen I smoked weed, drank and had over a 4.0 GPA. I did volunteer work and hung out with senior citizens. I also hid in the classroom after school making out with whomever I had been dating that week.

I did a lot of dating. If I could give my past self a piece of advice, it would be to hold off on dating until my thirties. Not very practical, I know, but it certainly would've helped if my brain had been a bit more developed before I dove into those kinds of relationships.

Why am I sharing all this? Because when I look back on the turbulence and wonder of it all, I feel like I would have been so happy to have a loving, accepting, empowering human being tell me that I was okay, that all was well, that I hadn't screwed up my entire life because I had sex too early or with the wrong person. It would've been amazing to hear that just because I failed a test I wasn't a failure, and that a failed test score wasn't going to follow me around like the bogeyman.

It would've been helpful to be reminded that I was allowed to be messy, to make mistakes, to fail, to try things that scared me, and to wear what I wanted. (Although I *did* in fact wear what I wanted to wear, I always felt like I was doing something wrong).

In short, I would have felt so supported if someone made it clear that I wasn't inherently flawed.

My parents were loving and supportive—and still are. My mom is still the person I call whenever I am truly thrilled about something. I know she will share in my enthusiasm. My dad is someone who believed I could do anything (and still does)—which included riding motorcycles at seven, driving excavators at ten, and carrying five-gallon buckets of dirt two miles, uphill—in the snow, both ways—as an eleven year-old. No, really it's true. Uphill both ways. That's possible when working with my dad, in the middle of the wilderness. Which is still his office to this day.

He treated me as if I were strong and capable, quite literally from day one. This message didn't always go in that way as a young one. I was often intimidated by what he thought I could do. But to this day, I am someone who thinks I, and anyone else, can pretty much do anything they decide to do. No matter how physically, mentally or emotionally demanding it might be. I learned this from my mom as well. She and my dad are both my role models for having a vision and getting it done.

But as much as I don't understand it, when I was a teenager my mom's sage wisdom and unconditional love and my dad's belief in me often just didn't penetrate the walls I had built up around me. It's so interesting to see this kind of dynamic play out with my clients. Teens who are deeply loved by their parents but who for some reason aren't allowing that love to seep in.

Until it does. Until, like happened with me, there is a melting, a softening, a gentle seeing that occurs, and without even realizing it they grow more open. More receptive and willing to allow themselves to be seen and loved for who they are in all their chaotic glory. (For me this happened through the work I did with perfect strangers at the University of Santa Monica, when I was nineteen.)

I love my conversations with teen clients where I share a bit about my own teenage experience. It allows them to open up to the insight that just because shit happens, it doesn't mean that *they* are shitty. Nor does it mean that whatever happens in the next moment of their lives has to reflect the current moment. The choices about where to go next are endless. We are constantly re-creating ourselves moment to moment. I love my work with teens, because I get to help them see that they are free, that they don't have to hold themselves to any particular set of perceptions or self-identification.

I truly love the process of holding space for a teen to feel into this truth for themselves. Not that adults don't have this ability, but teens seem to know it at a very deep level, often very quickly. It's as if they've just been waiting for someone to come along, tap them on the shoulder and whisper in their ear, "You are enough. You weren't made wrong. You have wisdom beyond measure within you, right now."

Many teens are at first very closed off and skeptical about this understanding. That's completely fine and understandable. Many of them are forced into a first coaching conversation.

As I'll share later, I'm okay if that first session is a "dry run" and they're not onboard yet. But I will not continue beyond that initial conversation if a teen isn't completely onboard. This is my policy. I don't make exceptions to this. If a teen isn't ready for coaching, I will not begin with them beyond the initial sessions. I am always doing what I can to support people—teens included—in taking back their power. Speaking what is true for themselves. Asking for what they need. Saying no when it is a no. Saying yes when it is a yes. Essentially supporting people in listening deeply to their own internal clarity and honoring it.

This is not an easy thing for most teens—nor for many adults.

So some teens come into a first conversation a bit shut down and dejected, but if you hang in a bit with them and take some time to create rapport—talk about music, movies or favorite foods, share your own challenges and the truth that you have ups and downs, and so on—they very well may begin to drop into their own knowing around the fact that they are okay. The fact of their wholeness. The fact of their resilience and wisdom. And once they glimpse it, it will feel natural for them to want to see more.

14

Undeclared

When I was in high school and we were all in class going through the process of picking our majors on our college applications—and trying to do so by deciding what we wanted to do in life—I had a little bit of a meltdown. I couldn't find any job on the list that I might want to do. I knew I wanted to do something in the field of personal growth and spirituality, but I had no idea what that meant, and I certainly wasn't seeing it bundled up into a nice employment package.

I snuck out of school, went down to the pizza parlor and sat on the benches outside. My best friend's mom, who was one of my favorite people—Bernadett—walked by then returned and sat down with me. When she asked me what was up I told her what I was going through. She looked at me and she said, "Aila, you know what's amazing? You get to make up your career, get clear about what you love and just go and find a way to do it. It doesn't matter if you can't find it out there; you get to create it."

In that moment I felt so relieved and so grateful. I cried a lot.

I felt truly seen and encouraged by Bernadett, always.

Flash-forward to today, where my work is primarily with

teenagers doing personal growth work/meditation and facilitation, and I often say to my clients exactly what Bernadett said to me. I get to encourage them the way she encouraged me.

I talk about her, and I tell them that the thing that is in their hearts to do in the world, they will find a way to do it, even if they need to make it up.

Although Bernadett has passed away, in a very real way her wisdom and love are radiating to teens and people all across the world, not only through her children and grandchildren, but through the work I do as a coach.

15

What advice do you give to teenagers?

"The greatest gift we can offer each other is the framework in which to think for ourselves."

Nancy Kline

I don't give advice.

Well, I try not to—and I generally succeed. Occasionally something that sounds like advice *might* slip out of my mouth. I'm human, and it's natural to want to share a "solution" to someone's "problem" if it occurs to me. But I do my best to avoid this for several reasons.

The most important one, based on my experience, is that unless an insight rises up organically within a teen, it's not likely to stay with them. If I give them *my* insight or advice, it's like sticking a Post-it note on their forehead. It's not going to stick for very long—if at all—because it hasn't bubbled up from their own heart and soul.

So the best thing I can do for clients is help them discover their own clarity. Every teenager I work with is fully equipped with their own wisdom and inner guidance. If I can slow down enough and create an open and safe space for them to explore what's going on in their lives, the answers often spontaneously emerge within them.

I vividly remember a period when I was deciding whether or not to drop out of college. I wanted to attend the University of Santa Monica, an unaccredited spiritual psychology program, instead of finishing my more traditional, "respectable" college education. I had already essentially decided I wanted to go to USM, but I was having a hard time getting behind the decision.

My mom and I were standing in the kitchen, and she asked me to think about going to USM and describe how it felt. I observed that I felt free and expansive. Elated and joyful.

Then she asked me to think about going back to Whittier College to finish school there. I immediately felt tight and constricted. Anxious and unsettled.

This may not have been the response my mom wanted me to have (although maybe it was; she is a pretty amazing human), but she completely supported me in seeing what was true for me. In asking me to *feel* my way forward, she created a space in which I could do just that. It was a clear, pure, and simple approach. And I made my decision from there to go to the University of Santa Monica.

I've learned to make most of my decisions from that intuitive, non-logical, inner-guidance-oriented place. It's not always easy to follow the guidance that comes from there, but whenever I do, I feel a sense of calm about the path ahead, no matter what unfolds.

What I want more than anything for my clients is for them to learn how to access their own information about what is and isn't in alignment with who they really are and what they want to do. Very often I see teenagers who have a clear idea about what they want, but who at the same time are receiving a lot of outer input contrary to this desire. This can be profoundly confusing. It can make them feel that if they follow their inner guidance they'll have to act against their friends and family, and that consequently they'll be abandoned and unloved.

Of course, this makes following their inner guidance much less appealing.

One of the ways to work with teens in this situation is to remind them that their relationship to their inner guidance doesn't have to be so black-and-white. When they are feeling stuck in a decision because of someone else's ideas about what they should do, they can learn to talk about it openly. You can help them navigate that conversation in a way that is supportive for them. This is a huge thing that comes up with all my clients. Every one of them. Luckily—because the way I see it, for a teen to learn to trust their own inner guidance, and to see that it can go hand in hand with having supportive, meaningful relationships, is one of the most important gifts they can have in life.

16

Client story: Rosie and the crush

"You do not have to be good.
You do not have to walk on your knees
for a hundred miles through the desert repenting.
You only have to let the soft animal of your body
love what it loves."

Mary Oliver, Wild Geese

Yesterday I had a session with Rosie.

Rosie is eighteen and has had a crush on Raven, a girl in her class, for about a year. Rosie found herself on a family vacation at the beach where Raven's family was also vacationing. They hung out on the beach together nearly every day. Rosie and I had a session while she was on this vacation, and in it she was telling me how much she wanted to have her first kiss, and how she wanted it to be with Raven.

I had been hearing about Rosie's crush on Raven for over a year and was familiar with Rosie talking herself out of making her feelings known time and time again. In response to this latest share I said with enthusiasm, "Go for it!"

Rosie is in a family who would completely support her decision to kiss another human being, whether it was a boy or a girl or any other gender identity. Rosie's grandparents, however, would not approve, nor would they likely understand why Rosie would even want to do such a thing.

This topic of teen sexuality, much less same-sex connections, is a charged one. It could be an entire book unto itself. I was tempted not to write about it simply because there's so much to say—it's such a rich area of exploration, with countless opportunities for teens and parents to deepen their own levels of self-acceptance and understanding of each other.

One of the most common conversation pieces I have with teenagers is around clarifying what they really want. It sounds like such a simple, "coachy" kind of thing to do, but it couldn't be more vital in my mind to help a teen understand how to listen to themselves deeply and cut through all of the noise that might try to keep them out of touch with themselves.

And when it came to discussing Rosie's figuring out what she really wanted, I admit that this was an area—teens grappling with gender identity and sexual preferences—where I felt like I had an advantage as a coach. I put myself through the ringer as a teenager and young adult, so I have lots to bring to the table. I often joke with coaches I mentor that, "You don't have to have had a rough childhood or upbringing to be a great coach for teens, but it certainly helps!"

(Steve Chandler is often fond of saying to coaches who have been or are going through some adversity or big learning opportunity: "That's going to make you an even better coach! That's going to help you serve your clients!" I'm not always a fan when he says it to me . . . but it's always true!)

My struggles with being attracted to both boys and girls from an early age quickly made me aware of the degree to which I was concerned about other people's perceptions of me—particularly how my parents saw me.

I'm not going to share about the many complicated scenarios in which I found myself while dating both genders—sometimes secretly at the same time—but I will say that when I got clear within myself that my life would only feel right to me if I started to listen to what I truly wanted and cared about, and didn't have to be ashamed or embarrassed, things felt simpler and much more clear.

I was able to make decisions without a weight hanging over me. I dated freely. In fact, when I ended up settling down with a gorgeous man and making myself appear oh-so conventional, I think my very outspoken, free-spirited self felt slightly disappointed. I'm joking a little, but it's worth noting that there was a part of me that didn't want to do what I *really* wanted to do—marry my now-husband—simply because it was also what other people might have expected of me.

That rebellious part of me is alive and well, and it never wants me to appear as if I'm conforming or doing things because other people want me to. And I also see that if I had stuck to that rigid way of thinking, I might have completely missed out on my beautiful relationship with this wonderful human and the amazing children that we now have.

I mention this because sometimes there's a kind of haze around what a teen wants if it happens to coincide with what their parents want for them too. The teen is put in an almost paradoxical situation where, in honoring what they want, they also feel like they're letting their parents "win." And because many teens struggle to create an identity that is separate from their parents, it can be tricky to help them see that their own needs and desires in this type of situation are what count.

So, going back to Rosie . . . In our conversation she told me again how much she desperately wanted to kiss Raven, but how at the same time she was afraid her parents would secretly disapprove (and her grandparents would disapprove without hiding it). She told me how she was afraid that one day, assuming it went well with Raven, she would be judged and cast out of whatever social circle she was trying to fit into.

I slowed her down, looked her in the eye and said, "But what does your heart really want?"

"I really want to kiss her . . . But what if she's not into it?"

"How could you find out? Maybe instead of going directly in for a kiss, you could ask her if she would *like* to kiss?"

Rosie said, "But what if she doesn't want to?"

"Well, then you would know, after a year of being in the unknown. Wouldn't it be great to know one way or another?"

"What will my mom think?"

"Rosie, what do *you* really want?"

She smiled and laughed as she said, "I really want to kiss her!"

"This is an opportunity to practice listening to yourself. It's not just about kissing Raven or seeing if she'd like to kiss you. It's about practicing listening to yourself, honoring what is true for you and knowing that you don't know what's going to happen—but that this is what feels right, right here and right now.

I could see her mind was made up. She said, "I'm going to do it! I always care too much about what other people think!"

I got a report back a few days later that Rosie and Raven not only kissed, but spent time walking along the beach holding hands, imagining a future together, talking about travel and college and all the things eighteen-year-old people should be fantasizing about.

Over the previous year I had shared a lot with Rosie about my experiences with kissing other humans, and about the freedom I found in simply honoring what was true for myself in any given moment, knowing that I could find a way to communicate with those whom I needed to—if I needed to—about my sexual preferences. I knew that the more I was in touch with what I really wanted, knowing that it was the only way for me to live a life that I felt in alignment with myself, the happier I would be and the easier it would be to communicate about who I am and what I want with those I love.

It took some time for Rosie to build up the courage to go for what she really wanted. She needed to deepen in her understanding that she could advocate for herself with love, and that she could honor her relationships with her parents and her grandparents and still be true to herself. I'm sure she'll have some difficult conversations ahead if, let's say, she brings Raven home for dinner and introduces her as her girlfriend. But Rosie will make it through that moment, and so will her family.

I've had the honor and privilege of sitting with many families together on group calls where my teenage client has decided to come out of the closet in one way or another. It's not always the right choice for a teen—it's not always safe, and it's not always something I would recommend. But when the stars align and there's an openness and gentleness and willingness on everyone's part to move into deeper levels of honesty and acceptance with each other, it is a beautiful thing.

As I mentioned above, the story I used in this chapter raises some "hot button" issues. But strip away these particular details and what this chapter is really about is helping a teen clarify what they want—independent of what others think or want for them. Helping a teen get clear on this is vital in so many circumstances, including what school to apply to, where to eat dinner, what to major in, what part to try out for in a play, who to invite to their birthday party and even what to wear in the morning.

I'm always on the lookout for the moment when I hear a teen talk about something they want and then quickly dismiss it. It happens in nearly every conversation. If you start to listen, I know you'll start to hear it as well. Not only with the teens in your life but with all of your clients.

And then when you hear it, what can you do? Offer them a space in which they can slow down and bring to light what it is that they really want. In doing so they learn more about how to listen to what they want, and how to honor that still, small voice that can help them be themselves in the world.

17

He's just not that into you

This week I talked with Sam about a crush she has on a boy from her class. She told me that she really likes him, they have a great time when they're together, she feels lit up in a way that she doesn't feel with other people, and she really, really, really wants him to ask her out.

This is one of the most common conversations I have with teenage and young adult women. They have a lovely experience with a guy and then assume it's up to the him to take the lead and move things forward.

I relate to this idea. When I was a teenager I read a book called *The Rules.* It was all about how to show up as a woman in the early stages of a relationship and do everything in what I would say is a contrived and manipulative way, with the goal of ensuring that the man quickly knows your intention is to get married. You're showing him what you expect if that's gonna happen.

At first sight this approach seems empowering for women. You set up the rules. You make sure the guy asks you out. You don't move in with him until the proposal is on the table. You make it very clear that you're in control of the process. This isn't the only book that emphasizes this kind of power structure. This advice is everywhere in our culture. Going to prom and homecoming are all about who's asking whom—in which case it's always up to the guy. Getting married is all about being proposed to by the guy.

This idea never sat well with me, and it's not something I subscribe to. I *do* acknowledge and appreciate the differences between masculine and feminine energy. And I do believe that at our best we are aware that we embody 100 percent of both kinds of energy and that we have access to both when needed. I want to be able to lift a car off my kid and access all of my masculine energy to do so. I want to be able to drop into my feminine self to receive gestures of love and intimacy from my husband. Both are part of who we are.

And while this feels relevant to this whole idea of who is asking whom out, what it's really all about is my relationship with myself. Am I someone who is going to go for what I want, or not?

Am I going to let myself move toward those things that light me up, or am I going wait for somebody else to make that happen for me?

Am I going to give myself permission to proactively create my life, or am I going to put that power in someone else's hands?

I love telling my clients the story of how I met and married my husband.

My husband is my best friend's brother. She introduced us in 2009, six years into my friendship with her. She actually called it. She told her mom one day that if he and I ever met, we would get married. Given that I was convinced I'd never marry, it was a funny thing for her to have said. In any case, when she saw the window—when he and I were both single—she planned a time for the three of us to hang out in a very casual way.

When I first met Dhiraj, I felt something inside me I'd never felt before. I was lit up, I was captivated, I was completely myself and willing to be seen and heard by this man. In fact, the first time we hung out we did a shamanic journey together, went out to Mexican food and then spent some time hanging out with his family, him playing his guitar and singing songs, me listening with stars in my eyes and butterflies in my stomach.

I left those five hours of hanging out feeling clear I would marry that man if I could. I even wrote it down in my journal when I got home: "I think I just met the person I'm going to marry. And, if not that, I just felt the feeling people feel when they know they want to get married."

A few days went on and I didn't hear from him.

And then a few more . . .

And then I realized the truth: I might *never* hear from him. So what was I waiting for?

So I called him up and asked if he wanted to play ping-pong. Over the course of the next three or four months I asked him to hang out probably once a week or more. About 50 percent of the time he said yes, and when we did, we had the best time.

My friends were a little dumbfounded by my behavior. You know that saying, "He's just not that into you"? I must've been told that a dozen times by people who were witnessing my process with him.

He never asked me out—literally, he never asked me to hang out once during those months. I could've made up so many stories about this. One of the most obvious ones: he just wasn't that into me. Or, I must not be his type. Or, anything else that would've slightly broken my heart.

But instead I decided to focus on the truth: that I really enjoyed my time with him and was committed to giving myself more of what I wanted.

I was committed to continuing to support myself in having experiences that lit me up.

I was committed to myself, and I was open to seeing where the journey took me.

It was quite literally over three months of us spending a lot of time together, getting to know each other, that little by little I wore him down (only joking there . . . a little bit!). And one magical day he sent me a message asking if I wanted to go see a movie. Only later did I find out that it was a movie he'd already seen: *Up*. But he knew I only watched animated comedies and made the sacrifice to see it twice. After the movie, he and I hung out in the theater parking lot, talking until 3:00 a.m.. I knew something had shifted inside of him. He was more flirtatious. He may even have put his hand on my arm or leg during the movie—I don't quite remember—but I could feel there was something opening.

The next day he asked me to hang out again. We spent the day watching Harry Potter movies and doing weird things like practicing prayer treatments, dancing and having lots of fun together. We kissed at the end of that night and have been together ever since.

I know Dhiraj would tell you that he's beyond grateful for my commitment to myself, for going for what I wanted, regardless of the feedback I got from other people at the time. We wouldn't be together today if I hadn't had (and still have) that commitment alive inside myself. In my mind there's nothing disempowering about it. I took a stand for what I wanted and I stuck with it. I didn't know where it would lead, but I knew that I wanted to live a life in a way where I had my own back—I still do.

Of course, I didn't want to push myself on someone who wasn't interested, but he was never not interested; the water was warm. And I often see now with the clients I work with that they miss out on the warm water—expecting or needing it to be sizzling hot instead; otherwise it's not good enough. Or they only think it's good if the warm or sizzling hot water is being presented *to* them instead of being created *by* them.

I encourage my young clients to go for what they really want in relationships, being willing to risk the good or bad outcomes. They don't need to rush—I didn't try to plant a huge kiss on my husband before I felt the opening on his end, but neither did I remove myself from his life. I kept engaging because it felt good to me. I stayed present in my heart to my actual experience rather than what my head (and other people) were telling me. I did need to overcome thoughts that I was doing something silly or setting myself up for disappointment. I met those thoughts with skepticism and curiosity, which was really helpful in letting them go and staying present to what I wanted.

In my view it's not just about how people show up in romantic relationships. It's how we show up to *anything* we want in our lives. It's a way of being, a way of living. It's a way of taking a stand for what my heart wants and being the one who says "yes" to that.

18

Really, don't give advice! (Does that sound like advice?)

I have other reasons I don't give advice.

For one, if I do I'm just adding my voice to those of the dozens of other people telling the teen what to do. I'm either going to increase the teen's confusion around decision-making or they're going to resent or lose respect for me. Or all of the above.

Another strike against the idea of giving advice is that I never want to tell a kid to do something, have it go poorly and then get a call from an upset parent asking me, "Why did you tell my kid to do *that*?" Or have the teen tell me the same thing. This isn't something that tends to be on my mind, but it's something that I see come up with the coaches I work with who work with teens.

There's a responsibility that goes along with giving advice, especially when you're in relationship with someone who is looking to you for guidance, someone who may not yet have learned to trust their own wisdom. I appreciate and respect the power and influence I can have as a professional coach.

I want my clients to take full responsibility for their choices. I know I'm not going to be regularly available for them beyond our coaching agreement, and I don't want to become someone they depend on for guidance. I want them to learn to access guidance within themselves so they can feel clear and confident making their own decisions; in fact, I want that for them from day one of our coaching agreement.

If I just give them advice, I'm sharing what I think would be right for *me* if I were in a similar situation. But that may not have anything to do with what's right for them. If as coaches we insist on a certain bit of advice, we might actually be encouraging people to do something they're not ready for, or something that isn't truly in alignment with how they're feeling. In this case what we're offering won't land in a real way for them. It might not even make any sense.

So I don't set myself up as an expert. I don't try to sound superior. The best way I can support teens in making good choices is by encouraging them to get in touch with their own intuition. I help them explore where their feelings come from, the difference between being grounded and being stirred up in their thinking, and the truth of who they are as whole and complete human beings, lacking nothing, unconditionally lovable, capable and worthy of pursuing anything that is in their hearts.

Again, part of my heart's desire in the work I do on this earth, is that I help remind people, teens included, to STOP looking outside for guidance. Or to stop SOLELY looking outside for guidance. To at least dare to consider that the insight and good ideas that *they* have about, let's say, what college to attend, are worth something. They do matter. That their gut feeling counts. That there might be agendas and influences happening in the world that are not necessarily supportive of people waking up to who and what we really are. That we are equipped with a wealth of knowledge that has no age requirement, and our well-being is present and un-damageable. That we do not need to be afraid. OF ANYTHING. We can stand fearless, or at least courageous, in the face of all the decisions and dilemmas this world offers and know that we have the guidance within to navigate our lives with grace.

This becomes possible, when we stop looking outside ourselves for our sense of okay-ness. Our sense of safety. Our answers.

My hope is that when I don't give advice to teens, I am encouraging them to take small steps in the direction of them seeing more clearly the wisdom and guidance that is always flowing within them.

19

What is your mindset in a session with a teenager?

I know I have made it clear that I see teens as having all the wisdom and insight they'll ever need inside themselves, but if feels worth repeating and emphasizing this, because I attribute any success I have in coaching them to this trust I have *in* them. I see that it's not always easy for coaches to recognize this wisdom in teenagers, and when they don't see it, this can create a difficulty in really serving them.

And I get it! At times the teens I sit with look so lost that it looks like they need rescuing from an outer source. But in truth, to sit with them, holding the mindset that they have what they need inside, it's easier to help them access it. And in accessing it, they get to experience something profound for themselves. They get to know themselves and their inner support system in a way that will serve them for years to come.

Like all of us, teens have an inner guidance system—a GPS that will help them navigate their lives, whatever comes their way. They possess an active and living intelligence, fueled by their heart, regardless of their situation or circumstances. My goal in working with teens is to help them realize this, and then help them learn how to listen to it.

When I sit across from a teen I don't make assumptions about what they can and can't handle, about what they're capable of discussing, or about how I need to "get them on the right track." I rely on my own instincts to help me hold space and support my client in exploring whatever they've brought to the session.

Listening to them, rather than my own thoughts about them is key. It's an amazing practice to take on as a coach and human. To see what it is like to truly lean in and listen without getting fascinated by your own brilliant thoughts on how to solve their challenges, but to listen to the meaning behind their words and the wisdom behind their actions. Listening to THEM rather to my own thoughts about them and what they are saying is one way I demonstrate to myself and to them, that I trust them and the wisdom that resides within them.

One reason I think teens resonate with me is that I tend to look at their 'problems' with a light heart. Not in a harsh way but with all the love and compassion I can muster. I love to smile when they're telling me about a big issue going on in their life. *This* is a reflection of my mindset, of the state of consciousness I am holding for them to meet me in. It's a place where they know they are much bigger and wiser than any issue that's going on in their world – or in how they are using their thinking. I am holding them in an energy that invites them to see that any issue is temporary and fleeting, and often simply a reflection of their own state of mind in the moment.

In a sense, I'm holding a higher vision for them, something that they naturally start to attune themselves to when they're ready and able. I don't get down into the trenches with them—that would just be doubling down on the "problem" and making it seem even more real, even more threatening and challenging, even more scary and insurmountable. Instead I remain open to what they're saying, without providing advice or my own "solutions." We simply talk through whatever issue they feel they are facing. And by asking them questions, reflecting back what I hear them say, staying neutral, non-reactive and compassionate, what happens is that they begin to have their own insights, their own moments of clarity with it. Their thinking starts to settle.

If I meet my teen client in the same consciousness that believes there is a problem, and I get worried with them, it just adds to the "problem." If I stay elevated—or as elevated as I can—it helps me encourage teens to see themselves and their experiences through a different lens. Often humor is the key, or at least a lightness and a gentleness in our work together.

When I stay connected to my deeper understanding of who and what they are and what they are actually up against (limited and often fearful thinking that they are holding a tight grip on,) and help them see what is really happening, that any issue is temporary, that the truth of who they are is unbreakable, resilient, creative, wise and resourceful, they tend to lift within their own consciousness. They tend to settle down and open to feelings of clarity and confidence, and they have new ideas for how to help themselves with whatever conundrum they were previously facing. A clearer state of mind changes everything.

20

What if you *DID* know?

When I'm sitting with a teen and I ask, "What do you think is the right thing to do here?" I almost always get a brilliant answer back, even if it follows an initial, "I don't know."

Sometimes when I hear that "I don't know" I'll ask:

- "What if you *did* know?"
- "What would you tell your very best friend if he were in a similar situation?"
- "If there was a way, what way would you want to take?"

(I've included a list of questions I often ask in sessions in the Additional Resources section at the end of this book.)

I do everything in my power not to overlay my own judgments or ideas about what they should do. I allow them the dignity of engaging their own process in discovering answers that will make the most sense to them—answers that will actually stick.

I might offer suggestions to see if certain ideas resonate with where the teen is at in a given moment. This can help teens understand and relate to their own inner guidance, with which they can then "test" my suggestions. In exploring new ideas and perspectives with me, they learn to become aware of their inner states and the feelings and ideas that arise from them. They learn how to say, "No, that's not a fit" or "Yes, that *is* what I want to do!"

The signals inner guidance sends each of us differ from person to person. It can take time and patience to sort them out and learn to trust that they're not leading us astray. As coaches we can create a space for teens to "test the waters" and learn what it feels like to listen to their own wisdom.

When a teen expresses to me that she wants to go for something, I ask why she wants it. What might this thing do for her? How might it add value to her life? How could it be helpful or supportive or inspiring?

These questions help her bring clarity and focus to her goal, which inspire a new energy and sense of engagement. Procrastination is no longer a thing. The "doing" part becomes obvious. Obstacles that at first seemed insurmountable start to dissolve. I'm not so much helping them find a way to get to their goal (though I will do that sometimes); rather I'm helping them connect with why their goal matters to them, because when they see this, the way forward becomes very clear.

I love supporting people in knowing in their bones that they can truly trust themselves. That even if an action they take doesn't go the way they wanted or the outcome is different from what they'd planned, they can trust that they will be there for themselves. It's the nature of their relationship with themselves that becomes very relevant in developing that trust.

Each outcome, a seeming endpoint, is really another starting point. We all get to start again right now, right now and right now. There isn't anything holding us back from making our next heartfelt choice. No matter how insecure or unworthy we might feel, nothing can stop us from making a choice that flies in the face of all of that. Whatever teens want—great grades, healthy relationships, the ideal college—is on the table for them if they're willing to give themselves a shot.

21

Client story: James and the panic attack

The other night I was talking on the phone with James, a client of mine who's a senior in high school. He's a straight A student who got into a very prestigious college. Yet he was dealing with what almost amounted to a panic attack because, as he told me, he felt unable to complete a research paper.

I asked him to share more about what was going on, and it all came out in a rush:

"I just don't know how to do it. I don't think I can finish it. I don't think I've ever been able to write. I don't know how I wrote my college application essays or even finished any of my classes, because I just can't write."

I slowly and gently said, "I want to give you a big hug!! I would be super-stressed too if I was believing all of that to be true." I saw him breathe a little easier, and I gently went on to remind him it wasn't the paper but his thinking that was creating his feeling. This rang true for him and lightened him up. I knew that I needed to keep talking to help him calm down even more and gain some solid ground within himself. So I went on to say a little about my own experiences of being in situations where my thoughts convinced me I had no idea how to do something—but how a wisdom boiled up from within me and helped me accomplish what needed to be done.

One thing that came to mind was my experience of childbirth, so I shared it with James. I've had three babies, and all of my labor experiences were filled with thoughts of, "I can't do this. I don't know how to do this. I'm not good enough to do this. I'm not intuitive enough. My body doesn't know what to do. I'm the only woman in the world who truly, truly cannot do this." These thoughts not only felt like problems—they felt true.

I remember during my first son's birth my midwife said to me, "It doesn't matter that you don't *think* you can; you're *doing* it right now."

That was a huge revelation for me. It brought about a moment of clarity in which I realized that most of the time my thinking is terribly flawed. Just because my thoughts *feel* true doesn't mean they *are* true.

And what's more, if a thought doesn't feel good or expansive, it's probably a great one to let go of as quickly as possible. At the very least I know I can benefit from taking a moment to question the validity of the thought.

In practice I prefer the first approach—simply knowing that if I'm not feeling peaceful and balanced it's likely due to my holding on to some thoughts that were innocently passing by, but which I paid too much attention to and allowed to play on a loop in my mind. If I invest time in analyzing these kinds of thoughts, I'm actually giving them *more* attention and allowing them to impact me even more deeply in the moment.

In any case, when I realize I'm fixating on some less-than-supportive thoughts, I know it's time to show myself compassion, because it actually hurts.

Every human being comes to the table with a mind and a consciousness that are receptive to all sorts of thoughts. We have happy thoughts, sad thoughts, angry thoughts, and uplifting thoughts. We have 70,000 to 90,000 thoughts each day. Some of them we like more than others. Some are more helpful than others. Some are complete garbage and should be thrown out immediately!

When we show ourselves compassion, we exhale. We let go a little—of the judgment, of the bearing down on ourselves. When we give ourselves permission to release our grip on our thoughts, we can see for ourselves that our state of feeling is directly connected to the quality of our thinking. Waking up to that can be so liberating. Our thoughts create our feelings—and our thoughts can be SO flawed and out of touch with reality. Knowing this—even when you're undergoing a massive meltdown—can create a bit of space and a new relationship with the thoughts coming through. And, it's not so much our thoughts that are the issue, but how we relate to them.

I offered this perspective to James: "You don't need to think that you can write the paper in order to write it. You don't need to believe that you're good enough or smart enough or capable of doing it.

"You can just write it.

"You don't need to try to figure out the source of all of these thoughts and why they are there. You can just begin writing.

"What would help you get started?"

He lightened up even more. He looked hopeful. He laughed. I saw him remember the truth about himself.

I asked him if he needed help with the paper or if he was feeling clear. He said he felt calm and able to do it but if I was up for staying on the call with him, it would be nice. So I did.

We began exploring ways that his paper could feel more

conversational. I took a few notes as we chatted and then sent him some text messages with the sentence-starters he came up with. He would have those to dive right into once we ended our call.

During our conversation he had several moments of reflection in which he noted that he had forgotten that his thoughts are not facts. He had forgotten that just because he doesn't *think* he's good enough, that's not necessarily the truth. And he had forgotten that he could take action *even* if he didn't think he was capable of doing it well. He could take action even before (or perhaps instead of) figuring out why he thought the way he did or why he was having these thoughts to begin with. As the conversation progressed James even laughed several times and said that his anxiety was essentially gone.

In this experience with James, it made sense to me, in the moment, to talk in a general way about where his experience was really coming from: his *thought-created* reality, not reality itself.

At other times, I know it makes sense to me to look more closely at thoughts that masquerade as beliefs, and tease them apart a bit. Teens aren't always up for this kind of inquiry and I find that it's not usually necessary. The more time I spend sharing with clients my own experiences of the temporary and flimsy nature of thought, the more they feel the truth of this for themselves. This can be very liberating for them. Rather than working hard to uproot and understand a dozen "negative" or "painful" thought strands, I help my clients, especially teens, to see that all thoughts, no matter the content, are temporary and neutral. A thought about what to eat for dinner and a thought about failing out of college, are made of the same "stuff." It's only when we cling to one thought and take it for a ride that we get stirred up and unsettled. If we can see that they are all neutral in their nature, we can relate to even the scariest sounding thoughts with more sanity and clarity. And even when we don't or we can't in the moment, it isn't a wrong. We are always doing the best we can given our level of understanding and consciousness in the moment. Always.

It's part of the perfectly imperfect human experience. I used to think it was of prime importance to always feel good and think "positive" thoughts. If you've ever tried this, you know it's not just a lot of work—it's impossible. We couldn't monitor the seventy to ninety thousand thoughts we have each day even if we made it our life's work.

Eventually I realized that I don't need to work so hard to manage my thoughts. The scary feeling ones, the angry feeling ones, the happy feeling ones, the ones telling me to be grateful—all of them are simply clouds passing through the tapestry of my consciousness. Sometimes they create a lot of unease, sometimes they don't. Sometimes I act on them, sometimes I don't. Again, depending on my level of consciousness in the moment, I have different choices available to me regarding how to respond to my life and my own thinking.

When we see thoughts as impersonal, we perceive them more objectively as unique flavors that are part of the ingredients making up the amazing, complex meal of life. When I'm less interested in the content of my thoughts, particularly the negative-feeling ones, they tend to flow through my consciousness without inducing trauma and fear, even if the content of the thinking has a tone of trauma or fear mixed in. This allows me to be more at ease with my humanness and my experience of life.

When I'm upset, I know that I'm having upsetting thinking. Sometimes just the awareness of this—"Oh, my thoughts are stirred up"—is enough to bring me back to that place of peace that always exists in the backdrop of my mind, that space of unlimited creativity, insight and love.

I believe that this place is who we are in our essential nature. This is what that backdrop is. This is what the thoughts move *through*. I've found it interesting to discover that the more I hang out there, the less I care if I'm there or in some other thought-created emotional experience. The more I hang out in the peace, the less I care if I'm having a peaceful human experience. I'm more okay with *all* of it. Sounds contradictory, but it is true for me. Everything can be embraced as part of the beauty of being alive. I am by no means perfect at accepting whatever I am feeling in the moment, but it is the direction I am always looking in. Remembering that no matter what my current "flavor" is, it will pass, because it is not the truth of me.

This might be one of the reasons I truly love working with teenagers. Teens don't tend to be obsessed with feeling peaceful or positive all the time. They are okay with their anger and their judgment—and so am I. I never tell teens they shouldn't be so judgmental or so triggered by things. I know that no matter how angry or upset a human is, there is a peaceful presence within them that is simply observing it all. There's no hierarchy in which peace is a better experience than anger. It's all part of the fullness of what it means to be alive.

At the same time, ironically, the more okay I am with a client's feelings of anger and frustration, the more I sit with them with no judgment but with loving and kindness, the more quickly those feelings tend to melt away. And then my client is naturally lifted up out of that state and into another.

22

Hope

"There is a crack in everything. That is how the light gets in."

Leonard Cohen

One thing I have found incredibly helpful in working with someone experiencing feelings of depression or anxiety or anything that has a low-level quality to it, is to encourage them to notice the subtle shifts in their experience.

In the summer of 2019 I heard a wonderful coach and healer, Scott Kelly,[4] talk about health in a way that I had never considered before. He said many brilliant, incredibly helpful things, but the one that stuck with me is that if we pay attention to it, we will notice that not only do our moods shift constantly, but so does the state of our health and the sensations that come with it. He talked about health as if it exists on a spectrum. We are never fully sick or fully well; we simply have physical experiences that are constantly shifting. Sometimes we're aware of them, sometimes we're not, but the reality of our physical health is that it continuously changes.

---

[4] www.scottkellycoaching.com

This went in deep for me. In all of my pregnancies I had a condition called hyperemesis gravidarum. Essentially it's nonstop nausea and vomiting. For me it was debilitating at times and came with an onslaught of mental and emotional turmoil. After two pregnancies like this, I was determined not to have another. Yet listening to Scott Kelly created a feeling of possibility around perhaps someday, maybe, giving pregnancy another go. And eventually we did—after three years of absolute clarity that I would NEVER put myself through a pregnancy again, I became pregnant with my son Arrow.

During this pregnancy, I experienced the benefit of paying attention to what Scott Kelly taught. I again experienced hyperemesis gravidarum. During some of the most painful and challenging moments of my pregnancy with Arrow (my now almost-two-year-old), I had thoughts of terminating the pregnancy. Constant thoughts of it. And then a still, small voice would creep in that would say something like, "Pay attention to the subtle shifts." Or another way I would hear it, "Look for the light coming in."

And I would, and it would give me hope and patience. It reminded me that the painful experience was transient and would shift. And so would those thoughts. And it did, and they did, always. Just a little at times—and sometimes in a huge swoop of relief.

And if I hung on to hope and was on a constant lookout for the shift, the light, a window opening, it gave my mind something to do rather than fixate on my discomfort.

I can honestly say that I think that it's because of this insight—that even the physical experience is temporary and subtly shifting all the time—that Arrow is here today.

I also received very timely support from Dr. Bridget Anderson, who is an incredible N.D., as well as support from Barbara Patterson.[5]

Both of these women showed up at timely moments to remind me of what I already knew to be true—that my experience would change, and the more hope I had, the more my mind was focused on the possibility rather than the current pain, the better I felt. Literally: *the better I felt*. That is the power of hope.

It's also something that I've heard the wonderful coach and teacher, Linda Pransky[6] talk about in a really beautiful way. Simply that we have the ability to look for an insight, to look for a shift in our mood, and in doing so we are essentially helping to create it, we are shifting our focus, and thus our experience.

This is something that I frequently offer to my clients. With hope, we are shifting the quality of our experience in the moment, which could be the difference between life and death, patience and suffering.

Which is huge.

That's what hope can do.

That is what understanding how we "work" as humans, can do. To know that our experience is not fixed and that we have a home base. We have an innate state of health and wellbeing that is the nature of who and what we are. We don't need to fear for ourselves if we find ourselves out of touch with this reality.

Being out of touch with it, doesn't change the fact of it.

Being out of touch with it only impacts our experience in the moment, but it does not impact anything that is REAL. And what is

---

[5] www.healnaturalmedicine.com, www.barbarapatterson.com/
[6] www.pranskyandassociates.com

real is our constant self. It is like the blue sky that is ALWAYS there, no matter the weather. No matter how crazy and scary and wild the weather, it cannot touch the ever-present, constantly there, never harmed, never leaving, blue sky.

One way I see obvious evidence of this truth in operation is that when we get cut, our body starts to heal, immediately. Without our trying. It has a pull toward health, not the other way around. Just like our minds. There is a pull toward balance and calm. Without our effort, it is happening. We have a natural pull toward a state of balance and inner calm.

23

Client story: Ann and acne

"How beautiful to know we create
our own tragedies."

Nick Cave

One of the things I love about coaching teenagers is when I get to see a teen "wake up" to something they haven't seen before.

Not long ago I had a conversation with a client I've been working with for several months. Anne, is a fourteen-year-old girl who really thought that having acne was a problem. It wasn't super-severe acne, which I know can be a painful experience for teens. In Anne's case, the slightest blemish anywhere on her face meant that she had a *major* issue.

The acne felt so emotionally painful for her that she'd feel compelled to stay home from school. She'd say "no" to hanging out with friends and refuse to have her picture taken. During these times she completely withdrew and ended up feeling very isolated and alone. All this, she told me, she did because of her acne.

In our conversations I showed her a lot of compassion and caring.

I made sure she knew that I really understood what she was saying. And eventually I said to her, in a very loving way,

"I'm going to say something that might sound extreme. Feel free not to take it seriously and just think it's crazy. Okay?"

She nodded.

"I don't think acne is the problem."

She looked at me without comprehension and said, "But if it's not my acne, what's the problem?"

"Well," I said gently, bouncing the question back to her, "what do *you* think the problem is?"

She thought about this for a minute and responded. "It's . . . it's the way I *feel* about the acne?"

I smiled. "Yes. You're getting closer."

"I don't get it! What do you think the real problem is?"

I said again, "What do *you* think the problem is?"

"Is it that I *think* it's a problem?"

"Oh!" I said playfully. "You're sooo close!"

Then, with a little frustration in her voice, she asked, "Well, if that's not the issue, then what *is* the real issue?"

"Okay," I began, "So what we've learned is that you have acne and you don't feel good about it. And you don't feel good about it because you think it's an issue. So now you have these thoughts that don't feel good running through your head. Now, everyone's always got a lot of thoughts running through their heads. It just seems to me that you think these thoughts about your acne are *worth believing*. You think they're true and then you behave like they are true."

She sat in silence as she processed this. Then: "So my real issue is that I *believe* my thoughts about acne being a problem."

"Yes!" I said, smiling.

She smiled back and I let her sit with the realization for a long while, after which I asked, "What do you think about all that?"

Her response struck me as really beautiful. "Well," she said, "that would mean that: **I don't actually have any problems.** I just believe the thoughts I have that *tell* me I do. *That's* my only problem, if I have one at all."

We both burst out with joyful laughter. It was a beautiful moment of awakening to something new and liberating for her. It was so touching to witness.

Seeing that light go on for her was striking. I know that things like acne and feeling overweight or underweight or a host of other things can feel truly burdensome and as if they are the source of our inner experiences. Maybe it's getting a bad grade or failing a test or not getting into the right college or just waiting a long time for a table to be ready at a restaurant. All of these things can feel like real issues.

At the same time each person experiences these outer events differently, and even the same person on a different day or in a different hour might feel differently about the same event, which means that in and of themselves they are neutral. They are essentially a *no thing*—that is true for our thoughts about them as well. It's not until we mistakenly grab onto an innocent thought or judgment passing through, that we get ourselves into some difficulty.

When we start to believe the thoughts moving through our awareness and see them as truths, we're giving them a lot of power instead of simply letting them pass by. So naturally they create a ripple effect within our bodies and we feel the impact of them.

We were made to think. Thinking is a major way, or perhaps *the* way, in which we relate to our experiences and process them. But so often our thinking is faulty and survival-based, disconnected from the ultimate reality in which we are safe, in which we're unconditionally lovable and full of potential, free to re-create ourselves again and again. In that ultimate reality, nothing defines who and what we really are.

Often our thoughts don't spring from a place of Truth within us. Instead they come from an insecure place, a fearful consciousness. Some may say our egos. But all thoughts, whether they feel positive or negative, are not personal. They are part of a collective consciousness, and wherever we happen to be within our own consciousness in that moment, we tune into the debris floating by on that frequency. Sometimes we get wrapped up in it. Sometimes we see it for what it is, and no matter how rocky, we can ride the waves with some grace.

Or we don't, and either way is okay.

Either way, our divine selves are intact, unimpeded. Just like the weather—rainbows, light showers, sunshine, turbulent thunderstorms—our thoughts are varied and complex. Sometimes they're beautiful and other times painful. But they are never the truth of who we are or what the nature of reality really is.

Just as the weather passes through the backdrop of the sky above us, our thoughts pass through the true nature of who we really are. That truth is always residing in the background, and it often comes to the foreground when we see thought for what it really is: temporary debris passing through the lens of our perception. Simply seeing deeper into the very nature of thought can lessen the grip we might have on any one thought, and thus create a more relaxed inner experience.

Grabbing on to a painful thought, believing it to be true, and then thinking we need to *do* something about it—in Anne's case, not go out with her friends or be seen in photos—is like believing a scary story about a bogeyman in our closet and acting as if it's true. Acne is never the issue. Our physicality is never the issue. Long lines are never the issue. The issue is always something thought created, that we have innocently glommed onto, something that we breathe life into and then sustain with our repetitive thinking. Or we simply make a decision from that misperception. "I will not go to school until my acne is cleared up." It's innocent and misguided. Once we see that we do this, the trick becomes learning how to *stop* doing it, if we want to stop. And it's really a process of bringing more understanding to how we create our experience of life, both our inner experience and what we chose to do in our physical world. Be with friends or be alone? Hide or shine? This is what I am aiming to help my clients understand.

With Ann, this experience changed her. I have been working with her since, and she is showing up to life in a much freer way. This is the possibility with coaching. It can put someone on a completely different life trajectory.

I was able to see Ann wake up to something truly profound for herself. I want to share this as a bit of encouragement to all of you coaches out there to not hold back with teens and young adults. Give them the possibility of having a completely new relationship to themselves and life. Treat them as if they are ready for deep impact. Don't hold back. Say what you see. ***Say to them what you would say about them to your own coach.*** I have used that advice for myself SO many times. I ask myself, "What would I tell Steve about this person? What do I wish they would see, or what do I wish they knew?" That's the thing to tell your client.

If I wasn't willing to go there with Ann, if I was only there to help her work it out on the surface level, as in getting better concealer, supporting her in telling her friends she needs boundaries around photos, practicing saying positive affirmations with her, and so on, I wouldn't have been doing her a service, at all. I would have been allowing my limited ideas about what teens are able to handle to impede her waking up process. The way I see it, what if I was put in her path at this time to say the truth to her as I see it? What if that were true of all my clients, for that matter, because they are ready? They want a deeper understanding? They want to wake up more?

They want freedom, and I want to help them move in that direction.

The truth is that there is no actual stress or anxiety in the world; it's your thoughts that create these false beliefs. You can't package stress, touch it, or see it. There are only people engaged in stressful thinking.

Wayne Dyer

24

The kids are alright

"There is something deeper than this "I" thought, and all other thoughts. That is truly who I am. There is a conscious, alive, intelligent, loving beingness here in this moment, watching all these thoughts arise."

Scott Kiloby

What my heart most wants to impart to teens and parents is that they are *okay – because I really believe this*. In years of working with people in psychological settings, sitting with the most distressed and disturbed feeling humans, I have seen over and over again that the experience of *not* being okay is the temporary one. It is created by the power of our thoughts, and as we've already discussed, thoughts are fleeting and unreliable. I do know that some people can become completely overwhelmed by their thinking and ideas about themselves and life, and feel unable to shake their painful perceptions . . . until they do. That process may take an hour or a lifetime, but what I know to be true is that wellness dwells within all of us. It is often just waiting to be seen, felt and acknowledged for what it is.

So when I am working with parents I help them see and feel the okay-ness of their teens in several ways. One of my favorite experiences is when a parent calls me because they're concerned about their child, and then in the course of our initial conversation they start to see that their worries about their child are simply a reflection of their own state of mind.

Oftentimes parents look at their child through the lens of their own low mood or distorted reality. They build up their child's transient mood into something catastrophic rather than simply noticing that their child is behaving perfectly natural for a human being. We all ride a variety of emotions throughout the day/week/year depending on the content of our thinking or what mood we might find ourselves in. What I seek to do with parents and teens is help them see that their mood or emotional state isn't a true reflection of who they are. I help them see their low moods for what they are: temporary experiences.

Moods are like the weather. Inevitable and varied. While some storms seem very scary, unpredictable, irrational, dark and gloomy, they are not actually indicating anything about the human being experiencing them. Similarly, emotions of all types ebb and flow, often irrespective of anything to do with us or the circumstances we're in.

I also know very well how nice it is for people to be present to their own well-being and to have thoughts that are uplifting—to experience "sunny days" as much as possible. But that's simply not required for experiencing a happy and fulfilling life. I know that when my son goes into tantrum mode, all I want is for him to return to balance. But at the same time I also know that he is sitting in well-being and mental health even when he's having a tantrum. There is nothing I need to do in that moment to fix him.

I could *add* to the energy of his tantrum by getting really worked up, yelling at him, shaming him, putting him in time-out. Or, similarly, I could force him to take deep breaths or meditate to teach him to regulate his own emotional state. But all of these activities on my part—even the ones that seem positive—are often attempts to bring peace to *myself, to ease my own worries about his well-being.* If he is having a tantrum, he's simply being present to his own experience and not having a lot of thoughts about it. With toddlers and teenagers, this is often why their emotional experience is so full on. They are not judging it as wrong. They are simply in it. Allowing it.

If Arrow asked me, "Hey mom, can you help me re-balance when I start to freak out?" of course I would offer him support and some ideas about how to be more comfortable. However any "advice" or help I would offer him would be prefaced by a conversation where I do my best to impart to him in two-year-old speak that even when he is in a big emotion, **he is safe**. Even when he is feeling anger, he is okay, and there is truly nothing wrong with him. I wouldn't want him to take helpful strategies for avoiding and shortening a tantrum to be misunderstood. To think that it's wrong to have huge feelings or that, even worse, there is something wrong with them.

In her book, *My Stroke of Insight,* Jill Bolt Taylor talks about this beautifully. I am going to butcher it, but essentially she says that any emotional experience simply left alone will pass through in about ninety seconds. That's how quickly the rebalancing mechanism operates within our own being. When we start intervening with our thoughts and emotions—investigating them, digging deeper, looking for their roots— we often simply add time to the ninety seconds it would normally take that emotion to naturally and completely pass through us

I know that as a parent it can be tricky—not to mention heart-wrenching—to stand by and watch your child experience painful emotions passing through. At the same time, we can take comfort in knowing that their experience is not an indication of mental instability, or even that they need coaching or counseling. In fact, allowing teens to pass through this kind of experience can help them realize for themselves the true nature of emotions. Simply seeing teens as perfectly healthy and well-functioning as they go through these very human experiences can bring a sense of peace to the whole process for both parent and teen. Helping them understand a bit more where emotions come from can also lead to a lessening of fear and concern.

Teens often find it very relaxing when I tell them that it's perfectly normal and natural to have a variety of emotions throughout each and every day. I ask them to start to pay attention to this truth. To begin to notice the changes and how often their moods shift, often without any trying or problem solving. When they start to see the shifts and see how reliable it is that we do indeed shift, fear lessens. They see the health and the helpfulness that is built into their system.

When teens and parents see this a little more, the pressure can be taken off the need to always be up and happy in order to feel safe and okay. The fear can begin to lessen around those moments that feel hard and painful.

We are made to think, and our thoughts are varied in their intensity and their content, and we feel our thoughts. I share with them that the less they identify with or take as guidance or truth each and every thought and/or emotional state, the quicker they move through those thoughts and states, and the quicker they return to their state of well-being—or rather to their *awareness* of that state.

Because in truth that well-being is always there. We are always, alright. And so are the kids.

Your heart knows the way.
Run in that direction.

Rumi

25

Flexibility and peace of mind

One of the biggest conversations I have with anxious, stressed-out and worried teens is around flexibility. Not in their bodies—although that helps—but in terms of their own thinking. When I look deeply into what the true source of their anxiety and stress is, I usually find that they're clinging to ideas about their lives that *feel* real—but aren't necessarily so.

Ideas like, "If I don't get a certain GPA then I won't make it into the school I want to go to. And if I don't make it into that school then I won't have a chance at getting a good job. If I don't get a good job then I won't be successful or happy." Many of these teens can't imagine veering away from the straight line to which they've committed themselves. Because of this, when unexpected things *do* come up—such as a bad grade or a real gut desire to go in a different direction than they originally planned—they tend to feel that their lives are crashing down around them.

This line of thinking, or some variation of it, is often the underlying reason for procrastination, for not wanting to go to school, for skipping classes, for turning things in late, and so on. If you think that a mistake on a homework assignment or test might have catastrophic repercussions, you'll feel an overwhelming pressure to "get it right" when faced with even the smallest tasks.

So as I work with teens to open up, to begin to question the thoughts that feel so rigid and confining, they tend to relax and become more engaged and productive. The pressure is released, at least a little bit. I do this in many different ways, but always with the same intention: to help them see beyond their limited ideas about what leads to success, fulfillment and being respected by their parents and peers.

Often, I will share my own story of attending college for two years, dropping out, and then going back a few years later when I knew what I wanted to study. I graduated with my bachelor's degree when I was twenty-three and my masters when I was twenty-five. I also love sharing stories about people who tend to be incredibly happy and fulfilled in life, and then point out that they took a variety of paths to get where they are today. There are so many amazing examples of people who allow themselves to step off of their "expected" path and then find themselves in a place of true delight and living a life that has heart and meaning for them.

In the same way I often talk with teens about the people who most inspire them. The people they love to be around. As we consider their lives, we almost always find that it's those people who didn't conform to any specific set of ideas about how to succeed in life. They truly walked to the beat of their own drum.

In *Grit: The Power of Passion*, psychologist Angela Duckworth shares details of a study following the lives and careers of successful, happy people. To be brief about it, essentially the researchers found that all of these people shared a core, common experience.[7] It wasn't graduating high school, attending a four-year college or even obtaining another advanced degree. In fact most of them didn't have advanced degrees at all. What they all had in common was that they faced a lot of adversity. Poverty growing up, neglect, abuse, moving from one state to another, financial hardship, and so on. Most of them fell to the middle of the pack in whatever educational system they were in. The quality that they all had in common was *grit*. No matter the grade they got or the circumstances in which they found themselves, they kept moving toward the things that made them feel alive and inspired. They embodied passion and perseverance. They kept pressing forward. **They didn't think that low grades or other setbacks meant something catastrophic for their future.** They knew that they were the ones who would create their own satisfying, fulfilling lives.

They were flexible in their thinking. And being flexible in this way means we understand that our outcomes and circumstances don't determine our fate in life. Setbacks can provide opportunities to re-evaluate, redirect, refocus and come up with new ways of thinking, to create new pathways and possibilities to experience happiness and success on our own terms.

So when I'm working with a teenager who is full of anxieties, I look into how rigid their thoughts are about how they imagine their lives need to go for them to be happy and to get where they want to go. I help them see that their happiness doesn't depend on having a specific trajectory, a single pathway in life that will only lead to

---

[7] Angela Duckworth, Grit the Power of Passion 2016

success if they don't get a bad grade or have a change of heart. I help them create a place of flexibility and curiosity within their own consciousness about what is coming forward for them.

I have similar though not identical conversations with parents. For example, if I'm talking with a parent about how to best support their teen getting homework assignments in on time, I'll often ask questions about their expectations for their kids. What path do *they* want their teen to follow? I try to find out if they feel a flexibility within themselves that helps them hold an open, spacious space for their teen. What if their teen feels it's important to take a year off between high school and college? Or to study online, travel for a year, or go to a junior college instead of an Ivy League school? Go to a school out of state rather than one close to home? What if at age seventeen their teen wants to devote their energy to pursuing a music career or inspired business idea?

I have read extensively about unschooling. This approach to life and to relating to school-aged humans has helped me open up my own mind to how we learn, why we learn and why we don't, and how to question our typical ideas of success and progress, among many other things. It's been a personal area of interest of mine, one that has helped me support the parents in my practice in thinking outside the box in terms of supporting their teens, and in how to trust their teens' wisdom and unique path in life, even more.

Sometimes there is flexibility within the parents and their thinking, and sometimes there's not. I understand this. I have children myself, and even though they are currently quite young, I know what it's like to want them to hit certain developmental markers, not only for their own health, but as a way for me to feel like I'm doing a good job as a parent. This feeling within myself serves as a constant reminder that their path might look wildly different from my own hopes and expectations. Their happy lives might be connected to them doing something I've never even considered. (And I also know that their experience of happiness is an inside job regardless of the circumstances of their lives.)

A statement hangs on the wall in our house: "We are so flexible." This doesn't apply simply to the possibility that our day-to-day plans will change. It's a reminder for my husband and me that the more curious we are about who our sons are and what would really serve them, the more we drop our ideas about who we *think* they are and how they *should* be—and the more harmony we experience within ourselves and in our relationships with them.

We want them to go to school if it feeds their souls and their intellects. We want them to homeschool or even unschool if that feels more inspiring and uplifting. We want them to play sports if their bodies love doing so. We want them to learn computer coding if that's what energizes them. We want to hold space for them to drop out of school at fifteen and take a year to study basket weaving if that's what they're feeling called to do.

I know even as I write this that I'll get attached to certain ideas and plans as they grow up. It will be a practice of continuing to let them go, all in service to creating flexibility within our lives for my sons to be who they are (including their moods in the moment). Such a practice will also allow me and my husband to live a very rich and satisfying life right here, right now, staying present with who *we* are.

The statement on our wall also serves as a reminder that when things don't go our way, we are okay. Nothing real is lost. Our happiness is not dependent on anything outside of ourselves falling into place. In fact, when things don't go to plan and we get ruffled by it, it serves as a wonderful reminder to reel it all back in and remember the truth about where happiness, contentment and fulfillment really come from: within.

Our school system can be of tremendous service to our teens—particularly those who resonate with its specific, daily rhythm of learning and the social interactions that go hand-in-hand with it. For other kids, however, school can be a very painful and unhealthy environment, especially if they tend to learn at a different pace or are more introverted. Even if it's just that their natural biological rhythms keep them awake later and require them to sleep in longer in the morning—school is simply not a one-size-fits-all affair.

I recall thinking when I was in high school that if I could do it my way I wouldn't get to school until third period. That's when my natural energy kicked in and I felt receptive and open. I knew I wasn't alone in this. I longed for a school day that went from 10:00 a.m. to 5:00 p.m. In my case, the normal school schedule was something I could overcome, something to push through even though it wasn't ideal for me. But for many students it can be downright debilitating. In such cases I think it is wonderful for a family to really come together and creatively brainstorm ways to focus on well-being over anything else and see what creative possibilities might emerge. Even when everyone cannot get on the same page around goals and expectations, I've found that creative solutions can appear and improve things.

Very little in life is one-size-fits-all, even though we may have many voices in our lives directing us to follow well-worn, "sure" paths to success. The truth is that when we allow for greater flexibility in our thinking, we create space for our inner wisdom to guide us in the direction of what will truly fulfill us and be in alignment with our nature.

26

It was *just* my imagination running away with me

"Worry is the misuse of imagination."

Dan Zadra

I feel like I could write a second book around this topic. Twice as long and even more dense.

I say that because this is an area that I have looked at extensively for myself. Do we need to monitor our thinking? Is it just our imagination, or deep trauma rearing its head? Is it better to have positive thoughts? Are negative thoughts really an issue? Do we need to investigate the root of our thinking? Especially our repetitive thinking?

A few years ago, Dhiraj and I were sitting on our deck talking. I asked him a question that was a little bizarre—but not really, given that our conversations are usually bizarre and a bit whimsical. I said, "Hey, I wonder what I would know to be true about myself, my soul, my heart, the way humans work, if I used only my lived experience as a way of gathering that information. If I let go of everything I've learned through spiritual psychology and the three principles, through

116

countless books and programs. What if I could only look at what I know to be true through my actual experience . . . I wonder what I would really know?"

In classic Dhiraj fashion, he just looked at me and nodded and created some space for me to wonder. As we were sitting in silence, what popped out of my mouth was, "I *do* know something! I know that when I'm worrying I don't feel good and when I'm not worrying, I feel better. And I know that worrying is always future-based, made up . . . assuming that I know what is going to happen and assuming that it's going to be bad. I know that when I don't do that, when I stay more curious, more positive about potential outcomes or future scenarios, I feel better right here and right now. I think that might be all I know to be true at the moment."

When I reflect deeper on this, there are a couple other things that I also know to be true, but this one is a life-changer for me. It's an absolute life-changer. When I have the wherewithal to know, to wake up to the fact, that I am only feeling my thinking in the moment—and if my thinking is full of worry, I'm not doing myself any favors—when I can wake up to this, I can stop. Sometimes immediately, sometimes slowly. I can change my mind. I can see it was just my imagination running away with me.

Sometimes it helps to work with my imagination. I don't see it as ultimately necessary but in certain situations and at different levels of understanding it can help. I'm doing this right now with my five-year-old. If his mind insists on imagining a monster in the closet, why not put the monster in a funny hat, on roller-skates, holding a bunch of balloons? When he does this, he laughs and he feels less afraid. So why not use the gift of imagination in our favor, when we can?

Sometimes we can't and we're really lost in thinking. And that's okay, because nothing real is damaged. No real harm is done, except we feel bad in the moment, which again isn't in and of itself a problem. But when we can wake up to our choice and we feel our free will I do think we can work with our imagination, and sometimes it is helpful. It is freeing and creates a more enjoyable moment right here and right now. For my son to know this and for him to be able to do this for himself, means far less fear, more laughter, more carefree trips to his bedroom by himself to grab his clothes or his blanket. It means him being less gripped by made-up monsters, spending less time clinging to my leg as we inch our way into the bedroom to grab one of his beloved stuffies. It's life-changing.

Why not use our imagination in our favor if we are going to use it at all?

27

All about goals

I am not a coach who fixates on concrete goals.

In fact, the last thing I really want is to be an accountability coach. I know a lot of coaches work this way with teenagers, helping remind them of things they have to do, checking in with them about how those things are going, and giving them feedback when they don't meet their mark. There can be a lot of specific conversations around valuing commitments, structuring their time, improving their grades, and meeting the kinds of responsibilities every human being has to meet. I know this kind of coaching can serve people.

At the same time, I don't tend to do any of that on a regular basis. Yet my clients often meet their goals, or exceed them. Now, as coaches, it's almost a given that we will support our clients with goals in one way or another. And when I start talking with a new client, one of the first things that comes out of my mouth is often something along the lines of, "What do you want? Why are you here? What do you want to create or experience more of?"

My big-picture intention in asking these questions is to understand more about the person I am talking to in order to serve them as well as I can in that first session and in every one that follows. Sometimes our conversation turns to goals, and sometimes it goes in other directions. But for me, it's not about the past or the future. It's about right here and right now. It's about being present with my client in the moment. In an initial conversation, I might ask, "What would make this conversation meaningful for you?" or, "What would you really like to talk about?" And then we dive in. We talk about what's on their mind that day. We talk about their life and how they're feeling in their life. We talk about their understanding of their state of mind and how experience comes to life through them. There might be things they want to change, so we talk about those things. Right then.

So in terms of goal-setting, I am always open to talking about future-based goals, and when goals come up, I first want to check in to see if the goal in question is something that is truly heartfelt. Sometimes it's just not, and this introduces an entirely new challenge in terms of accomplishing it. For example, I know what it's like to set a goal when I'm in an insecure place in my mind. Let's say I'm worried about money for one reason or another, so I set some lofty financial goal. It's possible that my goal has nothing to do with what I really want and instead everything to do with trying to ease my financial anxiety in the moment. What might then happen as I start taking steps towards my goal is that I might find myself making choices that aren't in alignment with it, because *I* am not in alignment with it. It is a made-up solution to a made-up problem. I wonder how many of our goals might fit that category? In such cases, instead of staying fixated on the goal, I start moving away from it, which is actually a good thing, especially when I realize where I was within myself when I set the goal.

When clients find themselves in this situation, or when they're procrastinating or saying things like, "I don't know how," I slow everything down. I encourage them to get curious. I'll ask, "Is this what you really want? Are you still in alignment with this goal?" Because so often we set something in motion and then just go on autopilot from there, not realizing we no longer want what we initially set out to achieve. And as I share in the next chapter, I'm a big fan of "quitting"—in the sense that I think it's perfectly acceptable that our lives and goals keep updating as our self-awareness and self-understanding update. So sometimes it makes sense to "quit"—to let go of ideas, goals, and beliefs that are no longer serving us so we can create space to say YES to what is.

If a client really wants to set a goal, I will, from my natural curiosity, tend to check in with them about it in our sessions as time goes on. But I will also let them know that it's ultimately up to them to bring it into our conversations if it's something they want support with. This is one of the ways in which my approach is different from that of an "accountability" coach. I am not going to make a goal a primary focus of a session unless that's something the teen wants to do. I am going to trust my clients to bring up what matters most to them. If we go three months without talking about a goal they once shared with me, I might mention it—but more from a perspective of curiosity. As in, "Is this thing still important to you? How is it going? Would it be helpful if we talked about it a bit?"

I love sharing a concept I learned in one of Steve Chandler's audio programs called "Want To Versus How To." In that program, Steve points out that when someone is really clear about what they want, how to achieve it becomes very obvious.

In one session I had with Steve as my coach I shared that I wanted to put together a workshop for parents. It had been on my mind for months and months, and I finally brought it up with him. I told him I'd been thinking about it and writing content for it, but I just wasn't following through and actually doing it.

All he said to me was, "Aila, when you really want to, you'll do it."

I did not love his comment—at first. It felt like he was being easy on me and letting me off the hook.

But then I really felt into it and realized it was honest and true. It wasn't that I was lazy or unmotivated. It wasn't that I lacked commitment and focus. (All things I was judging myself on.) I have seen myself move mountains to create things I wanted. I have jumped into the unknown, doing impromptu speeches at holistic art fairs, at twenty-one starting and running a successful pet-care company with no business experience, moving to L.A. when I didn't know anyone there. I have done things even though they felt scary and overwhelming—and I've done them when I really wanted to. The thing with the program I was thinking of creating for parents was that it seemed like a good idea, like it could be helpful and of service . . . but there was not a lot of energy behind it. I didn't have a zest for it. Consequently I was procrastinating around putting it together.

The reason was plain and simple: I just didn't want to do it enough.

Procrastination around our goals, at times, can simply be an indication that something we think we want doesn't have much energy or "life" to it. We don't desire it as much as we desire something else.

Maybe there's a "competing intention." For example, let's say someone wants better grades and knows this means they need to study more. This might require them to wake up earlier in the morning, but they can't ever seem to do that. What's going on? It just might be true that they have another—much stronger—intention to get more rest. One obvious suggestion would be that they go to bed earlier. But for 99 percent of the teens I work with, it's not watching YouTube or Netflix that keeps them up late. Rather it's all the time involved in homework, athletic training, tutoring, part-time jobs, extracurricular activities, and so on. And even if it were Netflix or YouTube, that might be the one time in their day where they get to decide what to do; they get to let their mind relax and settle and integrate everything that happened during the day. It might be the one time they can chill out. In this sense, the inclination to relax might be something that ultimately keeps them in a state of higher mental wellness.

When I'm coaching someone around this, I don't necessarily see it as my role to clarify those competing intentions and help them drop the "lesser" one in order to align with what they really want. Rather, I simply want to call it out and discuss it. Because in this context, wanting—but not immediately achieving—better grades isn't always connected to a lack of motivation. Instead it can often be tied back to something in a teen's life having more of a pull over something else. Simply bringing this to light can help a teen feel into a helpful way forward. They have a wisdom that will bubble up when they are given some space to reflect, see what is really going on, and slow down within themselves.

Let's say a teen has a goal that is relatively straightforward, such as: "I'd like to get an 'A' on a test." In our session we'll talk about how they need to show up and do what they can to give themselves the best possible shot at getting that "A." I'll ask them about what they think they need to do. Study more? Wake up earlier to get quiet time to themselves? Curtail activities with friends for a week, or schedule study sessions with them? And we'll explore whether what they think they need to do is different from what they're currently doing.

We'll also look very deeply at the truth that whether or not they get an "A," their life can be happy and fulfilling and successful. I don't say this to "let them off the hook," but rather to put their minds at ease. Every high-performing athlete knows it's when our minds are at ease and we're in a relaxed state that we perform at our best. So when my clients want to do well on a test or give a powerful speech, I almost always go into a spiel about the fact that no matter how it goes, their lovability cannot be changed. Their respectability, their worthiness of love and support, are intact, regardless of their performance or outcomes.

The way I see it is that it's a shift in consciousness, a shift in our state of mind that makes behavioral changes happen. It's not so much about setting the alarm for an hour earlier. It's about being in that clear state of mind that gives you a feeling of optimism when it comes to taking steps toward a goal or dream or desire—whenever you happen to wake up. It's about being clear on the reasons you want to accomplish or experience something.

So my hope in each and every session is that I meet my client in a space of love and support, and that I help them lift up within themselves. From this space the challenges they're working with become much clearer, as do the steps they can take toward any goal they set for themselves.

Another note I'd like to add on to this whole topic of goals and goal setting is this: so often goals are used as something that we hold against ourselves. But since we're making up all the goals that we set, why don't we make them fun? Why don't we make them work for us instead of against us?

I love approaching goals from that perspective. Knowing that we can play with them, we can step in and out of them, we can experiment. We truly never know what something is going to be like until we start being in action toward it. Sometimes we realize that that action is not what we thought it was going to be.

None of us knows how long we're going to be on the Earth, and I doubt that anybody on their deathbed looked back on a life they begrudgingly led and said, "Well at least I followed through on my goals, even though they weren't right for me. At least I stuck with it, even though it sucked out my soul. At least I wasn't a quitter!"

Why not instead live a life you love, follow your heart, move on from things that aren't right for you, listen to your wisdom, appreciate yourself as you are, right now, slow down . . . and soak it all up, all that is here, right now?

28

I love quitting things

"In the end, only three things matter: how much you loved,
how gently you lived, and how gracefully you
let go of things not meant for you."

Buddha

Books that drain my energy. Jobs that suck out my soul. Projects that I started to please someone else. Relationships that are no longer healthy. Personal or spiritual growth programs that feel out of alignment.

Giving myself permission to quit has given me a lot of permission to dive into the unknown. To take risks. To follow my intuition or a playful nudge, fully knowing it might not go according to plan *and* that I am free to course correct if needed.

One of the biggest sources of anxiety I've seen in teenagers and young adults is their fear of making the wrong decision.

I didn't quite understand this fear at first, because I didn't grow up with a powerful attachment to following things through. I was encouraged to get in over my head. To do really hard things, knowing that I might not do them well and that I might even decide to stop at some point. I know that in many circles—especially in coaching—sticking with something you start is synonymous with being a kick-ass human. And there's a really beautiful intention behind teaching young people how to keep going when things get tough. I want my kids to learn how to do that too.

But I also want to send a message that feels a bit more supportive, one that acknowledges that sometimes we find ourselves on a path that seemed like a good idea at first, but which no longer feels like a fit. That's when the idea of getting brownie points for seeing things through no matter what doesn't make sense to me. I want my kids and the teens I work with to stick with things that feel right, that are aligned with them, that light them up, that they know are important to them, even if it's hard, even when it gets rough. I want them to know how to stay with things that truly matter to them.

But I also want them to learn the art of letting go of the things that don't.

29

Client story: Robert

When quitting means staying alive

One of the teens that I had the privilege of supporting was feeling suicidal. In fact, he attempted suicide and survived, three days before I met him. He was so worried about picking the wrong school, so worried that he wasn't going to make the right choice and that it would ruin his life going forward. Through our conversation I learned that for him quitting wasn't an option. In his family, once you'd started something, come hell or high water you'd finish it. So he was paralyzed with indecision. In one of our sessions, while visibly trembling, he asked me, "How can I know I'm making the right choice?"

I said to him with a lot of love and a big smile on my face, "You *can't* know! You're not at the school yet!"

It seemed obvious, but it came as a kind of revelation to him. He started laughing—and he laughed for a long time.

The observation really resonated with him. He knew that it was true. It's actually *impossible* to know ahead of time if what he's moving into is truly going to feel like a fit. But that didn't keep him from trying to know and working himself into a panic in the process. And, in fact, it's not the "not knowing what will happen" part that is the issue. It is assuming that if it is not the right decision that it's just something that he'll have to suck up and try to live with. That idea was the real issue. That was the thing that was paralyzing him and creating a huge feeling of overwhelm and panic within.

He and I both realized that his parents might not change their ideas about what it meant to stick with something you start, but within himself he found his own freedom to know he could choose a different way forward if it turned out that his college choice was completely out of alignment. He found a place of inner power and strength that came from knowing that no matter what his parents or anyone else had to say on the matter, he was willing to trust his intuition and his *lived* experience. He was free to quit if quitting meant staying alive.

And in his case it truly did.

He was so intelligent, so creative, so filled with beauty—but absolutely terrified of taking the next step for fear that if things felt wrong he'd just have to stick it out forever. The pressure of that felt too much to deal with, and he would've rather died than make the wrong decision. But when we took away those consequences of being trapped in a situation that turned out to be wrong for him, he immediately felt lighter, freer, more optimistic. He even started opening up to seeing that there are also other choices he could make if he wasn't enjoying his school experience. He could try new classes, join different clubs, live on campus or off campus. His creativity and his inner resources started waking up in him as he relaxed a bit within himself.

We all know what it's like to have a gut feeling that something's not right for us. An inner knowing that says not to get into the car with a friend of a friend. A nagging feeling that someone isn't being entirely honest with us. Our intuition offers supportive nudges, impulses that propel us toward a place to live or a class to take, or that tell us to go left instead of right when we're lost.

It is so freeing and beautiful when a teenager has the awareness that they have intuitive hits and gut feelings all the time, and that they are free to decide to move out of their current situation and into a different one if everything within them is calling them to do so.

These ideas often come up with some of the teens I work with when they're considering dating. Many of them don't even want to go on a first date for fear that someday down the road it might lead to a situation—whether it's about having sex or moving in together or breaking up—in which they won't have the courage to change directions if that's what feels right. This is such a huge topic of conversation between my clients and me, and it often leads to my asking them questions like:

"Are you willing to listen to yourself, at your deepest level, even if it means disappointing others and letting go of time and possibly money that you've invested in a certain path?"

"Are you willing to be labeled a quitter in order to have a truly meaningful and fulfilling life?"

In addition to teens, I've also coached many entrepreneurs, business owners and fellow coaches over the years. For them, too, this idea is often the magic elixir for allowing forward motion. Knowing that none of us is locked into a specific business model, niche, offering, price point or program structure is very liberating. We can acknowledge that it's very human to *want* to know how things will turn out, but we usually *can't* know. Sometimes what we think we want doesn't feel good once we get it. Sometimes we realize that the path we're on isn't taking us where we want to go. But we can't always know this in advance. In fact, our minds aren't designed to work that way. Trying to know the future and control the future is a misuse of our intellect. In my experience, it only creates suffering, stress and worry.

From my perspective, the very best I can do for myself is to make best guesses about what will be the right choice—and then adjust accordingly as I get more information. Life is a process of learning, and it is a beautiful thing to allow that learning to take place and create positive change in our lives. If that means quitting sometimes, I am okay with that.

There is merit in learning how to make wherever you are a beautiful experience, especially if you truly are stuck there—in fact, there is absolute freedom in truly knowing that we all have the peace and happiness we long for, right here, within ourselves, right now. We often try to find it by shuffling around our outer circumstances. I think it's wonderful to understand on a very deep level that it is here now, regardless of our life circumstances and even the thoughts we have. We can feel a peace that transcends it all, that holds it all.

There are several organizations focused on healing work that go into prisons and do work with the inmates, many of whom are there for life. The healing and the freedom that so many of them experience is truly inspiring and beautiful. It's right along the lines of the work that Viktor Frankl brought into the world through his work and in particular his beautiful book, *Man's Search for Meaning*. If you don't know of him and his work, look him up and dive in. For me, it's been life-changing and enhancing to take to heart his experience and wisdom.

And most of us are not stuck in our circumstances. We have the ability to move about in our lives in ways that serve us when we feel called to shift. We are here to create. To share, express, serve, and experience a full range of feelings and life events. We have something called an entelechy, that is unique to each of us. As I heard it shared at the University of Santa Monica, "the entelechy of an acorn is to become an oak tree. The entelechy of a human is not only to awaken but to be who we came here to be—our unique selves."

We all have qualities, traits, interests that are part of our nature. The things we were doing when we were five years old, when we would lose track of time and beg to be allowed to keep doing them until the sun went down. We don't "try" for them—they are just part of us.

For example, I love inspiring conversation about the nature of our souls, and my brother would rather eat roadkill. In fact, he'd rather create roadkill, going ninety miles an hour on his motorcycle, winding aggressively up and down our mountain roads. I, on the other hand, have been known to jump mid-flight out of cars that he has been driving before picking up too much speed.

In my mind, we are all MADE so differently. With little say in the matter. Why not let yourself move toward those things that naturally bring you to life, rather than the ones that scare the life right out of you? Why don't we let ourselves sing if we feel called to sing, paint if painting brings us alive, and quickly get off of a path that we mistakenly hopped onto before we knew better?

30

Life's curveballs

I have another personal story I like to share with my teen clients, because it was a turning point for me in terms of my own understanding around what we are equipped with as humans, and it comes up naturally in discussions about how to move through perceived failure or how to navigate curveballs that life might toss our way.

I played basketball starting in seventh grade, and because I lived in a very small town and went to a school that had thirty kids, I came off pretty well. I played on an A.A.U. (Amateur Athletic Union) club team and on my high school team, so I played year-round. I loved it. I wanted to play in the WNBA. When I was fifteen, I traveled to Australia and was able to play against a professional team, and even then I did fairly well. In fact, I did so well that I thought if I couldn't play in the WNBA I would move to Australia to keep playing.

Then, two weeks before I turned seventeen, I severed my ACL. This caused my skill level to drop by about 50 percent. My right knee hurt all the time, and before long so did my left knee. I ended up having four surgeries over the next two years. I went to Whittier College and played basketball there for a year, only to be in constant pain.

All of a sudden I had to course correct my entire vision for my life. At times I felt completely devastated, and at other times I had clarity that nothing was lost and that my life could be just as happy, just as fulfilling as I wanted it to be.

I decided to end my basketball career when I was twenty, shortly after my fourth surgery. This was so painful for me. It was literally like giving up a dream. Giving up a vision for my life and stepping into the complete unknown. Walking away from playing basketball every day was the hardest part. I loved the effort, the discipline, the connection to the other athletes. All of it.

There have been many incredible gifts in this experience, several I didn't see until years later. One of the most significant things about having my life change, was that I realized that none of us are locked into a set path, and if we deviate from a path we're on, it doesn't mean something is wrong. I see that I had the gift of thinking that basketball was my only path in life. I would play until I couldn't and then coach basketball until I couldn't. It was going to be ALL about basketball and it was comforting to think this way. It felt good and safe.

Having that option pulled away from under my feet gave me the opportunity to see that there are MANY things that bring me a sense of satisfaction and joy. There are many ways of engaging in life that light me up. And beyond all of that, I got to see that basketball was not my source of happiness. It was not—and nothing else outside of me would be. I was and am the source. Meaning, it comes from within me and through me, and can spill out to anything I might decide to do. But one thing I saw for sure it that it's not what we *do* that bring us happiness or fulfillment. Certainly there are things that are more interesting and in alignment with our values and natural interests, but within the range of what that is for each of us, I know there are literally dozens or more options for all of us. And in truth, the good feeling that comes with doing work we tell ourselves we love comes from within. I know many people who are doing work they say they love who are also essentially miserable or depressed most of the time. The work isn't the issue. It's not the source of the suffering *or* of the joy. And again, I will emphasize that I know it is so exciting to move toward work that feels in alignment AND I also know that if one door closes, there will be and are MANY, MANY other ways of serving and showing up in life that can be just as juicy and satisfying.

When I share this with young people, it typically does something for them. It takes the pressure off. It puts them into a more at-ease space and also tends to get them more curious about this whole business of happiness coming from within. And when we get to dive into that level of conversation, it's a very good day at the office.

Another big revelation I had related to basketball came in for me about eight years after I quit playing. I realized I hadn't stopped playing because of my injuries, something that I wholeheartedly believed, but because at the time I wasn't able to **accept** my new (decreased) skill level. Yes I was in pain, but if I would have simply slowed down to move at a pace my body could handle, I could have continued competing. I wasn't able to embrace the joy I had for playing at just any old level. I thought I had to be the best—or at least a whole heck of a lot better—in order for me to justify playing. What a painful, misguided idea I was holding onto.

When I realized this I immediately joined an adult women's rec team.

It was so fun! Yes, I was *so* slow. And I almost vomited after the first three minutes of running up and down the court. But I loved it so much. My husband watched me play and I felt the same thrill with him sitting alone in the stands in a huge, empty gym that I'd felt with a packed, standing-room-only gym when I played as a teenager.

Those feelings of exhilaration and joy—the love of the game— were in me all along, and they had nothing to do with my level of skill. My satisfaction had everything to do with where I was placing my attention. The more I focused on the feeling of being present to the ball in my hands and the women on the court with me, the more uplifted I felt.

This experience was a wake-up call for me in a lot of ways. It showed me that my feelings of fulfillment playing basketball really had very little to do with my skill, my fitness level, winning or losing, and making or missing the shot, but everything to do with what I was focusing on and what I was allowing to bubble up within myself.

My being a superstar for a minute as a high school athlete and then a complete "failure" in college didn't have to define the choices I could make in my life. If anything, the experience of my life plans shifting illuminated new paths to explore, and directed me on a path of inner healing and self-realization. The same usually holds true for my teen clients and the challenges they face when twists and turns become a part of life.

I also see many athletes and performers decide to quit because they are not the best in the group, perhaps after recovering from an injury or after joining a new, more advanced team. When I see someone in my practice is dealing with this, I love to get into it with them. I love telling them that even today, as a successful professional coach, I had to let it be okay that I might fall middle of the pack in terms of my success and skill level for several years, and maybe forever, in order to give myself permission to move into the profession. I even named my coaching school, Coaching Well. Not Coaching Masterfully, Not Coaching Brilliantly, but Coaching Well. There is a double meaning in there in that I see my work as helping coaches connect to their own innate wellbeing *and* serve their clients well. But it is was also a name choice to stand in support of myself, doing what I love, regardless of my status, so to speak. Regardless of my accomplishments. I absolutely want to help coaches and I pour my heart into my work, but more than that, I want to continue to be an example to the teens and children in my world, to do what feels so good to do, whether you are the best at it or not.

So many of us think that we need to be the best or not do the thing at all. I am all about encouraging myself and my clients to go do the thing they feel *called* to do, that brings them alive, that wakes them up with a pep in their step, even if they are the worst on the court or middle of the pack in terms of skill. Perhaps this mindset comes along with the territory of participating in our current traditional school systems that openly and emphatically reward students for receiving "good" grades.

I shared my experiences around this topic with one my teen clients a year ago and it was so soothing for her, as she loves to sing but always compared herself to her mom, who is a professional singer. My client is sixteen and had never sung for people, but she would constantly be singing in the shower and while she drove to and from school. Singing was her thing, but she always put herself down whenever she talked about her ability. I brought all of this up to her more than once, and I was able to see the light bulb go off for her, that **what matters is her experience within herself** while she sings, how she feels as she is singing—this is what matters and what she should base her decision to stop or keep going on. NOT what other people have to say or think about it. She heard this on a deep level. I know she heard it because ever since then she has been singing every chance she gets. She sings in the choir at school, she sings in her band, she sings at cafes, on YouTube, in the shower and in the car.

31

Coaching athletes

As I shared, I was an athlete, and I made a point of seeking out athletes to work with. Not everyone who works with teens needs to be an athlete, obviously. But as there seems to be a really high percentage of teens who do participate in sports and it's an area in which I have a lot of experience, I thought it might be useful to share some of the ways I help teens and young adults in this area. I've had the privilege of coaching high school, college and Olympic athletes across a variety of sports.

Playing sports was the thing that brought me the most joy in life and also one of the things that evoked the most pain and suffering within me. I bring all of this past experience into my work with athletes.

There are many ways that I offer support her, but the thing I see that makes the biggest impact is something I like to playfully call Confidence 2.0.

When I was sixteen I played on a team that traveled internationally. While we were in Australia, my team and I were deep into the playoffs in a tournament. We were playing one of the tougher teams and doing well. Prior to going to this event I had stood at the free-throw line for hours and hours on end practicing my routine and free throw. Now that I think of it, twenty-plus years later, I remember that routine like the back of my hand. I definitely put in, well, maybe not 10,000 hours, but I was working my way there. So here I was at this tournament and my team was down by one point with ten seconds to go. I was given the ball near half court, and as I started to bring the ball up the court I was fouled. The other team was really distraught as I made my way to the free-throw line with one second on the clock. I was having a great game, scoring many of our points. As I got to the stripe and did my tried and true routine, all confidence left my body. I felt the strength drain out of me. I felt the fear that if I didn't make this shot, I wouldn't have a future. I wouldn't be considered a viable athlete for any of the college recruiters to seriously consider. The stands were crowded, and within those stands were several people whom I wanted to impress, including college recruiters from all over the world. So as I stood there with the game literally on the line, the ten seconds I had to take the shot slowly winding down, I did my best to chuck the ball up toward the basket. Miraculously, it went in. We were tied.

I thought that would give me some confidence in my next attempt but literally the same thing happened. It was nice to know that we at least had a chance to go into overtime to win the game but it was also heavy considering that I could end it right there, and we would win if I made the free-throw. I tried to remember all the times I had made free throws. I did some visualization. I did some deep breathing. I practiced some gratitude simply for being there. I did all the things I knew to do, and yet when I went to take my next shot, it literally didn't even make it to the net, it fell about a foot short—I airballed. Anybody in the basketball world knows what that looks and feels like. When I look at that experience, I realize I was trying desperately to ensure that the outcome would go in my favor. The slowed-down breathing, the visualization, all the things that matter—but none of which ultimately made up for the concern I had about how I would treat myself if I didn't make the shot. We went into overtime and ended up losing by three, which knocked us out of the tournament.

This was a really pivotal experience for me as it highlighted the fact that there was nothing physical or mental that I could do to guarantee an outcome. I thought that with enough mental and physical preparation, there *was* some guarantee, up till that moment. Yet instead of feeling deflating, it actually felt freeing. I saw that the pressure to guarantee an outcome was me trying to avoid an experience that doesn't need to be avoided: the disappointment. The letdown. The tears. The sadness. It doesn't need to be avoided at all costs. I didn't know that then, but the realization of this slowly started to sink in.

When an athlete can see that there is value to practice, both mentally and physically, all of those skills matter and make a difference in the moment—all of them. No time is wasted when you're spending hours and hours in the gym or hours and hours with a mental skills coach doing visualizations, affirmations, gratitude practices, and so on.

However, what I started to see is that it sure is a lot of effort to try to avoid feeling like a failure, to avoid feeling disappointment or sadness. Now, I know sometimes it's simply a matter of doing the thing (visualization, mantras, etc.) in order to be the best you can at the thing, which is awesome. Which is why time spent practicing skills can be truly meaningful and supportive. But as a professional coach it's typically the players who are struggling in a significant way who come across my path. They're not taking it all as light and fun and joyful. They're not rolling with the punches. There is a lot of fear involved. It's life and death and high stakes. So Confidence 2.0 is acknowledging that no matter how much experience or practice I have, I might miss the shot in the moment. And every athlete knows this. Every athlete knows that it doesn't matter how many times you practice your serve or your cut shot—at some point it just might not work. So Confidence 2.0 is understanding that no matter how the outcome goes, you are going to be okay. Even with a tidal wave of disappointment or sadness, it can't destroy or harm you, and in knowing that, you're not going to let it take you down for too long or completely detour you on your path. You're going to stay in the game. You're going to stay buoyant and resilient. You're ideally not going to beat yourself up on the three-hour drive home. You're going to bring in some compassion, you're going to see it all for what it is: an outcome that means nothing about who you are, your value, how respected you are, what your future will look like, and so on.

When I'm working with an athlete now I do my best to remind them that participating in their sport is optional. It's a complete choice. In fact, maybe they don't want to actually do it at all? Sometimes I bring that up in a playful way just to really bring the point home that it is not life and death. That even if they don't get picked up from one college they might get picked up from another. It's helping them have eyes to see that even though they may want to win and perform their very best, the chances are they will do that when they're in a lighter state of mind, able to access the flow, feeling free and unburdened. I don't need to reference the hundreds of books that talk about the value of this. But they're out there, all pointing athletes back to the reality that being serious and stressed while playing often does not lead to the results that you really want. I find it especially fascinating to work with people who are very dedicated to inner practices while playing—visualization, deep breathing, etc.—and I think all of these practices are incredibly supportive . . . until they're not. Until they become the thing that an athlete does because they are afraid of losing. Often these practices can add a whole extra layer of pressure, as they did for me when I air-balled that free-throw.

To resolve that fear eliminates so much of the extra work that many athletes do to simply stay open. I find it especially ironic when I'm coaching an athlete who says things like, "I started to get really tight on the court, and then I started to do my breathing techniques, but those weren't working, so I got even tighter and tighter, so I tried some gratitude and that wasn't working, so I thought I must really be screwed here." What I see in this is an opportunity for my client to consider the possibility that getting tight is a part of the playing field. That feeling insecure is a part of the process. Because we are human beings who have thousands of thoughts passing through our awareness every day (and even every hour), our emotional state is going to fluctuate if we find ourselves particularly interested in one of those scary thoughts. The more we see our experience for what it is—fluctuating, fluid, changing moment to moment to moment—we can rest and ride through a difficult, tight-feeling moment, knowing that a new experience will be here shortly, even during a game or match.

My work with athletes has gotten more and more effective over the years the more I've pointed them in this direction and away from all of the rituals and practices. It's more about a deeper understanding of how humans operate that leads them to know what to do in the moment during competition or practice. It's an understanding that our bodies move in a freer and more skillful way when we're mentally less "gripped," when we are open to and not afraid of the variety of emotions that will inevitable flow through us without demanding that we always be in the flow state, and when we know that the outcome of a game or performance is not life or death, it's not going to affect who we are, how loved we are, and what we can create in our future.

Another thing that I find to be tremendously helpful is reminding athletes of the power of having a beginner's mindset. The moment they put themselves into the box of professional, collegiate or high-performance athlete, they tend to pile on a load of expectations as well. Of course they do tend to perform consistently well over time. But I always want to remind athletes that treating themselves like beginners, always open to learning, open to enhancing their form or technique, willing to make small tweaks even if it causes a down-tick in their performance for a short while—all of that helps them stay buoyant when performance dips.

I always recommend the book *Mastery* by George Leonard to clients who are also athletes. It's great for everyone, but the way he illustrates the learning process and the path of mastery offers an incredibly helpful perspective when athletes find themselves with the yips or some other sort of setback, whether through injury or otherwise.

It is also how I treat myself as a coach. It is true that I have a full coaching practice, and at the same time I'm always looking for ways to make a deeper impact with my clients, ways to become more present in my life and thus with my clients, ways to feel more at ease, to be more gentle on myself when a communication comes off the wrong way or when I don't perceive I've made as big of an impact as I could have. All of these instances, in my mind, are opportunities for learning and growth, rather than an indication that there's something wrong with my performance. Having a learning mindset versus a right wrong/good bad one when it comes to performance is very helpful. It's wonderful to have an athlete ask herself, "What can I learn from that loss? Or, what will help me improve?" rather than experiencing an onslaught of deprecating self-talk. This increases bounce-back, helps athletes stay in the game longer, and creates resiliency in the moment.

I find this to be especially helpful in parenting as well—for example, to get to say to my five-year-old when I spill my coffee or mistakenly put his dad's underwear on him, "I'm still learning!" Instead of beating myself up in front of him we get to laugh about a funny moment.

He gets to see me model humility and gentleness as a way of being with myself. This is also a great conversation to have with parents as well who have high-performing kids. Teens with performance anxiety can experience so much healing and support through watching their parents take the pressure off of themselves in a very ordinary, day-to-day kind of way.

32

Client story

Quinn and sex

"Speak the truth, even if your voice shakes."

Maggie Kuhn

A couple years ago I worked with a seventeen-year-old girl named Quinn. Quinn was struggling with a dilemma about whether or not to have sex with her partner. Many of the "normal" fears and motivations teens experience around this issue were present: what if I decide not to and he's upset about it? Is it too soon for me? What if I do it and regret it? Is he really someone I want to sleep with?

Our exploration went deep, and it led to a number of revealing conversations and email exchanges, with both of us sharing personal experiences and thoughts. Quinn—like many of my teen clients— appreciated that I could open myself up to her, that it wasn't just a one-way street of exploration. Maybe hearing my stories at times helped a little to normalize her own life experiences. As I've mentioned elsewhere, my goal is not to put myself on a pedestal, but to connect with my client and help them bring out their own natural wisdom. So when it makes sense, I am happy to offer parts of my own story if I think it will help my client.

At one point Quinn asked me via email to share more of my own journey toward being more honest about what I want and don't want. Below is my response:

> For as long as I can remember I've always wanted to bring the light and the love and the joy everywhere I go. Unless, of course, it was during a basketball game. Then I wanted to bring the heat, the pain, the intensity!
>
> In general, I always wanted to be the bearer of great news and warmth and sunshine and rainbow kisses. In my teens and early twenties I used to say, "I have no preference," when asked by friends or family what I wanted to eat, what movie I wanted to go to, etc.
>
> The truth is that in general I usually didn't have a strong preference. The even *truer* truth is that if I *did* have a strong preference, I would still likely choose to say that I didn't. I thought I was being a peacemaker and a very spiritually evolved person by not creating upset or conflict anywhere I went. (I have nothing but mountains of love for that younger yet misguided part of me.)
>
> In the past several years, as I've been coaching teenagers, I keep seeing the same pattern emerge over and over again, where my clients are struggling with knowing and accepting what they truly want and are afraid of upsetting other people if they share their desires with them. Whether it's a choice about what college to apply for, whether or not to quit a sport that their parents have paid

big money for them to play, to say yes or no to a date, to having sex, to what to do on a Friday night, etc.

It's a huge thing—simply getting clear about and communicating to other people what you truly want. Territory I know all too well.

In the past ten years, I have looked at this within myself and discovered a major flaw in the thinking that led me down the path of withholding my honest desires, or even of simply being honest about what my experience with something was.

Being honest, being true to yourself, can be as simple as saying, "No I didn't like that movie" or, "I was actually scared out of my mind when I went on that roller coaster! I nearly passed out!" (Who cares if my "rollercoaster" was the teapots at Disneyland?)

Speaking in this way is just simple, honest self-expression. But for some reason it was terrifying to let it slip out of my mouth.

I even realized that no matter how challenging my life felt to me at the moment, I would try to find the silver lining and *only* communicate about that, rather than bringing up the dark, scary, petrifying cloud that was also a big part of my experience.

The flaw in my thinking—and I see it in my clients' thinking as well—is this idea that I am *responsible*, and even the *creator* of other people's emotional experiences.

That's a *big* misconception. And to take it just a little deeper: I believed that *I* was good or bad based on what others were feeling around me.

If I brought a happy story to them, I brought them

148

happiness. I was good.

If I had bad news, I brought them sadness. I was bad.

Of course, I couldn't be more wrong. This might seem like what happens in reality, but it's definitely not the full story. If it were, we'd all be screwed. We'd all be victims with no power to choose how we feel or experience our lives. Thankfully this is not the case.

I've told you about my baby, Rowan, who, in 2013 died during childbirth. In the weeks and months and now years that followed her death, I have had ample opportunity to know the truth that we are not responsible for how others feel.

In the beginning, just after she had passed, whenever I was asked about whether I had kids, I would hesitate. Do I say "yes" and share her story? Or do I say "no" and pretend that she wasn't the most AMAZING, IMPACTFUL, LIFE-CHANGING EXPERIENCE OF MY LIFE?

What I found myself typically doing would be to silently size up the person asking the question, determine what kind of emotional capacity I thought they had, whether or not they were in therapy or had a good support system, and then say "yes" or "no" accordingly.

The truth is, typically when I said "no" my response was coming from that younger, misguided place inside of me. I was misunderstanding my own power. I was believing that if I shared about Rowan's life I would be, once again, the bearer of bad news and was, in fact, bad. I would create a negative emotion within the other person. Even if I chose to also share the millions of silver linings about my baby—when someone has just learned about a baby passing away, at times it can be hard to take regardless of any positives.

Now that I'm pregnant again [which I was at the time I wrote the email] I get asked all the time, "Is this your first baby?" Now I know that for the sake of my own well-being I can decide how to answer questions like that based on what *I* want to do. Do I want to invite a complete stranger into my inner world at that moment? Or not? Sometimes it's healthier and simpler for me to make interactions with other people as short as possible.

What I've learned time and again is that I truly *don't* have the power to *make* anyone feel anything. That's a big realization and one that is not comfortable. Because when you think about it in this way, you realize that **no one else has that power over you** either. I'm responsible for my inner reaction and response. I'm the only one who can impact the way I relate to my own thinking and feeling. I get to interpret every piece of information that comes my way and decide how I think about it, and if thoughts come in at warp speed, without my input, then it becomes true that I am the only one who can decide how I react or respond to those thoughts. How I think about the experience, or my thoughts themselves, determines my emotional response.

The same is true for other people and their reactions to me—or rather to their thoughts about me and my story. If this weren't the case we would all be victims of each other. If someone told us a sad story we'd have no choice but to cry. If it was a funny story we couldn't help but laugh, even if we weren't in the mood.

But of course that's not the case. We aren't at the mercy

of other people in this way. And I know this now more than ever.

When I share my story about Rowan with some people, they well up with love and compassion. For others it ignites tremendous pain and suffering.. And the same person might react differently to the same story if told it at a different moment in their day, depending on their state of mind.

But if my story were really the *cause* of people's emotions, everyone would be affected by it in the same way. In reality, different people have different thoughts about it and thus create different inner experiences for themselves.

In the same way, as much as I want to control the way they think about me, my life and my stories, I can't. Believe me. I've tried. That is *their* responsibility, their opportunity for growth, their choice—whether they know it or not.

Quinn, I know this is a bit heady, but if you can feel into the message behind my words, I want to encourage you to feel into this for yourself. To play with the possibility that listening to yourself, your desires, your needs will be much easier, if you take the impending doom off the table. If you let yourself get curious about what might happen, rather than pretending you know. It can be so scary to speak your truth, but it's a more meaningful way to live and it leads to incredible intimacy with those in your life. He will be better for knowing the truth. You will be better off for having shared it, whatever it is.

I know you are trying to make this decision, and it will become much clearer for you if you can set down the negative future fantasies and simply acknowledge what is true for you—and communicate in whatever way you can.

Quinn—to complete this massive email!—here's a quote I just love:

"Speak the truth, even if your voice shakes."

~Maggie Kuhn

When I work on this concept with clients, it naturally leads to them feeling freer in their lives. They learn to honor themselves more as they understand they can choose how they want to connect to the people in their lives. They can make choices based on their inner knowing and intuition, regardless of whether someone else may create a negative story inside themselves about it and feel angry, hurt, or disappointed. It can be very liberating for my clients—for all of us—to know we are not the cause of anyone else's upset.

They also get to live in the mystery more. They don't have to pretend that they know how someone will respond to them and what they're about to say or do. Even more, they don't have to try to figure it out ahead of time—something that can be quite stressful if they feel a lot is hanging on what they decide.

This doesn't mean that my teen clients are abandoning consideration for other people's feelings. There are times when it might be inappropriate to bring up a certain topic, or when there are more effective ways of expressing oneself. But all too often people learn to suppress their own needs out of fear of upsetting someone else, and that usually doesn't serve anyone. In fact, I've learned that people can be surprising—they often welcome honesty and openness. It even prompts *them* to be more honest in expressing themselves.

Many teens I get to work with learn to know that they are free to say "no" to sex, knowing that doing so may embarrass or empower their partner, depending on how their partner interprets the "no."

They are also free to say "yes" to the college they truly want to attend, even though it may be three thousand miles away from their family, and even though their decision might "create" sadness in their parents. Of course, it might just as easily inspire their parents to travel more. The parents are responsible for their own reactions.

In short, the teens I work with are learning how to live in a way that is in alignment with them knowing and trusting themselves and their inner guidance. Sharing this concept with my teen clients and feeling the liberation it creates in them is a powerful and uplifting experience.

33

Client story

Tiffany and procrastination

I was recently in a coaching conversation with Tiffany, a fifteen-year-old client, around her resistance to turning in homework assignments on time. This was something she'd been struggling with since the fifth grade. It was a major source of stress between her and her parents: she felt they badgered and pressured her constantly about it, and in response she had a lot of anger towards them. Both sides were exhausted by the constant battles around the issue.

As Tiffany and I talked, we began digging deeper into what this experience was like for her. What did she feel stood in the way of her turning in her assignments on time? She wasn't sure herself. Did she naturally procrastinate? Was she finding the work too hard? Was she overwhelmed with the number of assignments she was dealing with?

Together, we slowed down and got curious. Tiffany remembered that in the fourth grade she was frequently called out as one of the smartest students in her class. She won several reading and arithmetic awards that year. She also, as it turned out, simultaneously lost two of her best friends because they were jealous about her academic

154

achievements. In fact, she was mocked by the friends she loved every time she was publicly acknowledged for her academic success.

Now she was struggling as a sophomore. She didn't understand why she couldn't get herself to commit to a study schedule or simply turn in a paper on time. She was late with everything.

Her parents had initially sought out coaching for her to help her be more disciplined and set up a better schedule for herself. But as Tiffany and I continued to talk, it became clear that she was already *incredibly* disciplined—at procrastinating and distracting herself. In fact, given her intelligence it was hard work to make sure she didn't stand out in school. She was doing a great job at failing and making sure she was never bullied again. *This* was her motivation. By not turning in assignments on time, in her mind she was protecting herself from losing friends and being publicly humiliated. And she was succeeding at it, but at the cost of doing her best in school.

In this sense, she was actually kicking butt at supporting herself emotionally. She was winning at keeping friends she loved. She was excelling at being a heart-centered human being.

The truth was that life for her at that moment wasn't about grades; it was about connection and friendship. The conclusion she had drawn from her fourth-grade experience led to an approach to life that had actually helped her get and keep what she really cared about: friendship.

So the work Tiffany and I did together was around letting go of her respect of the thought that if she did well academically she'd automatically lose her friends. Once this idea was questioned and brought out into the open, she began to relax and open up to new possibilities. She soon saw that "friends" and "good grades" weren't mutually exclusive. She could have both. She could achieve her academic goals and also maintain strong, meaningful friendships.

We spent quite a bit of time discussing this, really clarifying new choices she could make and new behaviors that she could test out in her life. Our discussions touched on many different aspects of what academic success meant to her, and why it was important to her. We talked about the truth that there are teens who have fulfilling friendships *and* good grades. Especially with human beings who have an emotional intelligence beyond that of a fourth grader. Friends and good grades are not impossible to experience at the same time. They are something she could create. This meant talking about practical steps she could take to move toward what she wanted, including creating the kind of schedule that would serve her academically, as well as making time to support her relationships and personal well-being.

Within a few weeks of our working together in this area, Tiffany developed a simple and productive mode of studying and getting assignments in on time. It was a process for her. She had some old habits to break but she stayed on the path. Best of all, she still has her friends. In fact, she's enjoying those relationships more now that she's no longer worried her friends will abandon her if she starts to shine in school.

Procrastination or skipping school, turning assignments in late— that kind of behavior is almost always connected to something much deeper than the simple labels that gets stuck onto kids: lazy, slackers, unmotivated, etc. And as a coach it can be tricky to have all sorts of great life hacks to share with them about how to "fix" those behaviors and have them show up session after session, making no visible effort to implement them or change. But if we can look a little deeper as coaches, we can see that fixing the behavior often doesn't solve the reason they are doing the behavior. The actual fix, isn't about learning how to show up on time. They know how to do that. The actual solution is looking for the wisdom operating within them, to see how the behavior is serving them. What the payoffs are for them (and they might be invisible at first). It's about slowing down enough to really see how the behavior is helping them in some way. It's about being in a non-judgmental frame of mind as a coach, assuming your client is doing something from their wisdom and looking for ways to help them understand themselves more and see new possibilities for themselves.

34

Client story: Angela and rage

A bout two weeks ago I had a coaching session with Angela, a sixteen-year-old girl who isn't originally from the U.S. Over the previous few months she had been dealing with a lot of rejection and discrimination from people in her life, including those whom she thought were her friends. So when she came to me she was feeling angry, full of rage, hurt, and lost. She wanted to do something significant, something rash, something that would empower her, in order to reclaim a sense of being in control of her life.

It made sense to me that without taking some time to reflect and heal, the kinds of experiences she was having could lead people to seek vindication or payback. Fortunately a relative directed her onto a path of healing and self-reflection, and to Angela's credit, she followed it.

One of the biggest sources of pain in Angela's life, she told me, involved a boy she'd had a crush on years before. You probably remember what it was like when you first had a crush. For most of us it's a rush of powerful emotions that we don't know what to do with because it's our first time experiencing them. This boy had been Angela's first crush and was someone she'd allowed herself to be vulnerable with. Unfortunately, he had publicly rejected her.

I'm familiar with the pain of rejection and unrequited love, as no doubt most of us are. I don't know what it's like to have those feelings mixed in with being treated as if I don't belong, but I do know a bit about the process of healing. I know that healing from loss from tragedy, from heartbreak, from deep sadness and regret can happen, and I understand the value in being proactive in this healing process if there is a lot of suffering going on, and trusting in our system's natural pull toward balance to support us along the way.

When I look at the world, so much of the pain and violence going on makes me wonder if it's all related to—and fueled by—deep, overwhelming pain. My sense is that much if not all of it is. My hope is that helping myself and others to heal and look toward our resiliency and wellness is my own small way of standing for and cultivating a more peaceful world. I hope that doesn't sound grandiose, because it's not intended to. Rather, it's just an honest and humble acknowledgment that there is pain and suffering within humans in the world, and that all of us can contribute to healing. The more of us who can facilitate this kind of inner freedom for ourselves and others—especially young people—the better off our world will be.

In Angela's case, during our sessions as we began to slow things down and together looked at where her pain was truly coming from—her painful thinking, her judgments of herself and others—I got to see her bring immense compassion and kindness to herself as she began to let go of her respect for the ideas about herself and others that were painful . . . I watched her reclaim some of her own power to stand for herself and for her own worthiness and lovability. I supported her in finding actions to take—such as inviting her friends out and asking her new crush to the movies—that would help her demonstrate how capable she was of leading a life she truly loved, no matter what setbacks, rejections, or low, scary moods came her way.

Part of that process for her was beginning to acknowledge that at times people's behavior toward others is not great. It is not always kind or compassionate. But instead of making this mean something is wrong with *us*, we can see that if someone is seeking to hurt someone else, they themselves are likely in some pain,. At the very least, they are out of touch with their natural sense of well-being and compassion for themselves and others. This is something that can be SO liberating for teens to see—to stop taking other people's poor behavior personally, and to start seeing that it has everything to do with the state of mind of the other person, and not them.

As we continued working together, Angela shared with me that when she'd first come to see me she'd felt like all was lost and afraid for herself. But now she understood that she had a big, bright future ahead of her, mostly because she was choosing to support herself when she felt rejected, to reaffirm within herself her worthiness when other people appeared to question it.

One of the mantras I had her work with is something I first heard as a teen from Dr. Wayne Dyer: "What other people think of me is none of my business." (And something I like to add on: "When I am feeling down, what *I* think of me is none of my business.")

This is a concept we can all take to heart. It's not an easy one to lean into, but it's well worth trying on for size. At the very least when we stop worrying so much about what others think of us, we can quickly release many of the unhelpful thoughts that keep us from feeling compassion and support toward ourselves. If we are willing to drop our concerns around other people's perceptions and appreciate that how they see us in the moment is a reflection of where they are at within themselves, we can take all opinions and reactions from others with a grain of salt.

35

Bullying

Bullying is tough. It's a painful experience. Many of us have been on one side or the other of bullying, teasing and feeling better than or less than.

When one of my clients is dealing with the experience of being bullied, I often share something that happened to me when I was younger.

I was always a bit outspoken in what I chose to wear. I'd often find myself in skirts over pants and tie-dyed shirts and bandanas. I shaved my head, dyed my hair every color you could think of, and was always experimenting with my external appearance. Coming from a teeny-tiny town, this caused me to stand out every now and again. When I was in sixth grade I got a Dr. Seuss hat—one of those really tall ones—and also a hat that looked like a beret. I really wanted to wear the Dr. Seuss hat but I settled on wearing the beret to school as it was a little more discreet. Not ten minutes after arriving, a much older kid grabbed it off the top of my head, called me a stupid weirdo and hid it somewhere in the school. All day she said insulting things about my appearance and told me she was doing me a favor by hiding my hat.

I felt really pissed and frustrated and also, of course, sad. Even at that age, I loved supporting people in doing what they wanted, being different and dancing to the beat of their own drum. So although I was sad, I also felt somewhere deep inside that I wasn't wrong. I was being myself, and it wasn't always easy.

I was a bit afraid of this teenager; it wasn't the first time she had picked on me. She was intimidating and had a very hard edge to her.

So although a part of me wanted to tell on her or yell at her or fight back, I was afraid to. I really, truly thought she would likely try to beat me up and I'd have to physically defend myself, which I would. And even at that young age, I believed in a nonviolent approach to life.

She never did return my hat, and on my way home, walking to the school bus, I saw her in the parking lot with her mom. She handed her mom what was likely her report card, and immediately her mom started calling her an idiot, a disappointment, and stupid.

My heart literally dropped. I felt compassion for her. I could really see that that age-old saying was true, at least in this case: "Hurt people hurt people." Or what makes more sense to me, "Hurting people hurt people."

I don't say this to dismiss anybody's abusive or destructive behavior, especially towards others, but it does give some perspective. So often the behavior that makes sense to us is behavior that we've experienced or become accustomed to.

I do think the motivation behind bullying or being harsh, abusive, critical, is complex and can point to many influencing factors. And one thing really makes sense to me: my behavior is not always kind or loving when I am not feeling kind or loving within myself. I did witness abusive behavior from adults in my world growing up, when those adults were in a state of overwhelm and stress. When they were in a more open and relaxed state, the same childlike behavior that set them off one day was totally overlooked the next.

What I really saw in this was that 'bad' behavior is not in and of itself the issue. The thing that we're actually seeing in the moment is somebody's state of mind and their relationship to it.

When I know I'm in a low state of mind, I know very well not to problem-solve an important issue with my husband. If I do try, we will no doubt end up arguing in some way. When I'm in a low state of mind I know that it's not a great time to think about my business. If I do anyway, without fail I start to worry and to make business decisions that reflect that worry.

When teens are in a stressed state of mind and they can notice it, they can do some damage control. They can decide to take a walk, to talk about it with someone helpful, to do some rebalancing rather than lashing out or sending text messages or Snapchats.

This is one of the biggest things that I discuss with teenagers. The importance of understanding their own state of mind and that of those around them. This gives them some leverage in how to support themselves when they're out of balance.

Understanding that others can experience a low state of mind as well gives them some perspective on what could otherwise look like really personally offensive behavior.

Our state of mind changes rapidly, often throughout the day. Some people talk about this in terms of "moods." We have lower moods—such as depression, anger, sadness, fear—while in between there are inner experiences such as contentment and equanimity. And then, of course, moods that feel lighter, such as joy and love and creativity.

This realization really flies in the face of what so many teenagers like to do, which is label themselves an "angry person" or a "depressed person" or a joyful person." Of course, someone labeling themselves a joyful person is wonderful, and something I would happily honor and encourage, however I think it's also nice for them to know that it's perfectly healthy and natural to move through a variety of emotions every day. So if they find themselves in a less than joyful state, it doesn't mean anything about them other than that they are simply having less than joyful thoughts, consciously or not, that are creating their experience in the moment.

And perhaps even more accurately, they are worrying about those thoughts, or not worrying about those thoughts, to greater and lesser degrees.

When I'm talking to a teenager like this I'll often use the example of me and my husband driving in my car with my dog, Oliver. Some days when we took Oliver to the park and he started whining and barking in excitement as we approached the park, we would laugh and appreciate his exuberance and the intense volume of his joy. Other days on the way to the park, Oliver would do the exact same thing, but for no good reason I would find myself shushing him and feeling annoyed and irritated by his beautiful, strong barking voice.

Oliver didn't change, but my experience of him was night and day.

Something that became so clear to me is that the only variable was my state of mind.

At the time I may have been fixated on my worried thinking about moving our home to the mountains in Northern California, or whether or not we would have childcare for our kids, and instead of being in a relaxed, more present state of mind, I was tense and agitated.

This had nothing to do with Oliver—and I certainly hope he understood that on a deep level every time I snapped at him to "Shhhhh!"

I also know that there are times when I have thoughts come through my mind that say things like, "What if I can't figure out how to have good enough internet to work at home (now that we live in the mountains)," and I get all stirred up and really worried about it. The thoughts start piling on: "I won't be able to nurse Arrow as much as I need to, I won't be able to work as much as I want, what if I can't be a great mom and a professional coach running my own business?"

In this state, I walk down from my office after a spotty Internet coaching session and pick up my son, who is stretching out his chubby infant arms to me, and as he's smiling into my face, my brow is ruffled and I am worrying about whether I'll be able to see him as much as I want to if I don't figure out this Internet situation. I'm actually missing the present-time experience of him in the moment worrying about missing him in a future moment. Crazy, I know! But something I have experienced time and time again.

And then there are times I have a thought like that go through my mind (wondering about my internet) where it's lighter and it feels less pressing. Certainly something I want to handle, but it comes into my system and I hear it and I see it and I feel it for a moment—and then I can relax around it, knowing that I will figure it out. That a solution will come forward and I don't need to fixate on it. In fact, that is a sure way to keep any creative, inspired ideas from coming in— fixating on a problem. So I relax. I walk down from my office, I pick up Arrow and look him in his smiling face and smile back and sit down with him and peacefully let him gnaw away on my finger as his new teeth come in.

Same situation, same thought about the internet, different experience—depending on my state of mind.

For me the most important thing here is to not punish myself when I am in a funk but to be gentle and aware of where I'm at. Again, to limit the damage to my relationships but to also let it be a gentler experience for myself. It doesn't feel good to be contracted or worried. It is often painful. Adding judgment to that situation simply doesn't make sense to me anymore.

Going back to my experience as a pre-teen with my goofy hat . . . Again, this is not about condoning behavior like that of the teen who took my hat, but it does give me a helpful perspective when it comes to this kind of acting out. Even though I was the target of that girl's negative remarks and bullying, it really had nothing to do with me. Not personally, anyway. She was in pain. She was likely fifteen or sixteen at the time, likely wanting to have freedom to express herself in her own unique way, likely wanting to know that she was lovable no matter her grades or her performance, and none of that was being reflected back to her from her parents.

It is so often not about the person who is the target of the bullying. And one of the most painful things I see that comes from bullying is that the person receiving it believes that there is something wrong with them, that they should behave differently to avoid being bullied, that they are wrong in some way, that they should tread lightly or change who they are. And that's simply not supportive or even on-track in terms of the reality of what's happening.

The person doing the bullying will find literally *anything* and *anyone* to pick on. Regardless of whether the person receiving the bullying is being authentically themselves or trying to fit in, it may still happen.

Another topic that often becomes part of coaching conversations around bullying is that of diffusing tactics. We talk about the idea that if a fist has nothing to land on, it doesn't actually hurt anyone. It's like when someone goes to fist bump you but instead you turn your hand flat into a high-five position. In reality it could look something like this, "Hey, Aila, your hat is really stupid!" And I reply: "Yeah I know. Just seeing what it's like to look stupid! I think I'm succeeding."

Sometimes comedy and self-effacement can be highly effective in completely diffusing a highly charged situation. When I brainstorm this with my clients, we usually come up with some pretty fun comebacks that may seem self-critical, but which are actually acts of self-empowerment. These teens are learning how to respond with intention rather than reacting out of fear or anger.

The other thing that often comes up when I hear about one of my clients being bullied is that I want them to know I'll do something about it—that they don't need to go through it alone, and that if someone is bullying them, not just for their own safety but for the safety of others, that person should be supported by being reported in some way.

Even seeing a deeper perspective, seeing that the person doing the bullying is often in pain, it doesn't mean that we don't do something about it. So often for someone who's going through life bringing a lot of harsh words and criticism to others, the wake-up call comes when they are called out and supported in dealing with their own pain, and in understanding a bit more about how their mental-emotional system works. For some people it's a real epiphany to realize that we don't need to act on every thought that we have. That our thoughts are not instruction guides. At best they are suggestions, and depending on how low our state of mind is, it may be better to simply leave them alone.

This can be a delicate topic depending on the clients' willingness to be transparent about it to parents and teachers. But it's something that feels so important to me—that my clients know they are not alone, that they don't need to go through it alone, and that it's really not okay to be bullied. I like to model and demonstrate what a healthy, supportive relationship looks like. That means telling them the truth, having their back and calling out unhealthy behavior when I see it.

36

Social anxiety

Many teens I work with have social anxiety, especially when it comes to meeting new people.

When I support a teen who's having trouble connecting with new people there are a couple ways it tends to go. In our coaching work, we might initially talk about things like what is thought and what is reality. We'll talk about the truth that we feel our thinking and often miss out on what is actually occurring between ourselves and others. Once we dive into this a bit and start to tease apart what's really happening within them, we'll often shift to focusing on the truth about them as a unique human being. We'll look at how deepening their appreciation for themselves, for the value that they bring to the people in their lives, the beautiful qualities that pour out of them—all of that good stuff—how noticing this about themselves can be helpful when it comes to social situations.

The other element I love to throw out there to them is around being more curious. This may sound like it's out of left field to them, which is actually a great thing! Teens love weird ideas.

First of all, when they're around new people, the truth is that the fear of rejection is so strong they often never consider whether or not they are actually *enjoying* their connection with the new person. They are often trying to be impressive, and so they have a lot of themselves on their mind—which is never helpful. Getting curious takes their attention off of themselves and puts it onto the other person, and that automatically creates more ease inside.

So their "curiosity" mindset going into these new relationships is "Let me ask a bunch of questions of the people I'm around. Let me see what it feels like to be around them. Let me take the focus off of myself and put it onto those I am with. Let me get less self-centered and more 'others' focused. Let me try to learn about these people by getting curious about who they are, noticing what I notice about *them*, how they feel to me, how they respond to my engagement—and see what that's like."

I've practiced this for many years. I have come to really enjoy the true bliss and relaxation of having less of myself on my mind, because this allows me to be more focused on better understanding the people around me. I am able to be more present and to enjoy my experience of simply connecting and gathering data, so to speak.

So I share this with the teens I work with. I say, "See what it's like to take your attention off yourself and put it onto others, not only as a way of feeling better in the moment, but as a way of knowing if the people you're connecting with are people that you actually want to connect with. Sometimes we're so focused on ourselves, on our own anxiety about embarrassing ourselves, that we don't realize we might not even enjoy the person we're trying to connect with."

This is a process and a practice, but for many of the teens I've worked with, it's been really helpful in moving through social anxiety and the fear of not making friends. It's also supported them in making meaningful connections.

This is also my recommendation for new coaches who are experiencing anxiety around initial sessions. When you first start out working with clients (and, of course, even beyond that), the more attention you have on the prospective client, the more questions you ask, the deeper you go, the more helpful you can be. Less self-conscious, more in-service. And the more you can feel into whether or not you actually enjoy working with them. You are in fact interviewing them as much as they are interviewing you.

37

Get yourself off your mind

This idea sounded crazy the first time I heard Barb Patterson talk about it. "Get yourself off your mind"? Wasn't I suppose to fixate on myself? To think about myself until I was blue in the face, to make sure I was dotting my "i's" and crossing my "t's" and everything in between?

When I slowed down to feel into this invitation I saw the beauty and the magic in it. It felt like true bliss. The kind of bliss where you become one with everything. Where there is no more "I"—just a "being-ness." Just what is.

When I really looked at this for myself, I noticed that "getting myself off my mind" was something I was actually very practiced at. I do it naturally with my kids and clients, and with my husband more often than not. It happens when I dance and play, when I'm meeting new people or old friends, and when I'm curious about and focusing on the other.

It's often when I feel I have a life issue to solve that the opposite thing happens: I get very ME-centered, which is never a good feeling!

This is something I absolutely love to talk with teens about. There is a true relief that comes when they shift their attention from themselves—as in, "How am I doing? What am I feeling? What am I thinking? Am I on track? Am I off-track? Should I be doing more? Should I be hanging out with my friends more? Does my boyfriend really like me? What are we going to do during the summer? Are we going to stay together when I go away to college? Are my parents mad at me? How do I get out of this problem I'm in?"

And on. And on. And on.

This kind of mental rumination is so typical, and so exhausting. Some of the teens I work with have about a thousand thoughts about themselves that feel really intense and overwhelming before 7:00 a.m. Of course I know it *can* be helpful to reflect on life and the circumstances we're in, to create space and time for considering next steps. But most of the time when I see my teens thinking really hard about their lives, they're not actually looking for solutions; they are, in fact, simply worrying.

I invite teens to consider the possibility that when they feel like they're in a state of worry or fear they can see it as guidance to take their hand off the stove, so to speak. To give themselves a mental break and shift their focus to something else: friends and family, doing random acts of kindness, creating something for the fun of it, exercising, reading something uplifting . . . Anything that diverts attention from their thinking about themselves is actually an act of kindness *toward* themselves—and quite possibly the quickest way to solve any problem.

This process also points them towards the understanding that our best ideas often come when we are not thinking about anything important. They come when we are doing something mundane or methodical, like taking a shower. Why is that? I even joke with my husband at times when I'm really fixated on an issue: "I need a shower right now!" He knows it's a sign that I'm caught up in a tizzy within my own consciousness, that I'm looking for relief, for an insight and a good idea and, yes—I might just find it in the shower.

It can also be found gardening or cooking or running or driving or playing. Why? Because when we're not trying so hard, when we relax in our thinking, our minds settle down, and what is actually beneath all that thinking is a wellspring of wisdom. Wisdom that transcends our intellect and our problem-solving abilities. It's the source of those ideas that come out of left field.

This is an ongoing practice for me—letting go of really serious, intense thinking, ruminating, problem-solving, and instead doing something that gives my mind an opportunity to actually help me. This is a process of surrendering what I think I know and dropping into the unknown. I can do this standing in one place, while in line at the grocery store or in the kitchen cooking food while my kids run around my legs. It's something that happens within us, so our outer circumstances don't matter in the slightest.

But if all else fails, and if your shower is anything like mine, it tends to be the most consistent, tried-and-true space for absolute genius to flow through.

38

It's urgent!

Hands-down, one of the biggest topics of conversation I have with teenagers is around things that feel urgent. Whether it's getting homework in, texting back a friend, going to a party, telling someone how they feel, checking their social media status . . . all the way to things like being in a moment in a group of friends where a decision feels like it needs to be made—and *fast*—around sex, drugs, acts of rebellion, and so on. Urgency is a topic that I love to talk about with teens, because it's an area I've spent a lot of time looking into for myself.

I like to share with my clients this situation that happens nearly daily in my house (although, truthfully, less and less as I spend some time reflecting on this and how it works within my consciousness).

My one-year-old and my five-year-old are both hungry, asking for food, needing their clothes put on or taken off, our dog is whining at the door to go outside, there is food on the stove (likely burning), and my husband and I are standing in the kitchen moving quickly—me with a frantic energy, snappy, bumping into things, harsh, intense— and my husband humming a sweet song out loud, trying to gaze lovingly at me.

Suddenly I snap out of it. I realize that we are in two different realities. We're in the same moment of time, the same situation, the exact same circumstances, yet our inner experience couldn't be more different.

He is living inside of a reality where life is complete right now. All is well. There is nowhere to go and nothing to do that will add to the overall beauty that is available right here and right now. He is aware that things can look urgent, but that it's truly an inside job whether or not to take on the thoughts and feelings that go with the way things look. It's a choice—once we see that it is a choice.

I recently had a coaching conversation with Aaron Turner, a wonderful coach and facilitator, [8]and he said very casually, as I was describing to him the above situation, "Sounds like you've had a habit of thinking that your urgent thoughts are valid."

He went on to share that I clearly have many thoughts that go through my mind that I don't give so much credit to. I could see this to be true; for example, when I have a fearful thought pop up about something I'm about to do, it typically doesn't stop me for a second. I see it and cast it aside. This holds true for several other emotionally charged thoughts.

But urgency . . . urgency was a blind spot for me.

I've had certain degrees of insight around this throughout the last couple decades, but becoming a parent brought it to the forefront in a punch-you-in-the-face kind of way.

I remember making a choice when I was a teenager to jump in the car at 11:00 PM to drive to my boyfriend's house. He and I had gotten

---

[8] Please see: www.onethought.com

in a fight on the phone, and he had ended the call without a resolution. I felt afraid, sad, overwhelmed . . . I thought that if I didn't fix it right away, things would be over between us. So I broke all the rules that he and I had with our parents and I jumped into the car and drove to his house. After a lot of emotional, unproductive talking and processing, I ended up staying the night with him—which was, again, against all of our family rules. I didn't make it out in the morning before his parents woke up, and I was caught. It made a bad situation way worse because we had breached trust with our parents.

Even later that day I thought that if I hadn't acted on that feeling of urgency I would've avoided a lot of additional suffering. If I had just taken a breath, had some faith in the connection that my boyfriend and I shared, reflected on the reality that if we couldn't go through a tough moment as a couple, that perhaps our relationship wasn't going to make it very far anyway . . . If I had slowed down and reassured myself, I know I would have woken up with a clearer mind—and of course an eagerness to connect with him. But I wouldn't have acted with such rash urgency.

When I share this story with teenagers, they always get it. They can see so clearly that it's illogical to act on an urgent feeling. It doesn't make things better. Or even if it does make things better for a second, that feeling is so fleeting. It becomes a habit of living life in a way where it's scratching one itch after another, never really ending up satisfied with the depth of life that is available when we slow down.

What I like to share is that when I have the feeling of urgency it's simply an indication that I am out of balance. That I am not in my right thinking. That my thoughts are not to be trusted. In that kind of situation, damage control might be slowing down and asking myself if I need some support, if I need some comforting, if I need to be reminded of some fundamental truths—like that everything is okay. That, literally, if the house isn't burning down, there's nothing that needs done in a hurry in this moment. Asking myself if I need support is my way of waking up from the dream, from the illusion that I was temporarily caught up in. There are many other ways of waking up, but this is one thing that my wisdom often brings to my mind in those moments.

I can slow down, sleep on it, take a breath and then, later, have a clear mind to do whatever I am about to do with much greater productiveness and thoughtfulness. It helps preserve my relationships. It helps preserve my mental health and well-being. It gives me access to a feeling of happiness, a feeling of peace that has nothing to do with what's occurring in the physical world but with what is always occurring and available within—if I tune into it.

For me, slowing down solves all things. It gives me access to the highest resources within my consciousness. It connects me up with the fundamental truth of who and what I am and what the nature of reality is. And when I am connected there, there truly is nowhere to go and nothing to do.

And of course, kids need to be fed, diapers need to be changed, school is going to start at a certain time, clients are going to be in my zoom waiting room. Yes, all of that is true, but to move through life in a constant state of urgency is literally skimming the surface of what is available. If I can slow it down and see what's really occurring, I get the greatest gift of dropping into the moment and feeling the depth of connection and true-life experience that is available right here and right now. And that is true for all of us, including teenagers.

If they can be supported in seeing that urgency or stress or overwhelm or habitual thinking, including ADD and ADHD and OCD-type behaviors like cutting, drinking, smoking, binge-eating, under-eating—all of those behaviors that feel compulsive—if they can see that when they are in a moment where there's something pulling on their attention and it feels urgent, that is the moment to seek out inner and outer support, not a time to "scratch the itch" so to speak.

It's not the time to jump in the car, pick up the razor, text a girlfriend . . It's actually a time to slow down, to recognize an imbalanced mind, and to allow things to resettle within. It's a life-long practice, but so worth waking up to, little by little.

I'll often share with teens that one small baby step in that direction is turning your phone on silent and turning off ALL notifications on all of your devices. They often can't even imagine doing this. Not even for an hour or a day. They are bought in—hook, line and sinker—to the idea that they need to respond with great urgency to other people's urgent energy, or they are mistaking a quick response time for being a good friend, a reliable employee, a responsible kid, etc. They are forgetting that they can be all of those things while still creating uninterrupted time in every day to simply be in the fullness of where they are.

They ask me why they would ever do something as horrible as leaving their friend "on read." (I first had to ask what this meant, and in case you didn't know: it means reading a message from someone and not responding right away, even though the sender might get a notification that the recipient read the message.) I then explain that the answer to that "why" is everything. It is life-giving and life-changing. It's the difference between living a life where you're constantly on to the next thing rather than dropping into the here and now—where happiness, peace and contentment live.

We all know what it's like to make a plan to hang out with a friend, only to have that friend constantly check their phone. When that happens to me, I like to joke with my friend by either texting them a simple, "Hi! I'm right here! No need to look any further." Or say to them, "Hey! What am I, chopped liver!?"

I don't know any teen or parent who doesn't have a meaningful experience when they consciously decide to put down their phone, or put it on silent, and simply be present with themselves or the people they are with.

So again, why is this so important? Because your attention is valuable. Right where you are, right now. It's a wonderful thing to be able to consciously decide when you want to tune into other people's worlds, and not have them constantly knocking. ALL. THE. TIME. If it really is urgent, whoever is trying to get to you will figure out a way. AND 99.9999 percent of the time it is not, and it only takes your attention away from the moment you are in. It creates fractured attention—and likely an unsatisfying relationship with the present moment—with the people who are in it with you, and with your own connection to the beauty of your inner experience.

I turned my phone on silent and my notifications off about ten years ago. Best decision I could have made for myself on the path of living with more presence and in a good feeling of peace and calm.

39

Social media

I didn't have social media growing up. I didn't even have my first cell phone until I entered college. I didn't send my first text message till I was about twenty-four years old. I'm still relatively new to all things social media, and I do my best to engage minimally.

I entered the realm of social media slowly. These days, Facebook and Instagram are the only two platforms I check in with somewhat regularly. In my own experience with it, I see that it's truly a minefield in terms of what any person might take in while innocently perusing their friends' profiles or scrolling through their feeds. There are news stories, posts, advertisements and lots, lots more—loads of unplanned, unanticipated and unpredictable input pumped directly into the scrolling brain. I learn about tragic events happening all over the world that I rarely have the ability to do anything about other than send a prayer of love and support.

The long and short of it in my opinion is that unless it's used with great intentionality, it's not something that is overall a health and wellness enhancer. In my experience, if I don't use social media in a very deliberate and self-aware way, it tends to drain my energy. It's not uplifting, and it doesn't add value to my life.

Having said all this, I'm not issuing a blanket statement that social media should be avoided at all costs. I don't assume that it would be best if kids got off it altogether. But I do tend to ask my clients about their tendencies on social media. I'm genuinely curious as to what they feel about their engagement with it. If it seems like they are being negatively impacted through their involvement—whether through comparison with others, pressure to reply to every comment or "like," fear of missing out, or whatever else it might be—I like to slow our discussion down and dive in with them.

I recommend the movie *The Social Dilemma* to every teen and parent I talk with if concerns about social media come up. This film does a great job of showing something of the addictive nature of social media and its elements of instant gratification and predictive programming. It also dips a toe into the devious side of the Internet and how it can be used to manipulate people, turning them from being purely human into mere consumers stuck in a bubble of common opinions and ideas; this tends to create an isolation effect and a closed-off mindset when it comes to connecting to people with different thoughts and ideas.

For my own part, after watching *The Social Dilemma*, I decided to stay on social media while doing something for myself to help counter what I could see happening. I started to click the "like" button for things that I didn't technically like. I engaged with posts that weren't necessarily in my comfort zone. I did these things with the intention of expanding my perception of reality and popping the bubble that I might otherwise be stuck in when engaging with social media. Too often we get stuck in a vacuum in terms of the information we absorb, only taking in what we already agree with. I'm not afraid of seeing things that don't resonate with my beliefs. In fact, I enjoy the process of learning about other people and why they think the way they do, why they behave the way they do. I don't particularly enjoy debating, but I do love open, honest conversations with people from all walks of life.

I'm saying all of this simply to acknowledge that my personal involvement with social media has informed my thoughts and opinions about it. I don't think it's all bad. It can be a wonderful way to connect to community and experience ideas we wouldn't ordinarily have access to. For example, I have found tremendous value in being connected to other women experiencing hyperemesis gravidarum during pregnancy. I don't know anyone in my "offline" life who's going through it, so it's a great way of getting support that might otherwise not be available. I also have friends who have participated in bereavement support groups through Facebook that have been incredibly healing for them.

Back to teens: I've shared that if it feels like they are having a negative experience with social media, I get curious about why. One of my clients recently told me about an app called "How We Feel," and we explored the idea of her using it as a check-in for how she feels prior to using social media, while she's using it and then when she's done. It seemed like a simple way for her to feel her own intrinsic motivations around engaging with these platforms. I share with some of my clients that I use a timer. Anytime I get onto Facebook I set a timer for ten minutes. When it goes off I either decide to set it again or to close Facebook. It's my own way of being conscious of my engagement.

I also like to share that the reason I'm on social media is to amplify joy, inspiration, hope and love in the world. I use it to connect with close friends and family. Occasionally I'll post something business-related, but I'm very aware that the quality of my life is enhanced through human connection, person-to-person, voice-to-voice, and that's where I put most of my attention, not only personally but professionally.

I also love feeling that if the Internet goes down, I would still know how to create a client and serve humans. I want the coaches I work with to know that too, and that's why I put such a huge emphasis on building a practice through personal connection, and on building relationships in real time.

There is so much research about the impact of social media on mental health. I have read pages and pages of content related to this issue, but for me it comes back to being with a teen in the moment, tuning them into their own wisdom about what would support them in utilizing their precious life energy. I ask questions about how they wish they would engage with social media. I ask about whether they'd like to be done with it all together or take a break for a while. I float out ideas to them about how I see other people using it, as a way of expressing creativity and love. I talk about the fact that I post on social media all the time but I don't feel obligated to go back and see how my post is doing, or to reply to every comment or "like." In fact most of the things I post I never go back to look at. I have notifications off on everything, including my email, so it's always with my own intent that I am tuning into anything through my phone or my computer. It's not because I'm being pulled in by a ding going off.

A part of this conversation also tends to go toward another

element of mental health and wellness. This is a conversation around input and output. It's the same thing as food and water and fresh air and anything that I put on or in my body. It's also music, entertainment, books—anything that goes into my mind. All of it has an impact, and slowing down to become mindful of what that impact is is super helpful.

Furthermore, from my own experience I know the quickest way to get myself out of a low mood or a feeling of drudgery is to create something. To serve someone. To share love and gratitude with someone else. To express myself in some way. Social media can be an all-consuming process, but if we can be mindful of the fact that we're there not only to consume but to express, we can be mindful of keeping the balance.

Part of my process has been to wake up to this again and again, to become aware of when I am slipping into an unconscious pattern with social media (or anything else) and using it more than I want to, or when I am starting to feel the icky feeling of comparison creep in. When that happens, I take a break. I take the apps off my phone. I stop, because it's all *optional*. And perhaps simply sharing these perspectives with teens, gives them access to new pathways they can take as well.

As a coach, understanding and using your own experience of participating with social media and the ways in which you use it to enhance your life—as well as the pitfalls you've fallen into with it—will go a long way in helping the teenagers you are working with.

40

Friendship fruit salad

We are impacted by the people that we spend time with. We could devote chapters and chapters to issues around teens and friendship, but this is observation comes up more than any other when talking with teens. For better or worse, who we are with regularly influences us in some way.

Even knowing this is an inside-out world, the truth is that when I'm hanging out with people who are consistently pessimistic, negative, competitive, angry, there is a part of me that quiets down— or feels the need to speak up louder than I'd like. There's an internal response, just as there is when I'm with people who are optimistic, supportive, inclusive, generous and kind. In the latter situation, part of me relaxes, opens up, feels more seen and safe and encouraged.

This is neither good nor bad—it's just the facts.

One of the stories I love sharing with teens in challenging relationships with friends or partners is this experience I had when I was in third grade.

My teacher had us all bring in ripe, beautiful pieces of fruit of all kinds—pineapples and mangoes and strawberries and blackberries— and we mixed it all together and created this gorgeous fruit salad we were all so excited to eat. But right before she served it to us she pulled out a visibly rotten banana and started opening it up. She was about to put it into our beautiful fruit salad. We all started shouting at her to stop. She did, and asked us why we wouldn't want it in the salad. There was already plenty of other delicious fruit in there—what difference would one rotten banana make?

After a very animated conversation where we yelled out our responses, she very neutrally and calmly talked about how we have the ability to be someone who adds nourishment and beauty everywhere we go—or to be someone who adds stinky, rotten banana energy everywhere we go. The truth was, she said, we do impact each other, for better or worse.

I probably share this story monthly with teens I work with. It's so simple, and the point is so obvious—and sometimes it really needs to be said.

I work with so many teenagers who feel a sense of obligation to be there for their friends all the time—morning, noon and at 2:00 a.m. Constantly available, always on call. They want to be there, they want to show up, they want to be good friends, reliable and helpful.

So it can come as a huge relief when we get into a conversation about the truth that their friends might need a different kind of support. They might instead need counseling or coaching or mentoring. There's nothing wrong with a person going through a time of great need. We've all been there in some way. But—it's not necessary for a fourteen-year-old to be the person whom another fourteen-year-old relies on for emotional support, especially around topics such as family violence, rape, heartbreak, feelings of failure, and so on. That kind of relationship is not actually helpful for either teen.

When I point this out, it's obvious. It's a breath of fresh air.

In my mind, friendships are a bit like social media. When engaged with intentionally, they can be nourishing, fun and uplifting. When they're not, when we slip into behaving in ways that seem obligatory and out of alignment with what feels natural and right, we can get ourselves into sticky territory.

As always, it comes down to helping a teen trust what is nourishing them and adding value to their lives, and to be courageous and willing to acknowledge what is not. They don't have to judge any of it, to make it wrong. They just need to see things for what they are and how they make them feel.

Parents and Families

41

Parents' expectations

When a parent reaches out to me about working with their teen, hope is already on the table. They perceive their teen as needing support in some way, and they think I might be able to help. As we engage, I listen to the parent with an open mind and heart. I help them relax and feel more calm and clear. I even look for ways in which they might be imagining problems where there aren't any. Sometimes this is indeed what's innocently happening, so if our initial conversation helps the parent realize their teen is doing fine and doesn't actually need the kind of support they were seeking, that's a win in my book.

If a parent does want me to work with their teen, I communicate how I've seen coaching help. I share details about the process and how it can support teens in discovering more about themselves and engaging with the world. I tell parents that I don't see my role as giving advice. I also explain that I don't have a "magic bullet" system for helping teens achieve more in academia or create better relationships, but that I support them in finding specific approaches that work for them. My goal is to empower their teen to discover the wisdom within themselves that will help guide them not just through their current situation, but throughout their entire lives. My intention is to support a teen in understanding more about how their mind and emotions work and how to support themselves when they are feeling low.

The most important understanding I wish to create is that if I work with their teen, the parent must be open to letting their child have the experience be all their own. In practice this means that if the parent has something they want to express or talk about regarding the coaching, they approach me and not their teen. It's vital to allow the teen to dive into the coaching experience unimpeded by parental ideas about what should be worked on or discussed. Any such agenda would make the coaching process more about what the parent wants, leaving the teen in the familiar space of figuring out how to respond to other people's expectations rather than honoring their own intentions and inner guidance.

So this kind of agreement with a parent allows the teen to feel freer and more open, to show up more fully. They can feel they're in a safe space without an agenda from me or their parents dictating what needs to happen. They know that I am there for them.

When a parent tells me they want their kid to achieve a perfect score on the SAT, my conversation with that parent tends to go very deep, but my first question is always, "Does your kid want that too?" If the answer is yes, I tell the parent that I will work with their teen around that goal, and that in my experience preparing and setting up a good plan of action, along with clear, intrinsic motivation and sound inner-support, is how one achieves heartfelt goals. The teen is then supported in knowing that whether they get a perfect score or not they're still completely capable of having a wonderful, happy life.

The "win" lies in learning how to take consistent action toward something that they want. If they learn this, I consider it a huge success. If they are kind and gentle with themselves no matter what their score is, that's a cherry on top. When I explain this to parents, they tend to feel in alignment with it because they know that there's a lot of love, support and wisdom in the approach.

Going for a big goal like a stellar test score isn't ultimately what my coaching is focused on. And I am not shy about communicating that. I tell them it's more about drawing out the resiliency, competency, loving and wisdom in each person I work with. I see the chance to improve grades and achieve goals as ways to facilitate this inner development. **Before I take money from a parent I make sure they understand this and are in alignment with it.** Big goals *can* be achieved, but success is usually temporary in the sense that another goal will soon come along. So what I'm really about is creating a lasting difference, an inner transformation, that remains way beyond my work with the client.

I've discovered that when a parent understands this focus, they usually start to care less and less about their kid achieving specific goals during our work together. They understand that while I value the goal and the outcome, I place a premium on their child's relationship with themselves and their learning experience. In fact, when I tell parents, "I want your kid to know that they are unconditionally lovable whether they achieve this goal or not," it sometimes shakes something open within them. They see that they can offer love like this not only to their teen but also to themselves. It can become a new way of being.

It's the most beautiful thing in the world to offer that kind of gift to a person.

I also want to be very clear that the way I coach is not always what a parent is looking for. Sometimes they really do understand my approach and values, and yet what they want is for the kid to have an accountability partner, a coach who guarantees they will stay on track to get the grade or the job. That is not me. As I shared, I care about reaching goals, but I want the work I do with my clients to transcend short-term goals and to have a deeper focus. A focus that will support a kid in having a happy, fulfilling *life*. Sometimes that means achieving goals; sometimes that means they get clear inside that the goal wasn't ever what they really wanted, and they find the courage to pivot and focus on what they really want. If the primary goal is an outer goal, we might miss the more important opportunity to help a teen find their voice and advocate for what they want, which isn't always the scenario of them deciding to drop out of college to start a flower farm. Sometimes it is them realizing they were holding back and aiming too low.

I had a client several years ago who was diagnosed with several learning disabilities just prior to us meeting. She was a junior in high school and was having a hard time feeling motivated. There was more to the story, but to be brief, I was essentially hired to help her get her energy flowing again and get motivated to take the steps to apply for college. She was looking at small, private schools for college because she thought that was what she needed to do. After a few sessions it came out that she really wanted to be a surgeon. (Binge watching Greys Anatomy for years on end, may have played a role in this!) She became an absolute ball of light as she talked about why she wanted this.

To make a long story short, after several conversations around the truth that she might need some extra support with studying, the deeper reality was that she could let herself go for what she really wanted. She could risk failing. The alternative—living a life that wasn't at all interesting or on track for her—was literally draining the energy right out of her.

Flash forward several years: she is right on track to become a pediatric surgeon. It has been a complex journey, but one that she says feels worth it, and one that she has energy for.

42

Client story: Timothy

"I'm slipping"

Recently I had a session with Timothy, an incredibly driven person who strives for excellence. We've been working together for a year. About six months before I met him, Timothy had been having suicidal thoughts and had checked himself into the hospital. At that time his whole life had been geared toward getting into medical school, and he had been an absolute badass when it came to all things academic. However part of his breakdown came about because of the pressure that was mounting within him to always be the best and never fail—which to him meant never living an ordinary life and always being exceptional.

Although Timothy graduated high school, instead of going directly to a four-year university for a pre-med undergraduate degree, he reluctantly chose to stay home with his parents and study at the local community college. He didn't feel emotionally equipped to fully engage in a full-on college experience. This choice felt fairly devastating for him; he saw it as a sign of weakness and thought that because of it his life wouldn't be as good.

Lately Timothy had been doing well. He was showing up for classes, engaging with his friends and having meaningful insights in our conversations, but in our recent session he told me was having a big dip downwards. He said to me, "I'm slipping."

When I began working with Timothy, one thing was very clear: he was capable of so much, but the fear that his performance would slip and he would lose his friends and the respect of his family was killing him. Although he liked the acclaim and notoriety he received around his many awards and accolades, they were a burden as well. He felt like he was constantly trying to prop up an image of himself—and it was getting too heavy.

In fact, in the month prior to his hospitalization he had gotten a B on his report card—and everything started to crumble from there. He started lying to his parents, he became afraid of going to school, and he was petrified at what people would think of him if they saw him as "average."

Through our conversations we started to tease out his ideas around who he was, and to then strip away all the identities he was holding onto that were not truly serving him.

He also started looking for evidence that he was loved regardless of his performance—and he found it. He had supportive friends. His mother was a nurturing presence for him. He could see that these relationships would not disappear if, for example, his grades slipped.

His dad loved him, but he was a different kind of presence in Timothy's life. Timothy was highly motivated to please him, because his father was very critical if Timothy didn't perform perfectly on a test or get an outstanding grade on a paper. He checked on Timothy's grades almost daily. If Timothy slipped a percentage point on a grade, he wasn't allowed to go out with his friends for at least a week, sometimes longer.

I did many sessions with Timothy and his parents throughout the year, both individually and as a group, because it seemed like it would be supportive. (This is something I will do on occasion—above and beyond my normal check-ins with parents—when I feel like it could be helpful.) When I talked with Timothy's dad I learned that he felt it was his duty to show his son what it takes to really succeed and be who you want to be. This meant not having fun and not making mistakes. It also meant self-sacrifice, and constant self-punishment.

In this case I definitely had a different value system, but we found our way through it. Timothy's dad was open to seeing the ways in which his expectations and behavior were hard for his son to cope with. He was willing to be coached around this and receive feedback—and to his credit, he really worked within his own consciousness around his long-held ideas of what success looks like, and what being a "good" parent looks like.

I frequently reminded everyone in this family that success is waking up each day. In Timothy's case, when he was having suicidal thoughts, simply waking up could have been taken off the table altogether. But he made the incredibly courageous decision to go to the hospital instead of taking his own life. Success was that he was alive—and that was true regardless of whether he went to school and became a doctor, whether he studied art or biology, whether he worked in a bike shop or a flower store . . . Success was being alive. It took tremendous strength of heart and courage to stay on the Earth. The more everyone saw that, the more relaxed everything became, and the more playful and connected they could all be.

So, back to this recent session. As I mentioned, Timothy had been doing really well for around six months or so: taking classes, showing up on time, working a part-time job, and staying on top of things. But when he showed up to the session he said, "I'm slipping."

These words are not unfamiliar to me. Many of the teens I work with have shared feelings like this. Things are feeling better and better, their lives seem to be going the way they want, they are feeling the way they want . . . and then they hit a moment where they worry that they're starting to go backward. I knew enough about moments like these to ask Timothy a few basic questions right away. I asked if he was smoking weed, drinking more than usual, staying up late, and so on. He immediately laughed and said that he was staying up way too late because three of his best friends had come home from college. "Late" meant until two or three in the morning—and he had to wake up at eight to go to work. One side effect of this was that he was behind on a school assignment (which he turned in right after our call) and on a work project.

As we talked, he began to notice that his feelings weren't indicating that his life was falling apart—only that he was exhausted and wasn't seeing what was really going on within himself. He was having familiar worrisome thoughts, and instead of seeing through them, he was making them true and then fearing for his life. From here we went into a conversation around the truth that even if he slipped all the way back down to the very bottom, to the worst he'd ever felt, he had already shown that he could count on himself to seek support as he had done before. Even in the worst of the worst moments, his guidance had pushed him into a hospital instead of onto a bridge. He understood this, and saw that because of it there really wasn't any value in feeling afraid. There was no logic in it. In fact, the more afraid he felt, the harder those low feelings were to deal with. But when he wasn't so afraid of them, he relaxed. He lightened up.

He could see, too, that we all have cycles, and that simple *rest* really changes everything. Taking care of our bodies tends to help put us into clearer states of mind, and this in turn makes it a little easier to take our lower moods and "negative" thinking in stride.

As it progressed, our conversation was filled with lots of laughter. Timothy remembered the truth about himself and how his system works. This reminded him that he is resilient, and that he knows what to do to support himself. For example: sleep! eat! drink water! Know that moods of all kinds are inevitable. Let it be okay to make mistakes, to turn things in even if they're late, and to apologize and repair when deadlines aren't met. Stay out of the cycle of self-punishment and instead sink into deeper levels of self-compassion.

By the end of the session Timothy and I were sharing TikTok videos and laughing our heads off.

One additional note on this topic:

When teens understand a little about the nature of thought and its impact on their emotions, it's simple to lead less of an "emotion-based" life in terms of decision making. I know I say this a lot but this is one of THE BIGGEST conversation pieces I have with teens, especially when they find themselves not doing the things that really matter to them.

"I'll do it when I feel like it," or, "I don't feel up for it."

These are clues for me that they have forgotten a truth about how they can relate to their thoughts and feelings. I seek to help them remember that even though at times you may not feel like doing something that is important to you—which is bound to happen, even with the most wonderful projects in life—because of your commitment to yourself and your fulfilling life, you simply do it anyway. You stop *not* doing things that matter to you and start being one with your word.

As a nice by-product, being one with your word is a sure way to help self-esteem and confidence soar. It's a very empowering way to live.

The trick is to get clear about what you want. At times, that's the hard part. But once you know it and understand a little about how our thoughts and emotions are linked, and once you learn to stop making decisions from an emotion-based space, it's in the bag.

All that said, when I am in a very clear state of mind and am doing my most productive thinking, if it still makes sense to me to stop doing something, then that's a time to decide whether I want to switch schools, change careers, and so on. When it comes from wisdom, from inner guidance. From a clear place within. Letting emotions make our decisions makes for a very haphazard, stop-start kind of life, because emotions are up and down and all around all the time! There's a metaphor I really love that relates our emotions to the surface of the ocean. Sometimes the waves on the surface are really intense and choppy, sometimes they are HUGE and all-consuming, and sometimes they're calm. But who we REALLY are is the stillness beneath the waves. Below the surface. The calm. The spaciousness. The depth.

43

How and when do you coach parents?

I coach parents in our first conversation. What I mean by this is that my intention is to be helpful right then and there, knowing I may never actually work with their teen. I don't make that first call one where I talk all about myself and my credentials or my coaching style. If they ask about those things, I tell them as quickly and succinctly as possible—as in ten to fifteen seconds—and then I ask them how I can help. I ask what is going on that has them reaching out for support for their child, and then I dive right in and offer support.

As part of my enrollment process I have a conversation with the parents/payer first, and then the teen. I also include two sessions for parents in my six-month programs with teens. Sometimes those two sessions aren't quite enough and parents and I enter into a separate coaching agreement outside of my work with their child.

When I coach parents my goals are similar to the ones I have with teens. I encourage parents to slow down and become more present to what's going on inside them. I try to help them see that whatever they're feeling is a direct reflection of the thoughts and judgments they're holding onto as truths. Sometimes our perceptions are spot on; sometimes they are flawed. The thoughts they hold about their children, flawed or not, affect the way they feel toward their children.

Most parents also benefit tremendously from realizing they are not alone in their concerns or in having feelings of fear, inadequacy, or whatever it may be. The same is true about behaviors they want to change, thoughts they want to let go of, and feelings that just don't *feel* good.

Whatever the case, they are not alone, and there's a certain amount of relief that comes with realizing that more often than not, *everyone* has experienced or is experiencing the kinds of experiences they have.

Let's say I'm working with a teenager who tells me, "I don't want to be the jealous girlfriend! I want to be calm, cool and relaxed when I see my boyfriend with other girls." I'll say something like, "I can be the jealous girlfriend, too! I can be a jealous wife! Whenever I start thinking that my husband's behavior with someone else is a threat to me in some way, I feel jealous. You are not alone in that experience."

Or maybe a parent says to me, "I don't want to be the overprotective, nagging parent. I want to be super-relaxed and chill, more like a friend." I tend to respond, "Sometimes it's our job as parents to be overprotective, at least until we see that it might not be as necessary as we initially thought. I can be super-overprotective and nagging as a parent. Like when my little boy is riding a bike and I think he's going to harm himself somehow, I can totally feel overprotective. If I start really believing the thoughts fueling those feelings I might even add to them by looking for evidence as to why he's in grave danger riding a bike. I will probably nag him, 'Put on your helmet! Don't forget your kneepads and elbow pads!'"

When a parent's experience becomes more normalized,

something very relaxing occurs, and the two of us feel more connected. Rapport happens. Within that connection it's easier to then take the next step forward, which involves reflecting on the reality of their behaviors and feelings and exploring the thinking that gives rise to them.

Renowned basketball coach John Wooden, once said that he never criticizes a player until he's sure that player knows they have his unconditional care and support. I've carried that sentiment with me ever since I entered the world of coaching and facilitating. Coaching, of course, is not about criticizing our clients. But my takeaway from Wooden's comment is that it's a wonderful thing to approach my clients from a foundation of respect, love and connection—and it's so important and helpful for them to be able to feel this from me in a genuine way.

Clients often come to us when they're feeling vulnerable, so I take time to create a space of warmth through my emails, my tone, my words. I care very little, if at all, about being perceived as somebody profound and filled with wisdom; that's actually how I want my clients to see *themselves*. In fact, the less I think about myself in our sessions, the more I feel I can help the person in front of me.

And just as with teens, I know that showering somebody with my own advice and wisdom may be completely pointless. It may land on them in unhelpful ways, or not connect with them at all if they're not open to and resonating with it. But if I simply show up with the intention of loving and caring, and from that space I share whatever occurs to me in the moment, I typically hit the nail on the head. That is, I'm most useful when I trust my own inner wisdom in working with clients, rather than foisting my own thoughts and advice on them.

This is a process for me that involves slowing down within myself.

The higher I go within my own level of consciousness (meaning the more present I am), the more neutral I am within myself, the more at ease, the greater my access to a whole different level of thought, insight and wisdom in the moment. I don't need to try. I don't need to have a plan. I don't need a strategy or a tactic or an agenda. I can simply be present and ready to meet the person in front of me right where they are. When I empty my mind I am free of any agenda, and actually able to hear what they are saying. I'll be listening instead of waiting to talk. I connect with them in a deeper way and provide a space that feels good to both of us.

44

What is your mindset with parents?

In terms of my mindset when working with parents, I start with some basic assumptions.

Parents are the best. Every parent with whom I have a conversation—regardless of circumstances or personality or even their relationships with their children—wants to do the best they can possibly do for their kids, or they wouldn't be looking for coaching support. Behind every parent's action is a loving intention. Yes, sometimes I do need to dig in to find it, but that's my job. I assume every parent wants their child to be happy and successful. From my perspective, a parent's intuition trumps my thoughts about what is right or wrong. They are a child's guardian until that child no longer needs a guardian. This must be respected in my mind. At times this means I don't work with a family, because I see we would be working in opposite directions. I don't want to be at odds with parents. I have learned the importance of this through rough-and-tough experience. It is important to me to be transparent about what my values are up front and to see if there is an alignment with the parents. Are they in support of their child living a life that is meaningful, balanced and heartfelt, fully themselves, filled with growth and learning? Or not?

And if not, I am happy to refer them on.

Parents are meant to be the parents to the kids they are parenting. I don't think there are any accidents here. *Sacred Contracts*, by Carolyn Myss, is a wonderful book, one that has influenced the way I view relationships and their perfection. It helps me trust the wisdom behind the relationships. It has helped me see the resiliency and wisdom in children and the parents they come in with.

I will also add here that when I don't feel aligned with the ongoing actions of a parent toward their child, I make it clear that I am not the right fit for them. If there is physical or verbal abuse—really, abuse of any kind, based on my sensitive standards of what constitutes abuse—I refer them on. If a parent or parents are ready to stop the behavior and want support mending a relationship, I am all in for that. This is my personal choice as a human and a coach. Everyone can decide how they navigate these delicate scenarios.

Parents are doing the best they know how to do. Any parent who is actually in conversation with a therapist or a coach is already winning. They want to have a better relationship with their teen, and they want to feel happier and more balanced in their parenting. They want their child to thrive. I know that just as teens do, parents also possess a perfect wisdom within themselves. That wisdom is motivating them to receive support and can help them respond to whatever's happening with their child. I have the utmost respect for parents who are looking for additional support.

This is the mindset I bring into my coaching with parents. These sessions support both teen and parent. The more that parent and child are attuned to their true selves, aware of the wisdom and goodness that they are, the better it is for everybody.

45

Helping parents connect with their teen

I have behind the scenes intel that is always helpful when it comes to supporting parents in connecting with their teens. Through hundreds of conversations with teens and young adults over the years, I have the huge benefit of knowing how desperately they want to be seen, heard and acknowledged by their parents. They crave attention. They crave truly being understood. They want to know that they are important to their parents. And most have no idea how to ask for this or to let it in. I have yet to meet a teen who doesn't want a more meaningful relationship with his or her parents. Knowing this from the get go gives me a leg up when supporting parents. I know that even if the door to the teen looks shut, or locked or even boarded up, it is not. There is always, always hope to repair and rejuvenate a relationship. Always. When a parent is willing to see it as a process or a game even, when they are willing to drop their ideas about what is right and wrong, and get into "experimentation-land" with new behaviors of their own, a lot of magic can and does happen.

When a parent is having a hard time connecting with their teenager, one thing that seems to be really effective is to encourage them to take a lighter, more flexible approach. This means getting creative and temporarily setting aside all of the less-than-effective ways the parent's been using until that point—but which seem to have become more habitual than useful.

For a lot of families this means no more trying to "talk things through" when people are tired or hungry or in low moods. It means doing a mood check before opening up *any* meaningful conversations.

All of us are receptive to course-corrective feedback at certain times and all of us are closed down at times. I'm sure you can find examples in your own life. Teens are no different. But the tricky thing is this: it's usually when we're in the heat of it all that it seems like our brains tell us it's a great idea to try to talk things through.

If your intention as a parent is to truly be heard and come to a mutual understanding, then it really is about choosing your connection time wisely. And sometimes it means tilling the soil ahead of time.

When a parent and teenager have such a contentious relationship that there is literally never a good time to talk—or at least it appears that way—I might give this little exercise to the parent to try out for a couple weeks and see if it creates more rapport.

CONNECTION EXERCISE: ACKNOWLEDGMENT FIRST

It goes a little bit as follows. I'll tell the parent: For one or two days, or maybe a week, catch yourself before you give any course-corrective feedback or check-ins. This might be stuff like "I'd like you to do your homework before you turn on your iPad" or "How's it going in math class?" or "How is it going with your friends?" or "You didn't eat enough of your food" or "I need you to make breakfast" or any of the stuff which is totally appropriate and reasonable, but which can tend to be the *only* way that a parent and a child are connecting. (And when it *is* the only way, it can create a lot of negative feelings in a teenager around their relationship with their parent.)

The exercise, then, is to see if a parent is willing to give their child three acknowledgments, compliments, words of appreciation, praise, gratitude, etc., before giving *any* course-corrective feedback or check-ins. *Three*, each day before anything else comes out of their mouth. It's kind a like if you want to eat less sugary foods, it's not so much about cutting out the sugar, but adding in a bunch of vegetables, eating them first and then noticing if you're still hungry.

Three acknowledgments before anything else is said. It takes trust. It takes patience. It takes a commitment to creating a warm and meaningful relationship. It takes a willingness to have things go poorly, to have commitments broken, to have a bit of a mess start to form in a bedroom or to leave chores undone. But it's a process of reprioritization, and the mess, if there is one, is typically temporary.

Most parents desperately want a meaningful connection with their teenager while *knowing* that they are doing their best to support them in becoming independent, successful human beings. Often, it seems the latter takes precedence and completely squelches the former.

This is not about dropping a parents' parenting, but simply sprinkling in some new behavior that might create a much more meaningful, graceful experience for everyone. Most parents find that, lo and behold, things still get done. The laundry eventually gets folded, homework gets done, and so on. It might take a few days and perhaps even a week for a teenager to start to take responsibility for their own life, and isn't that really what teaching them to be responsible is? Letting the balls drop for a bit, and letting them pick them up and then seeing what support they need if they want to keep those balls in the air?

CONNECTION EXERCISE: THE SANDWICH

The variation on this exercise—and sometimes the two versions can go hand-in-hand—is to see if a parent is willing to do what I like to call The Sandwich. It's when they really do need to say something to their teen, or at least they feel like they do, and it is course-corrective or a bit of a check-in, but they say it sandwiched between some acknowledgment and appreciation. It could sound like this: "I really appreciate the effort you're putting into getting to school on time. I know it can be hard and you're doing great. Can you text me if you notice that you're going to be late, so I can plan accordingly? Again I really appreciate the responsibility that you're taking around your schedule. I know it's not easy, and you're doing a great job." This replaces the common practice of shouting in an aggravated tone, "Would you just text me, like a normal, caring human being would do, so I don't have to wait on you, Every. Single. Day!"

CONNECTION EXERCISE: FLY-BY BLESSING

The other exercise I call is a Fly-by Blessing. Doing this for a few weeks can work wonders for building rapport with a teenager and parent (or your partner if it feels relevant). Rather than sitting them down and having a long, *meaningful* talk about something important, it's more of a light approach. The approach is one that teens often respond really well to, because it's about meeting them in their world and at their pace.

It goes like this: When you know you need to have what feels like a tough conversation with your kid about a class that they're failing, you could simply meet them in the hall of your house, and as they're walking by, when they least expect it, do a Sandwich. "It's so fun seeing you excel at violin, it's amazing the way that you show up and participate. I'd love to support you with your math class and the grade that you have going on there; I noticed it's a D. Wondering how you're feeling about that? By the way, I love being your mom." Then pause and listen.

It's about finding a way to normalize unconditional love. It doesn't need to be this big old, serious sit-down talk to make sure your kid really hears you. It's more about meeting them in their world with a quick and simple comment or expression of caring. A drive-by blessing is as easy as saying, "You're doing a great job," as they get out of the car, or simply saying, "I see how much you're trying," "I love your style," "You are such a beautiful person," or, out of the blue, "I'm so proud of you." Drive-by Sandwiches are great too when something needs to be said, but a drive-by blessing is something that can happen all the time, any time, and it is like making a deposit into a relationship bank account.

This is about helping your teenager feel the unconditionality of your love and caring for them. Showing them that it's not attached to any accomplishment. It's not connected to them doing anything well or achieving something. It simply is.

When my five-year-old does something that he is proud of—let's say, winning a race with his dad—I will emphasize it as I say, "Looks like you're really proud of yourself, that's awesome! I am proud of you too! And what I'm most proud of is that you let yourself run and have fun!"

I'm always aware of doing my best to tease apart his feeling good about himself from his performance. Of course, it's a beautiful thing to feel a sense of accomplishment and achievement. I can relate to that, absolutely. But so much of the pain that I see teenagers in comes when they forget about the other side of the story: that they are lovable even if they fail. That they are worthwhile even if they don't measure up to some status quo or beyond. I do believe that as parents it's almost like they need us to continue to reiterate it over and over, because for so many of them it's like a firewall is built up within them that needs breaking down. They can't take it in at first because somehow it's become embedded within their own consciousness, this idea that they only deserve a carrot when they have completed a task.

In my mind, parents and coaches can do a lot of good in breaking that pattern. It enhances mental health and well-being, which naturally enhances performance.

Not that this is a book about enhancing performance; I am sure that is obvious by now. It is a book about enhancing well-being, noticing it, magnifying it and appreciating the implications of doing that. Appreciating that it tends to make us wiser, more resourceful, more creative, and more willing to take risks, to do things that look hard, to risk failure while knowing deep in our bones that our lovability is never at stake.

46

How do you relate to parents, especially when they think that their teen is a hot mess?

"Having a mind that is open to everything and attached to nothing seems to me to be one of the most basic principles that you can adopt to contribute to individual and world peace."

Wayne Dyer

I relate to parents with respect and honor. I'm a parent myself, and I know it's a path of ministry and devotion. I honor the parents I work with, and the relationships they have with their children.

In practice this means many things. For one, I never pretend to know more than a parent, or to know what's best for them and their teen. I defer to them. While I share my best reflections, my experiences and my own personal insights, I never assume parents should buy into them or take them on as their own. I don't tell them how they should act with their child or give them advice about what they "need" to do. I will share ideas, such as the ones in the previous chapter, when a parent is asking for support. But I let them decide if they want to play with anything I share. I let them take their own growth and healing into their own hands. Just like teens, they have the answers within.

When I talk with parents about issues their teens are experiencing, I remind them that their child is an intelligent and wise being, perfectly capable of handling whatever is on their plate—even if "handling" it means asking for help. Their teen knows on a deep, intuitive level exactly what they're doing. While I remind parents that they're not alone in their worry about their teen, I will also share that the more they worry, the more they make their teen's issues feel more difficult to navigate.

On the other hand, the more parents can take a step back, get a bit more detached from their ideas of what is right, and connect in creative conversation with their teen, the better they are able to support them. This kind of collaboration between parent and teen in problem-solving gives teens the dignity of their own inner wisdom. When parents do their best to honor this capacity within their teens, and when they allow their child to contribute to the conversation, everyone tends to feel a greater sense of peace, empowerment and connection in the relationship. This kind of big moment, where all might feel overwhelming and chaotic, can be used as an opportunity to practice seeing the teen's wisdom, beyond their chaotic behavior and emotions. It's an opportunity to see them through the eyes of your own wisdom and unconditional love as a parent. It's a moment that can be transformational for everyone, if there is a willingness as a parent to lean in closely with a lot of openness and gentleness.

Of course it's not always easy for parents to let their teen collaborate in an important decision-making process—much less lead it—because teens often make mistakes. It takes trust. But while it's true that common sense should always be in play, it's also true that when we let teens fully engage in a conversation around a meaningful issue, both parent (and coach) can allow them the space to find the way to their own inner wisdom. Directing the teen to act or think in a certain way may at times feel convenient or expedient, but guiding an individual to a deeper understanding of their own innate capacities is far more powerful, and has tremendous long-term benefits.

Mistakes will be made, for sure. But I have to believe that the point of life is to not be perfect at every turn, not to have everything go well all the time. I'm not sure *what* the point of life is (though I have my ideas) but the overall goal can't possibly be to have everything zipped up perfectly tidy every step of the way. If that were the goal, then every parent of every toddler and teen would be failing miserably—and I know in my heart that we are not.

Messes and mistakes and failures are only moments. And with each of those moments comes a choice of how to respond and how to be in the next moment. We can build a lot upon what's learned in those moments. I love the quote, "Failing is not the falling down, but the staying down."

I might add that it's okay to stay down for as long as you need to recover and to build your strength back up. There's no wrong way to go through this life. Our worthiness and our lovability is inherent even if we look like a hot mess each step of the way. This isn't true just for teens, but for parents, coaches and everyone else. In fact, understanding this for yourself will make it easier for you to help the teens in your life.

One of the ways I feel like I support parents the most is by reminding them that their kid's path in life and whether it looks "successful" or not is not a reflection of who they are as parents and how well they did raising their kids. I really believe that each person who comes into the Earth does so with their own personality, their tendencies and their soul's purpose.

Not to get too woo-wooey, but I am woo-wooey.

47

Separating performance from identity

My husband and I were both very high-achieving in different areas—me academically and him athletically. Those achievements for us were a part of our journey, but they certainly didn't define us, and at times they created a sense of dependency on our success for the inner experience of "okayness." I needed to keep doing well in school or I believed I wouldn't be liked and I wouldn't be okay. Just like my husband with his athletic career. If he wasn't winning tournaments, at times he wouldn't feel great about himself.

I share this because I can see that often there is this assumption that if a child is doing well in different areas in their life, then it means that they are feeling well and are thriving within themselves. That's just simply not always true. Luckily, we can see through this illusion that being successful (or failing) means something significant about who we really are. Seeing the truth of this as parents can do wonders for our relationships with our kids. A more sane way of looking at how well I did in school would have been to see that I have an aptitude for academics some of the time—and some of the time I don't. With my husband, he had a lot of athletic skill (and still does), and some of the time he won, and some of the time he didn't. This takes identification with the performance out of it. It separates out who we are from our performance or our experiences.

Truth be told if I had a B on my report card and my mom went into some sort of overdrive mode demanding that I seek out the support of a professional coach or homework coach, it would've put a lot more weight on that B—rather than seeing it as something that happens. If I had gone to her and said, "I never want to get a B again. Can I get some support with my study habits? I think there's something I'm missing that could make it easier," well, that would've been a different story. And I have to say, I've never had a parent come to me telling me that their kid said something like this to them. It's usually the other way around. A parent is making up a scary story about what a B or a C or a D means, feeling afraid of that story, and then trying tactics of their own (like taking away phones, limiting social time, hiring homework coaches or professional coaches, etc.) to try to get their teen "back on track." Again, all of this is so often done with the best intentions in mind. But also often it is not coming from a teenager worrying about themselves, but from a parent looking at their teen's performance and making assumptions and drawing conclusions.

This is a process of inviting parents into a whole new reality around what "doing well" looks like and means. It's about helping them open their minds to the possibility that everything going well ALL the time isn't necessarily winning in life. In fact, like I shared with my academic experience and my husband's athletic one, being successful can have a downside when it's not put in perspective. It can create pressure, performance anxiety, stress and overwhelm. In fact, I'll never forget my first game as a freshman playing on my varsity basketball team. I was having the time of my life in the first half. No expectations, just playing wild and free. At the break, a friend of mine came up to me and told me she couldn't believe I had scored 15 of our 25 points. My stomach dropped. I didn't feel joy. I felt pressure. I started worrying about what was going to happen in the second half. I actually felt sick to my stomach and didn't even want to start the next half.

I know this is anecdotal, but it is something that I see with so many of my teen clients. The pressure to always be "good" and on track is just too much at times. It is the number one reason I see athletes and performers stop their sport or craft. They love it, but the way they are taking in the onslaught of praise and mistakenly associating their identity with their performance is too painful.

And on the flip side, the sheer panic and worry that many parents (and coaches) bring to teens when they are acting irrationally (skipping classes, staying up till 2:00 a.m. chatting online, drinking at parties, sneaking out with the car, etc.,) is not helpful either. These great big reactions on both sides of the story are not wrong; they are normal and make sense on some level. But I see an opportunity here to support parents in slowing down within themselves and getting a bit more neutral. Seeing behavior and results as only a small part of the story.

Instead of seeing good behavior as an indication that things are going good and bad behavior as a result of things going bad, drop the good/bad perceptions all together. Your kids are good. You are good. I am good. I do stupid things sometimes. I do great things sometimes. None of the things I do mean anything about who I ultimately am. None of them define my future. Or yours or your teens.

Being neutral with a teen when they are going through something challenging gives them a chance to feel into their own experience. To see that it doesn't define them. They don't need to be afraid of their highs or lows. Of their wins or failures. These events are literally just moments of time that are passing by—if we let them. And we get to be new in this moment. We get to be light and free and we can help teens with this by not overlaying our own heightened emotions onto their experience. And that's all it is. Experience. Good, bad, brilliant, horrifying. It's all neutral experience until we judge it and assign meaning to it.

I have seen such incredible magic happen when a parent sees their kid is failing a class and simply asks their teenager, "How do you feel about your grades? Are they what you want them to be?" I actually never ask a teen, "Are you getting good grades?" I always ask something like, "Are your grades what you want them to be?" It's a much less judgmental question, and it tends to lead to a very productive conversation about what they would like, how they could create it, and so on.

When a teenager feels a bit out of control—as in they don't know how to slow themselves down, set up study time, reach out for help, etc.—it can be amazing for a parent to step in and be supportive. And I think that support goes so much farther when it is 1) wanted, and, 2) created in collaboration with the teenager in a clear field of energy-free of judgment.

I have a family I currently work with where if the teenager gets a grade below a B, he doesn't get his phone for a week. He likes this. It feels supportive and motivating. I think it's really cool for a parent and a child to figure out a way to come into this kind of supportive agreement together, and I also understand that it takes a parent being willing to let go of their ideas about how their kids should perform in every area of their lives.

I'm using an academic example here, but I see this with everything, whether it's a kid playing a musical instrument, putting in volunteer hours, showing up for their job, and more. It's amazing when a parent can really take a step back and trust that their kid is being fueled and sourced by their own inherent wisdom, and that that wisdom—as they learn how to listen to it—will continue to guide them toward a meaningful and happy life. And it will be a complex life, one where the trajectory might not be straightforward. There might be dips and zags and zigs and detours along the way, likely just like your life, my life, the life of everyone I know.

And the more a teenager is feeling lifted up—as in, reminded that they can do it, they can go for what they want, that their dreadful, average or award-winning performance in the moment doesn't define them, that their life has purpose and meaning that will continue to unfold, that their lovability is not tied to their performance—the freer they will feel to take risks, to go for what they really want, and to fully engage in life.

48

Seeing your teen with fresh eyes

Sometimes I find myself saying to a parent, "What if there were no other kids to compare your own to? No faster learners or quicker runners? No one who's taller, shorter, less social, more social, kinder, snobbier? No kids getting into college through early admission or dropping out of high school? What do you think your perception of your own child would be?"

When I ask parents these kinds of questions they tend to laugh out loud. Something happens inside them that helps them realize they've not been seeing their kid for exactly who he or she is: unique, perfectly on time, perfectly sized, and possessing a perfect, unique demeanor. There can be quite a learning curve involved in wiping away preconceived notions about who their kid is and who they want them to be.

So the questions I ask parents invite them to see their kids in the present moment, just as they are. They open parents to honoring how their children are showing up in the world. Sometimes it becomes apparent that a child is struggling not because they're "inferior" to another student, but because the system they're in isn't nurturing their natural way of being and learning.

I love working with families who can tune into this understanding and start to see that a typical teen's life—going to school from 7:50AM to 3:10 PM, then doing extracurricular activities, then doing homework until 11:00 PM, then waking up at 6:30 AM for another round—isn't a one-size-fits-all type of deal. Some kids are simply crushed under this regimen, and understandably so! It's not a system that was set up to nurture the creativity, emotional intelligence and natural rhythms of every single human being. It's a "practical" system that was set up to operate as much like a well-run machine as possible. I know that theoretically we can all flourish under any circumstances, but for teens newly finding their way in this world, the expectation that they should be able to fit perfectly into a pre-existing system along with everyone else seems unrealistic. What's more, it can be quite demoralizing for the teen who struggles to fit into the system.

I've worked with many parents who ultimately find it freeing to let their imaginations run wild around how they might support their teens: online school, homeschool, testing out and taking the GED, starting a business, working from home or working overseas—to name a few different options. These unorthodox approaches call for their own unique learning styles to be honored, and often this is just what's needed to support a teen. And it can be very liberating for people to "feel" their way into creative ways they can go about life for themselves and their kiddos. It is not a one-size-fits-all school system, workforce or life.

I truly believe that the more tuned-in we are to what is serving and what is hurting us as human beings, the healthier we will all be, both individually and collectively. Of course, doing this for our kids is essential. It may not seem like it all the time, but they often look up to us almost as if we're gods, and they want to please us beyond anything else. So when we open our minds to different ways we can support them, we're effectively giving them space and saying, "I want you to be healthy. I want you to be happy. I want you to learn important skills in life. But beyond that, I want you to be yourself and to thrive. And I don't have a strong opinion on how that has to look. It needs to work for our family overall, but we can collaborate and find a way forward that serves you."

This conversation becomes essential when there's a crisis going on with a teenager. I've worked with many families in situations where their teen is severely depressed or suicidal. So the kind of conversation I'm talking about in this chapter can be life-saving. It can give options to a teen who thinks they don't have any.

At the same time, I don't think the conversation needs to be reserved for kids who are visibly suffering. It can take place within any family, at any time.

In a program I listened to about twenty years ago, created by Mark Victor Hanson and Jack Canfield (I believe it was *The Aladdin Factor*), they talk about doing a check-in with your partner where you ask, "On a scale of 1 to 10, how satisfying has this relationship been in the last six months?" Then you open up a discussion about what could be shifted on either person's part. Sometimes it will be behavioral things and sometimes it will be letting go of judgments or perceptual filters that are impeding an experience of love and grace together.

In the context of talking with teens, this kind of question can be asked around how they're currently experiencing their lives. One valuable way to phrase it so that it can open rich discussions might be something like, "How satisfying is your life right now in our family? In your school world? Your friendships?"

Then create space for everybody in the family to answer the question. This question honors the individual. It shifts any emphasis away from comparison with others to address individual needs. As well, if there are issues family members need to deal with, opening up this space for discussion can illuminate many new perspectives and solutions. I will often suggest this exercise to parents who are wanting creative and meaningful ways of connecting with and supporting their kids.

49

Lying

"If you could look inside the heart of any and every single human being, you would fall in love with them completely. If you see the inside as it really is and not as your mind projects it to be, you would be so purely in love with the whole thing."

Mooji

Lying is a huge source of frustration between parents and teens. I am a recovering liar myself. As a teen, my lies were usually more the simple, white-lie kinds of things that would reflect an effort on my part to maintain peace and reduce confrontation. They also served to help me get the freedom I desperately desired. Often the lying wasn't even necessary, but I was so afraid of not getting *my* way that it just became *the* way of doing things.

Fortunately I was raised by parents who trusted and encouraged me to make choices that felt safe for me. There were a few tough moments where my mom held the line and I was furious in the moment . . . and then secretly grateful hours later when the gut feeling she had about me not going camping at midnight actually resonated with my own.

As a coach, I've seen lying run the gamut, from teens changing their grades on their report card (been there!) to whether or not they are doing drugs, drinking, having sex, sneaking out, going to work versus going partying, and so on.

One of the ways I support teens in this area is by helping them understand how it feels for *them* to be lying on a regular basis. Does it feel good? Does it stress them out? I also want to explore with them their deeper, underlying reasons for lying. This lays the foundation for us to make progress in finding healthy and supportive ways to navigate lying. Without a teen understanding why it's important to address issues of lying—why doing so matters to *them*—there's not a lot of motivation to change the habit.

I don't judge lying as bad or good. Lying serves a purpose: it's a tool that children and teens use to help them get more of what they want in their life: more freedom, peace and cooperation, and less upset, friction and difficulty. What I *can* help kids understand is that there are other options available to them.

Earlier this month my five-year-old was nowhere to be found. My husband and I could both hear an odd clicking sound somewhere near the kitchen. When my husband went to investigate, he found Orion crouched down on the floor opening and shutting a tiny glass bottle that had some cookie sprinkle decorations in it. Orion was licking his finger and dipping it into the jar so the sprinkles would stick to it, then popping them into his mouth.

Now, in our house we essentially only have foodstuffs that he can eat as much of as he wants. We don't have anything that has processed sugar; in fact we have very few processed things. A pretty boring food selection for most kids, but it's what we have decided to do in our home to limit conversations around sugar consumption. In this case, those sprinkles were one of the few items Orion knew there was a limit on. We only use them when we're baking, and when we do have them out, we don't let him eat them by the spoonful, which is what he wants to do.

It was a fun moment for my husband and me—we were equally surprised and amused by our son's behavior. The first thing out of our mouths, said gently and with loving, was, "You don't need to hide from us!"

But at the same time I knew in the back of my mind that Orion *did* have to hide from us if he wanted to get what he wanted—unlimited access to the cookie sprinkles.

So I knelt down next to him and in a nutshell said, "Hey, I really understand why you were hiding. If me or dad had seen you, we would've told you to stop eating those. You wanted to eat as much as you wanted to. So it made good sense to you to hide. I really understand that. Even though me and dad usually say yes to things that you want, it is true that we say no sometimes. This was a good solution for getting around that! How about this: next time you want something like this, instead of hiding, let me know that you want it so much that you would like to hide. If you do that, it will let me know how much you really want the sprinkles. It will help me understand how strong your desire is and what it really means to you. And then we can figure it out."

This is an idea that I share with my teenage clients and their parents: having open and honest communication. It's not just about lying. It's about the reasons we have that lead to lying. It's about the environment we've created, consciously or not, that makes lying look like a good idea. As a coach, I often need to spend some time with my client sorting out those reasons and understanding what the underlying *want* is that sometimes leads to lying. The more honest and open communication is, the more it can help create a space in which the inclination to lie fades into the background. And when lying does come up—as it did with my son—it can be used as an opportunity to demonstrate what communicating and seeking to understand another person look like—rather than being punished, which can naturally lead to more lying.

And an update on Orion: He has truly taken that moment to heart. When he wants something that he thinks we will say no to, whether it is a toy, a third banana, my chap-stick, he will commonly say, "It feels really, really, really important to me to have this. It is SO important to me." This is him letting me know that he'd like to hide or lie because of how important it feels to him, but instead he's opening the door to a conversation where we can figure it out together.

Lying is a tool. Nothing more than that. It's not an indication that a person is inherently flawed or bad. It's a tool to help teens navigate their complex world. Teens often lie or hide things to save face. They are afraid that they will be judged by their parents, or that they will be punished. As a coach (and a parent), if you can help teens understand why they're lying—to see what they're trying to avoid and what they're trying to create—you may also help them discover ways through the experience without the lying.

The way of the miracle-worker is to see all human behavior as one two things: either love, or a call for love.

Marianne Williamson

50

Punishment

L et's take a moment to contrast this approach around lying to the idea of punishment. One of the main ways I see my teens lying to their parents involves grades. If a teen is traditionally punished for low grades, lying about their report card is, in a way, genius of them. Maybe it's because they know in their bones that they do not deserve punishment for simply being a human—they are flawed, but deserving of acceptance—and in lying, in their own way, they are giving that acceptance to themselves. Or they believe, mistakenly, that they *are* flawed—that they're inherently bad at math, or whatever—and they are lying to keep that a secret. Or maybe they know they didn't study enough because they wanted to do other things, and they need to hide the fact that they made a poor decision from their parents.

In all these cases the lying is serving a purpose. It's a kind of hiding, like Orion with his cookie sprinkles. And in many families it will lead to punishment once it's discovered.

There are countless studies around the effectiveness of severe to mild punishment, many of which point to the fact that punishment, especially physical, or any form that involves a withdrawal of love and connection, simply doesn't work. In fact, it tends to erode what otherwise could be a very supportive and meaningful relationship. And at the very least, the threat of punishment can inhibit open communication.

Imagine if parents could take punishment off the table. I know this might seem like a radical suggestion, but it can also be very exciting and lead to a much more lighthearted, playful, collaborative life experience for both parent and teen. It also supports creating a space of open and honest communication. For example, if a teen is hiding their grades from their parents, this makes it all the more challenging for the parents to support the teen in getting what they want out of life—the lie must be discovered and overcome first. The threat of punishment makes this process even harder.

Of course I don't have the answer for what will work most effectively every time and in every given family and situation. But just as you can support your teen client in understanding why they might be lying, you can also help their parents consider how they can go about creating what they want in their relationship with their teen. Punishment can seem like a logical choice, but with a little more thought, so can creating positive rapport between the two of them, creating trust and support and encouragement, and an energy that fuels thriving and expansiveness. In such a space, creative ideas can come in around how to navigate rule-breaking or failing to meet expectations. It could be as simple as asking a parent things like:

"If you were only seeking to understand more about your teen and why they did what they did, how would you approach her when she came home?"

"If you were only wanting to support her in knowing how loved and capable she is, what would your conversation with her look like around her drinking or sneaking out or having sex or failing that test?"

When a parent really understands that what you want as their teen's coach is also what they want at the deepest level—for the teen to be healthy and happy and successful in a way that matters to them—then the parent can be more open to these types of suggestions. If you go in guns blazing, lecturing them about how to parent, you'll quickly see that you're not creating any rapport, trust, goodwill or positive feelings. This is where my belief that parents want their kids to be happy, that they have their kids' best interests at heart, comes into play. It is not my role as a coach to supplant a parent in any way. It is to help the parent see new pathways for themselves in creating healthy, loving relationships with their teen, as well as a space for their natural knowing and wisdom to come to the forefront. If you can truly stay in the space within yourself as a coach where you trust the parent, then you honor their experience. When you trust the relationship between the parent and their teen and you move into a conversation from that space, you can be far more effective as a coach for both parties.

I think this is evident in what I shared above, but it is worth reiterating. When I am neutral within myself around hot-topic things like lying, I can serve with more effectiveness. When I put a blanket statement around it—"Lying is bad and should be stopped at all costs"—I lose my ability to serve my clients. I want to offer this up to you, fellow coach, because as you serve this demographic, teens will bring in all sorts of behaviors that just may expand your own ability to love unconditionally, to trust unconditionally, and to hold clear, neutral space. My life and my way of seeing and being has been forever enhanced because of my work with teens and their parents.

So, yes, I truly do my best to take the judgment off of lying and help both teen and parent see the motivation behind the lying itself. To help them see, in a neutral, non-judgmental way, the environment that created the need for lying to happen. To help them work together to create a *new* environment and culture within a family, where lying no longer makes sense. It can take time to create, and it's so fun when a parent and a teen are open to moving in this direction together.

It can be a really big learning process for everyone. To take punishment, reprimand, negative consequences off the table takes a lot of trust on the part of a parent to see that perhaps shifting into a different way of being with their child might be just as effective and also help create a more honest, supportive relationship in the process.

I do see punishment much like lying, as a tool used to help a parent get more of what they want, and in this case it might be comfort, the feeling that they are doing what they can to help mold or shape or curb their child's behavior. It's fueled by love.

It can also be pretty exciting for a parent to see that there might be another way to be in relationship with her kid, where love is palpable, in each stage of the learning process.

Often it makes sense for me to ask everyone involved if they would like to have a couple of group sessions. I tend to add these in pro bono to my six-month or year-long programs if I see a need for them. It can be really amazing to be able to discuss all of this together so that a teen feels safe to share why they lie, and so a parent feels supported in coming up with solutions that work for everyone to have a more open, honest and supportive relationship going forward.

51

Teens who know it all and who are always right

I actually like working with strong-willed teens. It's exciting, and as a recovering know-it-all myself, I see a lot of opportunity there. When I am faced with such a client, I do what I can to agree with them A LOT, making sure they know that *I know* that they know it all.

I am only kind of joking.

The truth is, I don't see it as a problem, them being a know-it-all. In fact, it worked for me for a long time—until I woke up to how much it was making me miserable. So with teens, I slowly, patiently, calmly ask questions of them about how being right and knowing it all serves them, or doesn't. How it improves their lives or makes their lives harder, with less joy, optimism and connection. This can come up when I hear them say something like, "I just know my summer is going to suck. Or I know that I am going to fail the test. Or I know that she was wrong and I was right. I know that I am going to hate it, whatever "it" is.

When the door gets opened wide enough through lots of questions and exploratory conversation around the topic, and they are sure I am not trying to fix them—because I am not—once they have shared with

238

me how it's not helping them be happier and feel good in life, then often I will share about one of the most profound things I've come across in my own personal healing journey. It's one of the biggest insights that has set me free within myself and created so much more peace and happiness in my life.

It was seeing how the bulk of my suffering was tied to moments when I just KNEW I was right: right that something should go a certain way, right that someone should behave a certain way, right that I shouldn't feel sadness, right that I need to do X, Y and Z to create happiness, right that I should know how to handle everything that happens in my life.

So much unnecessary suffering. And it shows up a lot of ways in my life, not just being a fortune-teller.

I see this day-in and day-out in my relationship my kids and my husband. If I'm feeling overwhelmed with them in a given moment, it's typically because I'm in a situation where I literally don't know what to do—but I am *unwilling to admit it*. My ego hates that moment! The overwhelm adds on as I try to navigate a hungry five-year-old, a poopy one-year-old and food burning on the stove.

Instead of simply slowing down and acknowledging that I have no idea how to handle the situation in the perfect way, I trudge along, bearing down on myself, serious and overwhelmed.

When I stop, take a breath and simply acknowledge that I don't know what to do, I feel a sense of peace. I usually laugh. A sense of calm washes over me and, often, along with it, clarity on what my next step needs to be. It's gentle and clear.

To me, this practice of admitting that I don't always know what to do, is an acknowledgment that it's perfectly OKAY to be in over my head in life. To have situations feel complicated and to know I don't *have* to know exactly how to navigate it. I can relax inside and ask for help from myself or others, even from Life itself. And sometimes just acknowledging that I don't know does the trick. It pops me out of my ego and into my heart—where all is well…and usually hilarious. I get to be humble in the moment which is a very good feeling for me. Where it doesn't matter how much or how little I know. Where I get to live in a space of being present to what is, trusting that I will know what to do, WHEN I need to know, and until then I can trust myself to navigate any moment of life. It doesn't always look pretty, but it doesn't have to.

This insight also opened up my eyes to how terrible I am at fortune-telling. My future predictions used to be filled with nightmarish scenarios, with me running scared in my life, alone and afraid! Completely forgetting that I DO NOT KNOW what will happen beyond this moment. This one right here. It has not been written, and what I can trust—and so can teens when you point it out to them—is that we have all survived each and every wonderful and terrifying moment of our lives up until right now. Every one of them. We found our way through. We conjured wisdom to guide us, even if it was rough. We found our way, and we can count on that the same wisdom that brought us right here will be there for us in our next "now" moments. It will be there, ready to be called on if we find ourselves not knowing what to do or what will happen. It's always there and always will be. We don't need to fear our futures. And if you are going to make up anything about the future, why not imagine it going well, or at least imagine a variety of scenarios, each one a real possibility, along with dozens of others that we can't begin to know exist? I do this with teens as a way of gently and playfully helping them see that it's okay to widen their perceptual filters and see beyond their ideas of how things "will" go. It's okay to step into a field of truly not knowing and to simultaneously know that all will be well, and is well, simply because wellness resides within. We try to predict the future often in an attempt to keep ourselves safe, to prepare ourselves in some way, not seeing that it only tends to create anxiety in the here and now. We do this when we forget that wisdom will meet us—and can only meet us—in the present moment. It has our backs, right now and in all of our future "now" moments, no matter how bleak or scary our minds make them up to be. Our minds don't always take our wisdom into consideration when contemplating the future, and that's okay. That's not our intellect's strong suit. But as we wake up to the fact of our innate intelligence we can practice seeing it and trusting it consciously as we find ourselves going down a particular path or into worry. We can feel into the truth of it, and in doing so feel a little more peace here and now.

52

Client story: Mary

The pressure to succeed

"Loving's really living. Without it, you're not living, boy, you're just getting up each day and walking around."

Ian Tyson
"The Lovin' Sound"

I started working with Mary about six months ago. At the time she was on antidepressants and had just come out of a period during which she'd felt incredibly suicidal. She was looking for more support, and she and her parents thought they would try out a coach.

In my first session with her she said she wanted to be a doctor or a lawyer, because that's what everybody else in her family did. She attended an extremely prestigious and unrelentingly competitive high school. Everyone there was expected to get high A's; anything less meant you were a bonafide slacker.

Mary was by no means a slacker. But she was experiencing a

crushing feeling of stress under intense pressure.

I could see quite clearly what was going on in her outer world as well as how she was using her thoughts against herself. I started talking with her in a light-hearted playful kind of way to get a sense of where she was at in her thinking around her path ahead, and to get an insight into where she thought her stress was coming from.

I shared about other pathways I've seen people take. Things like taking a year off after high school just to travel, going to the Peace Corps or AmeriCorps for a year, simply volunteering on a farm, and other options. Her response? She said she'd never consider doing something like that because nobody at her school would respect her for it. She felt locked in around this. She, like so many teens, put a lot of importance on the inner dialogue she had around what other people thought. It's almost invisible to some teens. Like it's a given that other people's perceptions are the source of their good or bad feelings, when in reality, it's all an inside job.

Over the course of the next four months I continued to support her in learning more about the true nature of who she is and the role thought was having in her experience of stress and overwhelm. I would also gently bring this conversation piece forward around different options she could entertain for herself. It was a dual approach, as most sessions with teens are, focusing on her understanding where experience comes from, as well as looking at her outer world and the choices she was making.

In terms of her outer world, I wasn't trying to convince her to take any particular course of action. That's not my role, and I don't want it to be; I don't want that responsibility, and it's not mine to take. What I explained to her was that our discussions weren't geared to having her choose any of the particular options that came up. Instead the point was to find a choice that really resonated with her heart and soul. Not a choice she felt *obligated* to make.

Nothing I said precluded her staying in her current high school, going straight to college afterwards, or anything else. Our conversations were really about her inner experience and learning to listen more deeply to *her heart* and less to her fearful thinking. And through the conversations she gradually saw that if she wasn't following her inner guidance and taking steps to honor what she was hearing from within herself, she might very well continue to experience depression, and possibly more suicidal ideation.

A part of her process was untangling her sense of self-worth from where she went to school and her career path. We talked about what made Mary who she was. The qualities that she embodied, her joyful spirit, her curiosity, her kindness, her humor, her playful way of being. Schools would come and go, careers might change, but the reason Mary is Mary has nothing to do with the temporary physical experiences that may come and go in her life. The essence of who she is is what makes her someone who is loved and respected.

A few weeks ago Mary and I met again, and she shared with me how excited she was about a state school she'd learned about. It had the kind of culture she was looking for and several opportunities to travel abroad as well. She told me she would never have considered it had she not stopped thinking that she needed to follow a prescribed path, but could indeed listen to her own heart and trust the wisdom within herself.

Mary was completely supported by her family. Her friends looked at her skeptically—but this was outweighed by the sense of freedom and joy she felt, something that had been missing from her life for a long time.

Mary's story drove home the point for me again: no amount of outer world success or notoriety can lead to an experience of satisfaction if there's not an inner alignment. People are often aware of this at a very young age, even if they can't put it into words. And it's often through their acting out, or depression or misbehavior that the deeper underlying issue or opportunity for waking up to this is revealed. I see a teen going into a sudden depression or an experience of overwhelm as really an opportunity to slow down and get curious. Especially for parents. When they can start to get curious about what is happening within their teen, rather than being *afraid* of what is happening, there comes the possibility for all of them to see the "crisis" for what it really is. And it is often something waking up with a teen. Something within them asking for attention and support. Something within them is yearning to be seen and remembered.

Sometimes it's about them breaking through to the understanding that they don't need to fit in to be loved. Sometimes it's understanding that their happiness is in-built and can't be found out in the world. Sometimes a crisis happens when they start to realize they are living their life for someone else and can't do it anymore. It's different for every one of them, and when it happens I see it as a gift. It's like a light-bulb going off on the inside, and they become acclimated to a whole new way of seeing. It's typically a blessing in every way when they are treated as if something amazing is emerging from within them. When they are seen as a soul awakening, and not as a human falling apart.

53

Divorce

I have a story I like to share with my clients, when it feels appropriate.

My parents divorced when I was around three years old. From everything I've learned and experienced since then, I think that in the end it was a great decision. They were creative and mature in the way they handled it. We did holidays together as often as possible, and the "kids swap" every weekend when my dad was in the area. Even though my parents had difficulties when they were married, and a few post-marriage, overall they did their very best to maintain a clean and clear relationship as we grew up. I never heard them speak one negative word about each other.

I cannot thank them enough for this. Even though as a small child I knew they had challenges in their relationship, they did not let any anger or frustration trickle into our conversations or their attitudes about one another when my brother and I were around. In other words, they let us have our own experience independent of theirs. They didn't try to shape our opinion about the other parent, either directly or indirectly, so I was not burdened by their challenges with one another, and because of this I got to have a very authentic relationship with both of them.

Even as I grew older and asked more questions about their divorce, the facts were filled with possibilities for them to judge the other. But when my parents spoke with me about their separation, they did so in a neutral way. I'm not even sure how they managed that, but they did. This enabled me to feel into my own experience with it.

I really like sharing this story with families who are going through a divorce. I like to share things like, "I'm so grateful for divorce, because it gave my family the opportunity to function in a much healthier way. Because my parents didn't impose their pain onto my brother and me, we got to live in a happy and free space within ourselves regarding our parents." It would've been much heavier for us had we needed to take on a lot of dialogue and pain from one or both of our parents.

Helping parents talk to their kids about divorce

Teens—especially young teens and adolescents—take their cues from their parents. So often a parent will speak to me with concern heavy in their voice around an impending separation or divorce. I know very well that what will make the biggest impact on their teen is the way in which the parents communicate about the divorce to them. If they tell the teen that something horrible is happening, that it's going to ruin their lives forever, then, yes, there is more cause for concern around how their teen will respond.

Imagine instead if they communicate something like this to their teen: "Your mom and I want to show you how important it is to be true to yourself in this life. We want to model for you what it looks like to make healthy choices. Right now, your mom and I have decided to separate, and even though our family will look different than it has, nothing real has changed. Our love for you is the same. We're just going to find new ways to spend time together.

"We've decided that I'm going to move into a different house. You'll have your own room there. A lot of things will stay the same, and a few will be different. Hopefully this will make things better for all of us. I want you to know that when things change it doesn't mean that anything is falling apart. In fact, it might just mean that things are fitting together in a more supportive way."

Of course, it's important for a parent to find their own words, and to tailor what they're saying to whatever age their kids are. But this kind of conversation doesn't need to be scary or heavy. It can be supportive for both teen and parent. It can be factual and optimistic.

I'm not saying that parents should hide their emotions from their teens. In fact, sharing their own fears or sadness can be great. Acknowledging that powerful emotions are natural gives a teen permission to feel them without shame. But there is a difference between a parent putting their own fear onto their kids and letting kids discover their own, clear understanding for themselves. The latter approach allows them to experience what it all means to them.

I do see the truth that typically what parents say to their kids tends to impact their kids, so if they're going to say anything that has an emotional bent, why not lean towards the positive and give them a leg up?

Helping teens with their feelings and thoughts around divorce

From what I've seen in all of my sessions with teenagers whose parent have divorced or are in the process of divorcing, the absolute hardest part for the teen is worrying about their parents—whether that's the parent who has left, the parent who is grieving, the parent who refuses to date, the one who's angry, and so on. Hardly ever in my experience—and I really mean this—is a teenager simply and solely processing their own feelings of loss.

In fact, it's the teens who are typically very quick to embrace a new reality and to understand that it doesn't mean anything is wrong or broken. The younger the kid, the easier I think it is for them to settle into a completely new experience of life. But even the older teens I've worked with through this generally discover that their own happiness and peace of mind are independent of whether or not their parents are together or apart.

I also love sharing with my clients and their parents about my current reality. Flash forward thirty-plus years and I live on a piece of property sandwiched between my parents, all within a fifteen-second walk. They both spend time with their grandkids as well as together, gardening and working on projects around our property. It's a very sweet life. In sharing about this I am simply offering a bigger perspective. Especially in the heat of a divorce there are a lot of potential outcomes that might not seem in the realm of possibility.

My own experience

Something else that I might bring up from my own past if it feels relevant involves a time when I broke up with someone I deeply loved.

He was my first long-term boyfriend as an adult, someone I respected and cared about. Yet before long I knew in my gut that our relationship wasn't right. It took me about a year to finally "complete" it. The breakup was really hard on both of us—one of the most painful things I've ever gone through, and it was not made easier on either of us, especially him, by my indecisive behavior.

When I was in the process of moving out of our shared place, I went to look for a new apartment. As I was meeting with the property manager of a prospective rental, I suddenly burst into tears, overwhelmed with the weight of what had occurred: I had finally broken up with this man whom I loved but needed to move on from. It felt like a huge moment in my life—and was also incredibly sad.

The property manager asked me what was wrong, and I told him I'd just ended a relationship. He said, "Congratulations!" And then he gave me a big hug. I had never in my life been met with that kind of reception when sharing about the news of a breakup. And I absolutely loved it. It made me laugh and cry even harder. I felt so seen in all the important ways. I felt acknowledged for what I had chosen to do—something that was so hard, but something I also knew was right. His reaction towards me helped me move through the guilt that was the main experience I was having and into that clear, good feeling of having made a choice to honor a deeper knowing within.

I've taken that with me as I've moved forward. Whenever I hear about a divorce or breakup, if I've "felt out the room" and it seems appropriate, I will say something like, "Congratulations!" And it is met with equal amounts of surprise and appreciation.

54

Orion's splinter

"If the only thing that people learned was not to be afraid of their experience, that alone would change the world."

Sydney Banks

My son is currently five years old. He never wears shoes. We live in the woods, so this is a bit problematic at times. Earlier this week he was playing on our driveway, which is filled with tiny rocks, and he got some sort of object stuck in his foot. A sliver or a tiny shard of rock or God knows what.

About six hours later, I noticed that he was limping. I investigated his foot and found a sliver beneath the skin. He didn't care much about the sliver. It was no big deal to him. It was certainly impeding his movement, but he couldn't really care less about it. Yes it was irritating, yes it was slowing him down—but it was no big deal to him.

I had a similar attitude: I wanted to see if I could get it out but I was not worried about it. I took some time with him where he reluctantly allowed me to investigate his foot . . . flashlight and needle and tweezers in my hands. I set up his favorite show to keep him distracted, and initially he was fine with me messing around to get the sliver out. But after about a half hour of me not making any headway, he was over it. The sliver was really deep and I wasn't doing any good foraging around in his foot. In fact, I was hurting him more and more.

My thought about it was that I would soak it in some Epson salt, perhaps put some baking soda paste or clay on it, and that it would start to work its way toward the surface within a day or so. I consulted my mom about homeopathic remedies to give him; we got some going and I was feeling good with the plan.

His dad had a different feeling about it. His dad wanted that thing out, now. We had a bit of a scuffle around it. The sliver was an issue in his world. He wanted us to get that thing out one way or another, no matter how Orion felt about it. He was worried about the sliver. He created horrifying images in his mind of Orion's foot becoming overwhelmed with infection and needing to be amputated, or of us taking him to a doctor and the doctor needing to cut it out. He was scared of the sliver. He heard that the sliver could be very damaging. And, of course, left unattended, that was possible.

So we were tending to it. My husband agreed to relax a bit around it, knowing his fear wasn't necessarily helping. Holding a struggling Orion down and cutting a hole in his foot to get out a tiny little bit of wood or rock started to not make sense to him either. Even though it was uncomfortable, we moved toward a more gentle approach. We soaked his foot multiple times and continued to give care and attention to him to help the sliver work its way out.

We didn't ignore the sliver and pretend it wasn't there. We acknowledged that it was indeed there and was something that needed to be supported—but it certainly wasn't something we needed to worry about or create an even bigger issue around.

I trusted Orion's body to know how to expel the sliver with some support. I knew that balance would be restored. I knew that he could live a very happy, healthy life even with the discomfort; he knew that as well and continued to remind us of that. The act of removing the splinter forcibly was definitely creating more panic and fear for him than the splinter itself.

Our experience with the sliver is a wonderful metaphor for a way of tending to any kind of uncomfortable inner experience. If we're not afraid of, let's say, anxiety, but simply acknowledge that it's there and tend to the anxious person (whether it's ourselves or someone else), the anxiety will work its way through essentially on its own. A bit of support—taking some deep breaths, going for a walk, asking for a hug—can be helpful if it comes from a place of understanding that the anxiety is temporary and fleeting. Anxiety is simply a reflection of a person's state of mind in the moment, not an indication that there's something terribly flawed within the human. In fact, anxiety, just like joy, is an indication that the human being is awake to their senses, that their consciousness is bringing to life their thoughts in a very powerful way. In other words, that their system is working properly.

I know this can sound a bit counterintuitive, but I see the power of this recognition playing out in my own life and in the lives of my family and clients all the time. It involves getting a feel for the truth that our feelings can't kill us, that we would need to decide to act on those feelings in order for any harm to be done. Feelings, just like thoughts, are completely harmless in and of themselves. Yes, they hurt. Yes, they're annoying. Yes, they might make us emotionally limp for a while, but we don't need to go rooting around in an invasive and unnecessarily aggressive way to try to "get them out," because they are not fundamentally an issue. In fact, the more panicked we are about an emotion, the more chaos, contraction and fear we bring to the experience rather than simply allowing it to pass through in its natural way.

I recently heard Dicken Bettinger[9] talk about cycles. The earth has cycles, nature works in cycles and human beings also have cycles. Obviously we see this with women, but he talked about our *moods* having cycles. If we look closely enough it tends to be true that each of us, to varying degrees of intensity and with varying degrees of impact, move through cycles of being in high moods and low moods. If we can appreciate the resiliency and predictable nature of these cycles, we can experience far less fear when we find ourselves down. If we know that it's in our very nature to eventually cycle into a lighter state of mind, when we find ourselves experiencing a low state of mind or anxiety or depression, we might see a bit more clearly that there's truly nothing to do, because there isn't an issue that needs fixing.

I've seen this in my own experience. I used to put in a lot of effort to shift my state of mind if I was low, and it took me some time to realize that my effort wasn't necessarily supporting me in coming back to a clear state. It was simply the nature of who I am, working as I was naturally designed to do, that did it. It has been very humbling to notice that my moods shift without effort, and I have clearer and better ideas as a result.

Going back to the sliver . . .

_____

[9] Please see: http://3principlesmentoring.com/index.html

I truly want to be more like Orion every day. He is not bothered by his sadness or anger or fear, or even a sliver in his foot. Yes, these experiences do make an impact. They might slow him down but he knows it's no big deal. It's temporary, it's a blip, it's part of life. It's part of being a human. He doesn't even question it. He's never once said to me, "Why do I feel so sad?" or, "Why do I get angry?" He's just in the anger as if it's the most natural thing in the world, and then five minutes later he's sitting on my lap giving me kisses. It's so easy to see the health within him even when he's distraught. He's not worried about his distress. He's not worried about his splinters.

What I do see is that he could become worried about his distress and his splinters if he sees his dad and I go into full-fledged panic mode every time he has one of those experiences going on. That would do the trick to put him on the path of worrying about these uncomfortable experiences, and thus worrying if HE'S ok or in fact, in need of fixing.

My hope is to get out of his way, and in doing so help him stay in touch with his health in the midst of splinters and all. To support his natural understanding that health and well-being don't always look the way that we think that they should. That perhaps a healthy minded person is someone who isn't afraid of their inner experiences (no matter what they may be)—or that even if they are, they're not afraid of that fear.

For me, the only way to see if these ideas have any relevance is to try them out and see what lands. And it has been a really beautiful paradigm shift in myself and my clients when we work from this perspective—really knowing that no matter what they're presenting, no matter how scary the emotion or the thought, their wholeness is intact. They have wisdom available to them. The proof is always in the pudding. For example, if they're in a conversation with a coach, their wisdom is allowing them to seek out support.

It's helpful to look for their wisdom, their health, and to point it out to them when you see it expressed. To fixate on their wholeness and to help them relax into it. A big part of creating that experience for a client is simply not freaking out about the "splinter," but trusting in their own built-in, resilient nature, and helping them see it as well.

ORION'S SPLINTER UPDATE: We applied bentonite clay to Orion's foot in a gentle and easy way. We watched it over the next week or so and his foot gradually pulled the splinter to the surface, to where it was visible under a thin lining of skin. One day I pointed out to him that I could see it and asked if I could try to pull it out. He happily stuck out his foot and let me gently tweeze back the skin and pull out the splinter, which actually turned out to be a small rock.

Coaches

"Don't be a magician—be magic."

Leonard Cohen

55

What we're really doing as coaches

One of the biggest stumbling blocks that coaches who work with teenagers have is that it can be easy to confuse a parent's or coach's expectations with what true progress looks like. And whatever the surface reason for this is, I think it essentially comes from a fundamental misunderstanding of what we're really doing as coaches. Or at least the way I see it.

As I think I've made clear in this book, I don't see my job as a coach to try to change my clients into more productive, more cooperative, more successful-looking humans. I ultimately see my job as a coach as an opportunity to help the person I am sitting across from see themselves more clearly. To see that they are not flawed or broken or needing to prove their worthiness for love and respect.

I see my role as helping my clients understand themselves more and connect to their gut feelings and intuition. To remind them to go to a mirror and ask themselves the important questions they want answers to, knowing that the answers reside within. To help them, if they need it, understand what it is they feel called toward and what it is they feel called away from. To help them learn how to listen to that and see themselves in a neutral light, free from expectation or obligation, and simply from a perspective of curiosity.

56

Our clients don't need fixing

Last year I was talking with one of my teen clients and she was punishing herself for turning her homework in late. She was berating herself for not keeping her agreements with her parents.

I asked her to take a step back, to look at herself as if she were looking at a stranger. In fact, I think the words that I spoke were, "Look at yourself as if you were an extraterrestrial from another planet. Be as curious as you can about yourself. What's really going on with this person you're looking at? Is she feeling overwhelmed? Is she feeling conflicted about where to put her energy and how to spend her time? What is she doing really well and where is she struggling? What kind of help does she need?"

When I started talking to her in this way, she started to cry. She could feel how critical and judgmental she was being to herself and how much compassion was available with a bit more neutrality.

I knew that her parents would want her to be more accountable. In fact, they would likely think that I was being a really great coach if their kid was showing up with greater accountability and reliability. I want that for my teen clients as well, but I also know that accountability and reliability aren't always available without my clients having a deeper understanding of who they are and what they really want.

If I go in all fired up, looking to help my client change into someone who is more reliable and more productive, I might miss the point entirely. I might miss the opportunity to slow down myself and help them slow down, to reflect within and see something more true and meaningful.

57

Trust the tissues

When my son, Arrow, was born, he was clearly in discomfort. For several weeks after he came out, he wasn't comfortable lying on his back. We couldn't hold him face-to-face or cradle him like you normally would a newborn. The only way he felt comfortable being held was with his back resting on our chests, with him looking out at the world.

When we laid him down by himself, he would scream—clearly from physical pain and not the emotional pain of separation.

So we held him—for the better part of eight months.

When he was about four weeks old we reached out to a local chiropractor. We didn't want to have anything invasive or intrusive done to him, but we wanted to see about giving him some support if he needed it. When I talked to the doctor about treating him, she said she'd be happy to help and knew that she could. We explained we weren't in a rush to get his body anywhere it wasn't ready to go, but we wanted to see, to make sure there wasn't anything truly wrong and that he was on the right track.

I felt fairly turned off, actually, by her certainty that she could help him. It's not that I don't appreciate confidence, but there was something missing for me in the way she was talking about him and his body. It was as if she knew intellectually what his body would be able to do, and that was the only thing that mattered.

Looking back, I should've trusted my instincts and not gone to see her. I'm sure she's a wonderful practitioner, but she ended up performing an aggressive treatment on him—in what I took as her attempt to make sure she got his body where *she* wanted it to go, and on her timeline. This, as I had tried to explain upfront to her, was not what we were looking for.

Even then I had a feeling that this is what many coaches/ healers/doctors/therapists do in an attempt to ease their own insecurities. They want to *make a difference*. This is a beautiful goal, but at times the change they want to make can come at the expense of their client's/patient's natural healing process.

We trusted Arrow and his body; we simply wanted to provide him with some support if he needed it. (And thankfully he wasn't worse off after our experience with her, but he certainly wasn't any better.)

I reached out to another healer in town, Dr. Dan, an osteopath/cranial sacral doctor who came highly recommended, and I remember my first conversation with him so well. I shared what Arrow was experiencing, and he said, "I'd be happy to visit with Arrow and see what his body is ready for."

This was so reassuring to me.

He trusted Arrow, and Arrow's body as well. He trusted whatever was occurring for Arrow and would work with that. He wasn't going to move too quickly. He was going to listen and tune in to what Arrow's next step was, if any, with his healing. He wasn't worried about pleasing me—the person paying for the work. He cared about helping my son, about creating a space where healing could happen if Arrow and his body were ready for it.

In other words, he looked at Arrow like we did—with curiosity and neutrality. None of us were in a rush to get him anywhere he wasn't ready to go. We weren't concerned about developmental milestones or markers, about being behind on some made up statistical chart, or being "broken" or "flawed." We saw Arrow as a unique being, completely perfect and with a wise, inherently healthy system and a wisdom that surpasses human understanding. We knew that physical or emotional crises are not necessarily problems that need immediate fixing. We want to tend to ourselves and our family and children, but with open, non-reactive minds and an appreciation for the mysterious energy that's working inside all of us.

We had a few sessions with Dr. Dan, during which he treated Arrow in the most gentle and helpful way. He listened to his body. He trusted his tissues—in other words, the inner wisdom inherent in his body. Over the weeks after the treatments, Arrow's systems started to unwind and we noticed a big difference. It was many months before his was a fully functioning little body, and I have no doubt that the work that we did with him made a significant difference in his return to health.

A few years later I started having my own sessions with Dr. Dan. I began this when I became pregnant with my fourth child. I experienced the same debilitating nausea and vomiting often associated with hyperemesis gravidarum (HG). I started seeing Dr. Dan every few weeks from the time I was about three months along and could actually leave my house without throwing up the moment I stepped foot in the car. Over the course of the next four months I had regular sessions with him, even though my symptoms didn't seem to be improving after each session. But what I did feel was a deep sense of calm and peace during our sessions. It felt right to see him. I was also doing several other things, including IV vitamin infusions, SeaBands, constant nutritional tweaks and adjustments, blood work, acupuncture, traditional chiropractic . . . anything I could to try to support my body through the process. Most of the other treatments I tried I had a very low tolerance for. They either exacerbated my symptoms right away, or I just knew intuitively they weren't a fit.

But going to see Dr. Dan never felt wrong. It felt absolutely aligned with my overall health.

One day in his office he asked how everything was going, and I shared that not much had changed in terms of my HG symptoms.

He genuinely and curiously asked, "Why do you keep coming back to see me then?"

I jokingly replied, "I trust the tissues."

He knew what I meant: I wasn't trying to hurry my system into a state that *I* deemed more healthy. On a deep, gut level I knew that what he was doing for me was making a difference even though I couldn't see it or feel it in a dramatic way. His work felt supportive in a way I couldn't explain. And I know that even though I was there for an acute reason, there were much broader positive impacts going on that I couldn't see. What's more, from a much bigger perspective, I trusted that whatever HG is in my life for, there's a lot to learn from it. I could write a whole book about that alone, but for now I will say that one of my biggest learnings, and something that has profoundly changed me, is the insight that my value as a human, a coach, mother, wife, daughter, is not tied to how much I can do every day and how well I can do it. There have been so many days where I've literally been unable to do anything but sit on the floor in a dark room, in a very still way, watching silly movies or listening to podcasts. I have always been someone who is up for doing a lot, who enjoys waking up early and getting things done, and who wants to do everything really, really well.

Without HG in my life I don't think I ever would've had the opportunity to know that my love-ability is not tied to how much and how well I *do* things. In the darkest moments of my time with this condition, I've had the deepest experiences of unconditional love spring up from my heart, completely flooding my consciousness. When I have physically felt the absolute worst, even with thoughts of pregnancy termination/suicide floating through my mind (simply as my mind's way of trying to alleviate the suffering), I have felt the most incredible love and compassion for myself and appreciation for who I am. This love, compassion and appreciation had nothing to do with anything that I was accomplishing or creating. It was completely and solely tied to my *being*, to who I am when I'm literally doing nothing but allowing myself to simply be still with a quieter mind. It's what's there (and what's *always* been there, unconditionally) when I'm not trying to be something more than I already am. When I am sitting in my presence, absent of any external striving or doing.

HG gave me the opportunity to have this insight because I couldn't do anything about the invisible thoughts that I used to take as truths—those familiar thoughts that would pop up in periods of rest and relaxation or even recovering from sickness or surgery or childbirth. Those thoughts would say, "Get up and do something! Don't waste the day! You should be doing more with your kids, with your work, with your life! You should clean that closet, prep that dinner . . ." With HG, instead of taking these thoughts as facts like I usually did and acting on them immediately, never slowing down enough to question them or to see beyond them, I had to sit there, unable to move, often in a puddle of nausea. And what I found is that the thoughts simply passed through my awareness. They had no real substance. Yet in one way or another they had been this background hum subtly running my life. HG left me unable to respond to these thoughts like a willing servant, so I received the incredible gift of watching them dissolve into nothing. I felt the fullness of my presence beneath them, and I saw the truth that I didn't need to do anything or go anywhere to truly be okay. To be love-able. To be enough. I could just sit there, still, quiet, and not contribute through doing. Just *being* was—and is—all that is required.

On a very meaningful level, I knew that Dr. Dan was working with me in a way that lined up with how I relate to myself and to the mental/emotional/physical challenges of life. I shared this with him (more or less) and he got it. He was moved and touched. I think perhaps because he felt seen by it too.

My intention as a coach is to bring this level of trust and thoughtfulness to each one of my clients. To "trust their tissues." To trust their process and not yank them into some other space even if it's where they are ultimately heading. I want to be an embodiment of trust in their process and reflect back to them the health that is already residing within them—even when they are in the midst of painful thinking and feeling. There is health and wellness. There is vitality. Right here right now. Sometimes I believe people enter into coaching arrangements to deal with an issue that might be a true gift sent from their soul, something that supports them in waking up to something even bigger than any of us could imagine. If we rush too quickly to get through it or past it, we might miss it. Yes, there might be shifts that can happen. There might be insights to have. There might be healthier thinking and behaving, and we can and will go in that direction with great clarity and intentionality. But we do so while trusting the process, the timing, the readiness of the individual. When I come from this place within myself as a coach it is a completely different experience from demanding that a client become something other than what they are right here and now.

I also never want my clients to feel as if I see them as needing fixing. I know this can subtly slip into the process—for example, when I find myself in some great, scrunched-up-face effort to get them to see something within themselves or wake up to their own brilliance. Sometimes they're just not there yet, and that's fine. So it helps me stay present in the moment, to look at them as if they are whole—because they are.

What I like to focus on is what the next, very simple, very gentle step might be. And very often that step, that insight, that awakening comes from them relaxing more fully into the present moment, knowing there's no pressure or expectation from me, knowing through a felt experience that there's no better destination to get to, there's nowhere to go, and that everything that they want to feel—the peace, joy, enthusiasm, etc.—is here now.

58

Changes that stick

I know it can be tricky at times to separate out my worth and value as a coach from my clients "performance." But as someone who truly wants to support people in living happy and healthy lives, it's absolutely essential to be able to do this. And it's also essential to redefine what success looks like within a coaching experience.

It's really important for me to be transparent with the parents I work with. To slowly and thoughtfully discuss expectations. To talk about what progress looks from my perspective—which might entail goal line or physical world progress. But more importantly for me is that my clients might learn how to say yes to things that feel right and no to things that don't. They might learn how to take risks, knowing that they are unbreakable, they might learn how to speak up for themselves, how to advocate for themselves, how to apply to colleges that they really want to go to even if they don't have the support of those around them, how to wear what they want, be who they want to be, come out if they are in the closet, stay in the closet if they feel pressure to be out . . . In short, success to me looks like my clients having their own back, appreciating the uniqueness of who they are and understanding that their worthiness is intact. That the very fact that they exist means that they were wanted here. They were intended.

Might I even say, they were created with great care and thoughtfulness.

This is an awareness that has huge implications if they can claim even a tiny glimpse of its truth. This understanding tends to handle procrastination, because it takes away pressure. It tends to take care of being more organized, because it creates priorities.

This is an inside-out approach that might be slower in some ways (not always), but in my experience it creates physical-world changes that actually stick, that no longer require pressure or willpower. I want the work I do within a six- or twelve-month coaching agreement to extend out for years and decades and centuries beyond that short little timeframe.

I don't want their work with me for six months to be the pinnacle of productivity and inspiration. I want it to be a working ground for tilling new levels of awareness, new insights, deeper self-discovery, a deeper understanding of who they really are, and an understanding of how their mind and emotions operate within the system of their being. An understanding of how their experiences are brought to life through their consciousness.

So if I am in a rush as a coach, trying to prove myself as "good" to the parents who pay me, I'm not being in integrity with what I truly believe helps people. I'm doing it for my ego. I'm trying to be good by other people's standards instead of what feels true in my heart.

And I *do* want to acknowledge that some people hire coaches to simply help on the "goal line," even if it's for a short time at first. It's really important for me to slow down in the enrollment process to get a feel for whether or not the thing that I am focusing on is the thing that the parents care about as well. And if it is, we can all have a very rich and meaningful, thoughtful, slowed down coaching experience together, and create beautiful, lasting changes that don't fade away the moment our coaching agreement ends.

59

The goal line and the soul line

One concept I always bring into my sessions with clients, especially my teens, is the idea that we are operating in two worlds simultaneously: The Goal Line and the Soul Line. This is a distinction I learned at the University of Santa Monica. I have since heard George Pransky discuss this concept as the Game of Life and Living Life, and Steve Chandler describes it as the Chess Board and the Chess Player.

The first is the physical world, and it may seem like the most obvious; this is the world we wake up to and work in and go to school in and so on. It is the world of polarity. Things going good or bad. Things going according to plan or not. We have what we want or we don't. There's visible, trackable progress, or there isn't.

Simultaneously, we're also experiencing our inner world, which in my mind is even more relevant than the outer one, in that it's the world we **feel**. The inner world is where we experience our thoughts, and thus our feelings, about what's going on around us. This understanding can be incredibly helpful for young people when they see it, when they begin to look in a more accurate direction for where their emotional experiences spring from—whether experiences of joy and fulfillment or grief and despair.

Our inner world is where we experience our state of mind. It's where we can move into a more neutral way of viewing our physical life *and* our inner world. It's where we can learn to transcend polarities and enter into an experience of acceptance, of learning, of growth and expansion as ways of being and relating to ourselves and our lives. It is also the space where we learn how to take responsibility for our experience of life, which is very empowering.

When we realize our experience comes from the inside, we also see that there is something we can do about it. If our emotional state came from outside of us, instead of being empowered we would be victims of all that happens to us and around us—and we are not.

With a focus on the soul line we can learn to slowly break the habit of living on an emotional rollercoaster, only feeling good when things are going well according to our ideas, and feeling bad when things go poorly.

We can wake up from this illusion and enter into a space that transcends the thought that our inner experience is tied to how things are going on the goal line. In this space we have the possibility of tapping into our true selves, of seeing ourselves and our lives from a neutral perspective.

In this space we know how to be curious, how to slow down before jumping to dramatic conclusions—or to any conclusions at all. In this space we are calm, patient, in touch with common sense and a genuine wonder about what each new moment may be bringing forward, even if that moment is not part of the ego's plan.

It's here that we can learn to listen deeply to a more grounded and trustworthy part of ourselves, one that has our backs no matter what, and which is fearless when it comes to life changing our plans.

I find it incredibly liberating to see the truth of this.

In this space I know that sometimes when my dog barks I am annoyed and sometimes when my dog barks, I laugh. It's my opportunity, looking in the direction of the soul line, to remember that my inner experiences aren't coming from my dog.

Because of this, we also have an opportunity to see the truth that when we accomplish a goal on the goal line, *it* doesn't create a sense of ongoing, never-ending fulfillment. It is often a very short-lived feeling of satisfaction and celebration. When, for example, an athlete wins a championship or a gold medal, you can see that this is a moment in time—a potentially *wonderful* moment—that is then moved on from. The athlete gets up the next day, possibly still in the wake of the success, but bit by bit the delight fades and a new goal emerges, a new destination to be strived for and reached.

When we look to accomplishments on the goal line to be our source of daily fulfillment and happiness, we are essentially going to a dry well for water.

When we start to look for a sense of fulfillment and wellbeing from the *inside*, a self-sourced reservoir, we're giving ourselves a real chance at a potentially more satisfying, meaningful and rich life experience. When we view ourselves as more than just goal-setters and goal-getters, but instead as multi-faceted beings capable of sensing peace and purpose regardless of circumstance, when we start to see each moment as an opportunity to turn within, slow down, get reflective, let go of striving . . . we can begin to tap into a wellspring of goodness that is not tied to anything in the physical world. It's a well that is never dry.

Of course, waking up to and remembering this is not a perfect process—at least, it's not for me. I have high moods and low moods that I occasionally blame on my kids or my husband or my work. I feel care-free and full of whimsy some moments and tight and edgy others. The powerful thing here, though, is waking up—sometimes slowly—to what is creating these shifts in state. It's not life going well or poorly. It's not my kids' behavior or the amount of money in the bank. It's not even more positive or negative thinking. The way I see and experience it, my state shifts as my intensity or my bearing down shifts within my mind.

Or said differently, when I am light-hearted about my thoughts— positive or negative—and take them with a grain of salt, even when literal shit is hitting the fan (which occasionally does happen with a one-year-old and five-year-old) I feel good.

When I am tense and really taking things seriously within myself about my thoughts or my outer-world moment (which I experience through my thoughts), when I am judging myself, others or life, when I am making dramatic conclusions or definitive statements about myself, others or life (which I have been known to do from time to time)—I don't feel great.

For me there is freedom in waking up to this. Waking up to **what** changes my state of mind and my good or bad feeling.

In terms of an experience of fulfillment and happiness, for me it's exciting to look at the truth that it comes from an inner experience, and perhaps it deepens as we grow our awareness of how we are relating to and experiencing our inner life.

More and more awareness in this area is a way of evolving on the soul line, as a chess player, as we live life. It's very lovely to look at what evolution on the soul line truly looks like. In my experience it's a simple, deeper enjoyment of life, regardless of how things are going on the goal line. It's feeling more peace, flexibility and love, within myself and for others. It's being more in touch with my natural state of being. Childlike, curious, caring, open and free.

Evolution here feels satisfying and meaningful, and it can happen regardless of goal line successes or failures. We can grow within ourselves, within our consciousness, and use life's challenges as opportunities to grow and expand our capacity for unconditional love, for tapping into a sense of wonder and possibility, for connecting more consciously to our essential nature—the space within, where the source of all feelings comes from. And in doing so, there's naturally a deeper sense of fulfillment, peace of mind and satisfaction that tends to be experienced more often.

With this perspective, evolution on the goal line can begin to take a different shape. Rather than trying to get something from the physical world (happiness, love, peace, etc.), our engagement there can become more of an expression of our creativity and our intention to make a difference, to give. When we wake up to the reality that accomplishments on the goal line don't magically create a lasting feeling of satisfaction or ongoing sense of fulfillment, but rather that those feeling come from within, we can relate to the goal line in a whole new way.

We can also relate to challenges and things not going according to plan in a whole new way. We can stop basing our sense of security, of wellbeing, of worthiness, on events in the temporary, always changing, physical world. We can begin to see the world for what it is: a playing field. A space to give, serve and create.

Looking at the goal line from the perspective of it being a place to create and to share and to give can be very liberating and clarifying.

Of course, we are on the Earth and have needs. Most of us, myself included, need to create a living and provide for ourselves and our families. AND there are endless ways to do this.

It can be very fun and uplifting to approach the goal line from this perspective . . . that it's the playing field, that it provides an opportunity for us to express ourselves and share what's in our hearts, to make a difference in a meaningful way, and to creatively contribute. When we stop looking to the goal line to give us the experiences that are not actually found there, such as love, safety and fulfillment, we can approach it in a whole new, much more expanded, playful and creative way, while meeting our physical world needs.

As a coach, one thing I'm very clear about is that I tend to put a premium on the Soul Line—on my clients' inner experience of life, on what's going on in their inner world and how they understand their own inner workings.

When somebody says to me that they want to get straight A's, get into Harvard and be at the top of the class—then maybe go on to be the President of the United States—I'm always incredibly supportive. I'll help them create pathways for these goals. I'll do my best to guide them to a vision and understanding of their abilities so that they see they really are capable of so much in life.

As a way of supporting them in achieving the goal, if it is really heart-felt, and supporting their overall deeper understanding of who and what they are as a human being, we'll also talk about the soul line here.

We'll get specifically into the WHY behind their goals, and especially about where experiences of happiness and fulfillment come from. We get to really dive into the motivation behind goals, what those goals mean to them and where they came from. In their mind, will it make them happy? Do they know a bit about where happiness and fulfillment really come from? Is it *their* goal, or is it perhaps their parents' goal? Do they know that even if they achieve the goal, they might feel the same as they do now? And if that is true, do they still want to pursue it? Does the pursuit and achievement of the goal allow them to express their creativity, their natural gifts, to share and to serve in ways that feel meaningful?

This can be an interesting conversation to have, especially for a young person. The takeaway I want them to get is that *their reasons* for doing what they are doing are incredibly important.

If going to Harvard is on the table as a goal because they feel it's what they are supposed to do based on, let's say, their family history, I'm going to ask a lot of questions about that. I'm going to encourage them to look deeper within themselves to discover if there are other choices they might make that are more aligned with who *they* are, how they want to make a difference on the Earth and the gifts they are here to share. I've worked with many people in their forties, fifties, sixties and beyond who, on reflection, felt they'd spent their entire lives barking up the wrong tree. Doing work to try to get approval or love. Taking on projects out of a sense of obligation or because it seemed like the right thing to do in order to be respected. Obviously none of us would ever want our teen clients to feel that way. Accomplishments on the goal line mean very little if they're not in alignment with the heart and soul of the person who's succeeding.

I see this as one of the greatest gifts we can support our young clients with—getting clear about what is actually available on the goal line: moments of delight, opportunities to give, serve and express themselves. It's wonderful to support a teen in getting lined up inside with what truly matters to them so they can start their adulthood with clarity on what would create a meaningful life going forward, as well as getting lined up and clear within about where true fulfillment lies. To help them connect with a vision and clarity on what a life could look like that would feel satisfying and worthwhile in terms of sharing their gifts, contributing in a way that matters to them, making a difference in a way that feels meaningful. Coupled with a connection with their own guidance system, an understanding of where they want to make decisions going forward from. From fear and other people's expectations? Or from self-sourced inspiration and joy? From a feeling of obligation or from a feeling of freedom? From their ego trying to feel safe or from a sense of trust in themselves and where their heart is calling them?

These are some of the questions we explore as a way of helping them get clear about what they really want, and how to make decisions going forward. It's also about helping them understand on a deep level that happiness, peace, fulfillment and ongoing daily satisfaction is an inside job that can start right now.

It's not out there, it's in here, right now.

Do you really want to look back on your life and see how wonderful it could have been had you not been afraid to live it?

Caroline Myss

Nuts and Bolts:

Creating a Coaching Practice

(Note: While this section goes into client creation and enrollment, I share additional thoughts on setting fees and creating programs in the Q & A section of this book.)

60

What does the enrollment process look like for teenagers into my coaching practice?

When adults pay for their own coaching, the enrollment process is fairly straightforward. Your enrollment and coaching takes place directly with your client. Agreements, goal-setting and more all occur within the context of the one-on-one relationship between the coach and the individual paying for the coaching.

With teens this couldn't be further from the truth, at least at first. It's true that once I've entered into a coaching relationship with a teen, there is a lot of overlap between the way I'll work with them and the way I work with adults. But the enrollment process is quite different.

I've learned through a process of trial and error that it's absolutely mandatory for me to talk with a teen's parents—or whoever is paying for coaching—**before** I ever talk with the teen. I went about this backwards for a long time. I'd meet with the teen first, and if we really connected and it felt like a good fit, I'd talk to their parents about my programs and fees. Sometimes this worked well. But when it didn't— when my fees weren't a fit for their budget, for example—there was disappointment all around. Even if I'd formed a bond with the teen and we had a sense of what we could create together, we couldn't move forward. So I've learned never to talk with a teen without discussing the coaching relationship with their parents first.

I've been taught to build a practice through service. This means my method is to serve a client first and then talk about money after a couple sessions if it seems appropriate and like we are a good fit for working together. But when working with teens, I serve the parent first. So when a parent asks, "How are you going to coach my teen?" I invite them in for an hour-long conversation about it, always, every time.

In that conversation, as I have shared in previous chapters, I'm curious not only about the teen but also about the dynamics involving the parent. How do they feel about what's happening with their teen, and how is that affecting the relationship? My goal is to support the parent in seeing possibilities and perhaps in feeling a bit lighter and more optimistic about whatever's going on. I give them support for working with themselves while they're going through whatever they're going through with their teenager.

Part of my intention in serving deeply in this way is so that when we start talking about money, the process and potential benefits of coaching all make sense to them. They see why I work the way I do, and they feel the value themselves from our very first conversation. I let them know that the way I work isn't a fit for everyone and it's okay if it's not something that feels right to them. If it doesn't, I will help them find a good referral, and I always do my best to make this happen for parents. I also explain that while it's premature for me to be talking about money for coaching their teen, I need to know it's possible for them to pay my fee and move forward if my initial conversation with the teen is helpful. That way, if the teen and I both want to move forward with coaching I know ahead of time that it's possible to do so.

Often, I understand at some point during my initial conversation with a parent that I won't work with their teen, for whatever reason, financial or otherwise. In these cases I aim to use our remaining time together to make a meaningful difference in my conversation with the parent. I coach them as if I've come into their life simply to lend some help in that moment. Regardless of the enrollment outcome, then, my heart feels very full and satisfied. If it's a yes, I talk to their teen and if after that, the parents, myself and their teen are all in alignment with working together, and the logistics and fees all line up—we enter a coaching relationship.

My programs are a minimum of six months and up to a year—sometimes longer with some clients. I started out my coaching practice with three-month coaching arrangements but saw after a few years serving this demographic that a longer period of time together created a deeper and more meaningful experience and more lasting impact. I've worked with several teens for four or five years, and it's absolutely breathtaking to watch them grow and evolve during that time. It helps me feel that in my own small way I'm doing my part to create a new generation of heart-centered leaders. Long-term work together creates long-term, lasting results, and that's what I want. That gives me great job satisfaction.

I know I talk about this ad nauseam in the coaching programs I run, but I do want to mention it here as well: my first five years of "trying" to coach, I did one-offs. I had no long-term programs and was ONLY focused on affordability. I was not focused on service in the slightest. I didn't see it this way at the time, but it became clear to me through my own experience of being coached that if I really wanted to help people, it meant creating a container around the relationship, where we were both engaged with and committed to the process together. So I do not do one-offs as a standard business model, and making the shift has changed my world. The year I made the shift from one-offs to three- or six-month programs, I worked about twenty hours less a week on average and billed $100,000 MORE that year. I am not one to fixate on making as much money as I can in as little time as possible, but I am one to focus on providing for my family in a substantial way, while being a mom and wife. I am one to fixate on creating high-quality coaching relationships instead of a fast and furious, haphazard coaching business.

Within the programs I create with teenagers I also include at least quarterly sessions with parents to continue to serve them and answer questions that may come up along the way. In my experience, including the parents is always valuable. The more time I spend with them the better. I have a reflection form as well, which the teen fills out around the halfway point of our program, and it goes to the parents. This gives the teen an opportunity to share their coaching experience with their parents. The form is also important because many teens don't discuss what they experience in coaching with their parents. The reflection form is one way for parents to get an inside look at what their teen is experiencing if they're not sharing a lot with their parents. I share an example of the reflection form I use in the "Additional Resources" section at the back of this book.

So my enrollment process with a teenager can cover a lot of

ground and be more nuanced than if I'm enrolling an adult client who is paying for their own coaching. It encompasses at least two conversations with the parent and one and sometimes two conversations with the teenager. I don't go fast. Quite the opposite: I go very slowly and seek to serve in a meaningful way for both parent and teen all along the way.

To break it down again: my process is to talk to a parent first, for at least an hour. If we agree to move forward, we schedule an hour-long session with myself and the teen. Once that session is on the books, and often before it happens, I put a second hour-long session on the calendar with the parents. I tell them in that session we will simply check in. I will share any insights I have around what may support their child and whether I think coaching together with me will be beneficial or not. I am very honest.

I know that parents are putting a great deal of trust in me as a coach and only want what is best for them and their child. If I feel in my heart that I am not the right person or that their kid is not ready for ongoing coaching, I tell them straight up. I give referrals. I love referring great people to great coaches and healers. I treat potential clients as if they were my family, and I come from that place of true, unattached caring, I make my recommendation on what I see may be helpful. If I found the session meaningful and transformational with their teen, I tell them that. I will say how incredible their child is, and I will also be honest about the opportunities I see for growth and healing. I don't hold back there. I used to and it wasn't helpful for anyone. I used to only share about what was wonderful about someone's child and was completely uncomfortable saying the truth about the struggle they might be having. It was with the invaluable coaching of Steve Chandler and Carolyn Freyer-Jones that I really saw I wasn't serving anyone by showing up that way when I reconnected with parents for that second conversation. I wasn't serving them or their teen. In fact, I was actually working in opposition to their child getting the support they were seeking.

So I make sure a parent knows that I will be upfront with them in that conversation about what I see is a good next step forward, and I will also be very curious to know if they noticed anything within their teen in terms of a shift in energy or mood or behavior following our session. Very often a teen won't talk to a parent about the session, which is absolutely fine by me. But I do want a parent to take note of any changes they may see, and I mention this to them in our first conversation once it's clear I am going to have a session with their teen. I don't expect a parent to come to that second call with me prepared with an answer about whether they want to work together. In all honesty, I might be clear it's not a fit on my end even if they are all-in.

So we meet in that second call to compare notes, so to speak. After that call, if I am a yes to moving forward, I will let them know. Sometimes they know right away if they would like to proceed— maybe even during that second call, and sometimes if they aren't clear, or I'm not, it means me or them talking to their teen again.

If and when they are clear it's a yes to move forward, I will clarify once again their expectations for the work I'll be doing with their teen. I'll slow this down and take time with it. It is so important. SO important. I want to feel at ease when I say yes to working with a family, knowing that expectations and agreements are clear and reasonable. I want to be in a place where I feel confident that I can over-deliver on their hopes. This is something to feel into for yourself. For a long time, I always felt like I was promising the world—and then hustling my butt off trying to keep up with my lofty promises. I would put unnecessary pressure on myself and on my poor teenage clients, trying to be impressive to their parents or trying to keep my unrealistic promises. Don't do this. Learn from me. It is SO much better for everyone for you to slow down this conversation with a parent and truly honor what they want and make sure it is in alignment with how you work and what you see is possible for their teen. Because you will have met with the teen by this time, you will have a pretty good idea about this.

Once we are all clear on moving forward, I ask them how they would like to pay. I get that handled in the moment, and I share that I have a coaching outline that lays out the coaching container I will be creating with them and their teen. I will reiterate the important parts of it right then (as in, I will have fourteen sessions with their teen and two with them over the course of six months), and I tell them I will send it to them when we get off the call. I will also let them know that I will go over the part pertaining to their teen with their teen in our first session. (I include a sample coaching outline in the back of this book in the "Additional Resources" section.)

I then set up the first session with the teen. I will often do that through the parent for that first one, simply for grace and ease, and from then on intend to do all future scheduling with the teen themselves.

I let the parents know I will reach out to them in a couple months, once I have done the mid-program reflection with their teen, and we will set up a time to reconnect for our parent session. I tell them they can reach out to me if something comes up that they want to talk through in the meantime.

A note here. While I will never work with a client who doesn't want to enter into a long-term coaching relationship, I am okay with a parent doing whatever they feel is necessary, apart from some sort of deranged manipulation, to get their teen to show up to an initial session, the one where we meet for the first time. From my point of view, a teenager doesn't know what they're saying yes or no to. So I am okay if they insist that their teen come to a first session. But beyond that it is 100 percent up to the teenager if they want to continue with me or not.

No matter how eager a parent may be, it's part of my business practice to only work with people who want to be supported and want to enter into a coaching relationship. And not only that, it is something that I feel very passionate about in a bigger way. I want to be part of the solution on the Earth of getting out of the dynamic of people having power over others. I know with parenting this is a slippery slope at times, and needs to be taken case-by-case in terms of what is best in each and every situation. But in terms of what I do within my coaching business, it is of the utmost importance to me that when we agree to work together, it's truly from a place of autonomy within a teenager, from a feeling within themselves that it would serve them and is something that they are willing to explore and experience.

I know it takes a lot of trust and faith on the part of parents to hold space for their child to find their own way through struggle and difficulty. Especially when that child is resistant to support. There is certainly a time and a place for stepping in and redirecting them, and a time and a place for stepping in and supporting yourself as a parent with your own feelings of discomfort and fear, while still allowing your teen the dignity of their own process.

61

The first session with a teenager

In a first session with a teenager, the first words out of my mouth are typically, "Are you being forced to be here?" I usually say it with a smile on my face—and in reality this is after we've said hello and done our normal greeting—but I love to ask this question because it calls out the elephant in the room.

If they say no, then I'll ask them simply, "Why did you want to do this?" And again no matter what they say, it's an easy gateway into more questions.

If they say yes, they are being forced, then I will remind them that they have no obligation to talk to me again if this conversation isn't helpful. I'll make sure that they really know this. In the sample I show in the next chapter you'll get to see this in action. You'll also see some of the questions I ask that get them opening up a bit more. If it's really just crickets on the other side I'll start with something like, "How's your day been today? What did you have for breakfast? What's that thing on your wall over there . . . ? The most mundane conversation can create a lot of rapport that is vital for making any progress with a teenager.

Sometimes I will ask if they have ever had a coach or therapist before. If they have I'll ask them how that experience was, if they liked it, if they hated it. I'm genuinely curious and I also use it as intel. I'll ask them things about their life. I'll say something like, "Can you tell me literally everything about yourself? I want to know everything! Who are your friends, do you have siblings, do you like school, do you hate school, what do you do when you get home from school, do you want to go to college, do you want to travel the world, what's your favorite subject? Sometimes I'll ask, "Is it okay if I just interview you?" They typically love that. And then I really slow down with this. If there's a moment where something pops up that is even slightly interesting or provocative, I will dive right in. I'll do my best to be reassuring and optimistic. I'll ask permission before I give any words that might sound like I'm trying to be overtly helpful. Like, "That experience with your girlfriend sounds rough, sounds like you are handling it really well. I went through something similar with my husband. Can I share with you about it?"

But more than anything, in that first session I want them to feel heard. I want them to feel good, and supported. Only then will they be open to a second session that could lead to some meaningful changes. At the end of the session, and frequently during, I'll ask if the session is feeling helpful. I'll ask how it's going for them. I'll sometimes make jokes like, "Seems like you drifted off for a second there; should we end now!?"

What teens really appreciate is authenticity and genuine honesty. Sometimes at the beginning of a session, knowing what I know about them through the initial conversations I've had with their parents, I'll jump in with something like, "Can I tell you a little bit about myself and why I coach teenagers?" They're typically curious to some degree, if they're not in a state of absolute stress or overwhelm. I'll tell a part of my story and share the epiphanies and insights that I had along the way that relate to them. I want to help them, so I want to give them hope in a way that's actually meaningful and related to them. I want to let them know that I've struggled. That I experience pain, that there are some things that have been really helpful for me. That they are not alone if they are feeling depression or anxiety or having panic attacks. That those experiences are transient and shifting and not an indicator that they are broken.

So I do my best to share things about myself that are relevant to them. They don't have a huge attention span for mundane conversation—actually, most people don't; adults are just typically more polite. But with teenagers, you really need to hit the nail on the head in terms of what you're sharing. This is one of the important reasons for the long initial sessions with their parent. Also, just to emphasize this, in an initial session with a parent, even if they show up to the call and ask me about my qualifications and my experience, how I work, and so on, I let them know that I am happy to share all of that, but what I would really like to do is to hear more about what has them reaching out for help, and I ask if we can dive right into it.

Ninety-nine percent of the time, this comes as a relief to them. Really those initial questions they might ask me are so they feel a sense of safety. They are seeking the feeling that they are making a wise choice by talking to someone qualified. That tends to get handled once we start talking. Then they feel safe, seen, supported and at ease. So I go right in if I can. If they press for more info about myself, I will simply give a 15-20 second answer like, "I had a coach as a young person and it changed my life. I have spent the last twenty years either learning everything I can about how to help teenagers or have been in the work of helping them. It's my favorite thing to do, and I receive so much satisfaction supporting families in having more peace of mind, more joy, more health and wellbeing, better communication between each other and all that great stuff that comes from coaching."

Notice I didn't go into the degrees I have (three) and all my on-paper qualifications. They don't really care about that. At all. They care about why I coach and if I tend to help people, so I try to go directly there. And not only for the parent but because, truly, the more I can learn about their teen the more I can help their teen and connect in a more meaningful way in our first conversation.

Back to the teens. In or near the end of the session I'll ask how it was. Were there any takeaways or anything that was really meaningful for them? I'll ask why. I'll get curious, because if they share something I truly want to know if it was helpful or if they are merely being polite. I will call it out if I think they are lying. I will let them know I care about them getting the help they need—regardless of whether or not I am a part of that. I genuinely want to know how they feel. I want to know so that I can take that information into my second conversation with their parents.

I'll let them know that if they'd like to talk again, we can, and often I'll tell them that I'm going to talk to their parents again about what working together might look like. I don't always say this to a teenager, but often they are curious about what the next steps are. So if they ask, I'll share the truth, and if they don't, sometimes I'll let it lie, because the last thing I want to do is put pressure on them to go home and think about it and decide if it's something they want to do. I truly don't want to do that. I want to let them steep in the experience and allow it to have its organic, natural impact without any future speculating.

As I mentioned in the previous chapter, once I've had the second conversation with the parent(s) we discuss if we want to continue. If the parents aren't sure about what their teen wants, I'll ask them to talk with the teen and get back to me. If they want me to talk to the teen about working together then I am happy to do that.

I will go into that conversation with the teen genuinely curious if they would be up for entering into a coaching relationship together. I emphasize that it's absolutely their choice, that I simply will not work with someone who doesn't want the support. I'll let them know that it would be us talking just like we did in our first conversation, only over the course of six months or a year or whatever we might decide. I also let them know I don't have an agenda and that it's an opportunity for them to receive support in any way that they will find meaningful. I explain I won't be reporting back to their parents and that in fact I only work with families whose parents have agreed to be hands-off in the overall coaching intentions.

In other words, I'll share with them the truth about what coaching together would be like and give them space to feel into what they really want to do. Sometimes it's a yes, sometimes it's a no. If it's a no, I'll ask them if they would like me to refer someone else to their parents. I'll explain that if they are looking for support it comes in many different shapes and sizes. I'll get curious about how they wish it was and why they think it wasn't a good match. Genuinely wanting to know, without a chip on my shoulder, does create a space where they are typically willing to be very honest. My intention is one of empowering a teenager to learn to listen to themselves and follow their inner guidance.

It's not about coercion or influencing them with my ideas about what is best for them.

In my first official session with a teenager after this process, when we are all on board with working together and are beginning a long-term program, it can look very much the same as our first initial session although it might be infused with a bit more enthusiasm now that we've all come together and agreed to go on this journey. I'll go over the coaching outline that I sent their parents, and I will let them know that it's completely up to them what we talk about in each and every session. We don't need to have a grand, master plan for where they "get to" in six months, simply a slow and steady, consistent coming together to reflect, to talk things through, to problem-solve and to help them trust, love and appreciate themselves more and more and more, bit by bit.

62

Exercises for intake

As I've mentioned already, I don't have a particular set of exercises I always use with teens, but the following two come up quite often during intake and also at times throughout my coaching programs with teens.

The Visioning Process

Sometimes in that session it will make sense to me to do some sort of visioning process in which I ask teens about different areas of their life and what they would like to be experiencing in each of them. What they'd like to feel within themselves and see out in their world in each area. I will often write down some of what they say, take a picture and send it to them. I emphasize that it's not a goal we're striving for, but more of a tool we can use as we come together and reflect on their life. I will pull it out from time to time to see what's relevant to them in that moment. I'll read it and ask questions like, "How's it going in this area? Are you feeling more relaxed around new people? If not, let's talk that through and see what we see."

So I use it in a loose kind of way when they might not have something on their minds when we get on a call. If we don't use this tool early on, I might use it later on in our work if it feels right. It's great for helping them see that they can be proactive in creating their life and their experience of life. The areas I'll ask about on these vary from person to person but typically cover:

- In your ideal world:
- How are you treating yourself on a daily basis?
- How do you treat your body?
- What are you experiencing in your friendships?
- How do you feel about school and how are you showing up?
- How are your study habits?
- What do your relationships with your parents look like?
- How are you being with yourself when you are stirred up or triggered?
- What do you do when you are out of balance?
- What is true about your thoughts and emotions?
- How are you feeling within yourself around all of the above?

1-10 Scale

Another tool I love to use is a 1-10 scale. I use it ALL the time. I make up what is on the scale given the situation, but a few I throw out often are, "On a scale of 1-10, 1 being you are miserable, just down and out, and 10 you are as content as you could imagine being, what would you say your average is over the last week?"

No matter what they say, I'll say, "Why did you give yourself that number? Why do you think you're that number? What stopped you from saying something higher? What would need to shift for you to be a higher number?"

When I do this, I am gaining an understanding of where they think their experience is coming from. It's one way of doing intake. I get to hear about their blind spots in terms of where they might be misunderstanding our human experiences. It's a very helpful tool. Often it leads to great, in-depth conversation around their relationships with themselves, their minds and their emotions. It can also lead them to seeing what choices they could make in the physical world to create more of what they want.

We talk about them being a creator rather than a victim. This is a huge revelation for many teens, that this is what they are. They can advocate for themselves, ask for what they want in every area of their lives. It does not always mean they get it, as we all know, but at least they have an opportunity to deal with reality, to learn how to navigate the situation, rather than sitting in a ball of dejection, feeling victimized in their lives.

63

Client story: Brady

Are you being forced to be here?

"Are you being forced to be here, or did you want to talk to a coach?"

"They bribed me."

"I hope you got something good out of it!" I said.

He cracked a small smile. "I did. After this I get to have my phone back after a month of not having it because of my grades."

"That's awesome! What a good deal! And just so you know, if you're not liking talking after a few minutes, you can just hang up on me and I'll let them know we had a good conversation but that we decided not to talk again."

"Okay," he said, sounding reassured and a little surprised. "That sounds good."

"I actually get to decide who I work with, and I only wanna work with people who actually want to talk and connect again after our first session."

"Cool. So my parents can't force me to talk with you again?"

"Absolutely not. In fact, part of what I work on with my clients—

including parents—is learning to trust their kids more to make the right choices for themselves. I want to help the teens I work with have more freedom. I want to help them create situations that they *want* to be in, not ones where they feel forced into things that aren't in alignment with them."

"Okay," he said again. "Cool."

"Why did your parents think that you needed to talk to a coach?"

"They think I need help getting motivated to do my schoolwork, and overall just have a better attitude."

"What do you think about that? Do you need help getting motivated or to have a better attitude?"

"I don't know."

For the past five minutes he'd been sitting back in his chair with his arms crossed, only intermittently allowing a smile to break through. Otherwise he was stone-faced.

I said, laughing, "Well, you look like a bright ray of sunshine to me!"

He laughed with me.

"Do you like the grades that you're getting?"

"I don't know. They could be better."

I smiled. "Are you working really hard to make sure that they're not better?"

He laughed again and said with a touch of defiance, "I just don't really care that much. I don't really get the point of school. I don't like people telling me what to do."

"I hear you on that. Most of the time I hated school when I was a kid. In fact I dropped out of college after two years. I went back later on when it was something I actually wanted to do. From one rebel to another, I totally hear you. What would you rather be doing with your time?"

"I don't know. I really like building things, like robots and remote control cars and things like that."

"That's awesome!" I said, with genuine feeling. "Can you move in with us? My five-year-old is obsessed with robots and remote control cars, and we break them so fast that there's almost no point in us buying them. We need an in-house mechanic! Or maybe you could make us an indestructible one. Do you have any of your own that I could see?"

He said nothing but got up and walked out of the frame of the video call. A moment later he was back with two very cool-looking robotic machines.

"Tell me about them."

It was like opening the floodgates. We spent the next forty-five minutes in his world, talking about things that he was interested in, about what he wanted to do with his future, how school might fit into that or not. We talked about how his childhood friends became obsessed with athletics when he didn't, so he felt like an outcast. We talked about the idea of him starting or joining a robotics club. He gradually sat up and pushed himself forward as he grew more and more animated. There was an increasing sense of optimism about him.

For my own part, I slowed down and really, genuinely appreciated his creativity, his ingenuity, his uniqueness. I didn't know any other thirteen-year-old who had a mind like his, and it was amazing to behold.

We went about five minutes overtime; at a brief lull in the conversation I let him know that we needed to wrap it up for the day.

"Do you want to talk again?" I asked.

He paused in thought for a moment, then said, "Yes. But I don't know what we would talk about. I don't know if I did it right."

I smiled. "This was great!" I said. "We'd basically do more of this—talk about whatever's on your mind. Or whatever's on my mind. I always have a thousand questions. There are so many things you brought up that I'd love to learn more about." I leaned forward and added, "This was a coaching session today. This is what it is. And from my side of things it was awesome. I loved getting to know you a little more. What about you?" I asked. "Was it helpful for you in some way?"

"Yeah, well . . ." He shrugged his shoulders and gave me a small smile. "I feel better. It's not what I thought it was going to be. I thought you were going to tell me everything that was wrong with me."

I laughed and said, "No, no, no. That's not coaching. In my mind, coaching is helping you appreciate who you are and learn to have life feel better for you right where you're at." I let this sink in for a moment, then added, "Do you want to talk next week? Your parents said that if we wanted to talk again we could set it up. Totally up to you, like I said, I don't want to talk again unless it's something that you want to do."

We set up a session . . . and it became the second conversation of over sixty I've had with him since then. A small note here. Given that he was clearly shut down when we started and opened up slowly over time, I wanted to set up another session with him prior to talking to his parents again. I got their go-ahead on this when I heard that their son was feeling very shut down. I knew it might be helpful. This isn't my standard practice, but it is something I am always willing to do when it feels right. I wanted some more time with him to feel out whether our time together could make a meaningful difference. I know our first session felt helpful for him but I wanted to make sure it wasn't a fluke, so to speak.

64

How do I get a teenager to commit to the work?

Coaches often talk about money as motivation for clients to truly commit. Payment often does commit coach and client to bringing their best to the table in a professional relationship devoted to personal development. I see the value in this understanding. But of course it can't work that way with my teen clients, because they aren't directly paying.

My coach, Steve Chandler, once shared with me that he had a client (also a coach) who said she'd never work with someone who didn't pay for their own coaching. When he shared that with me I said, "I'd have a lot less money in my pocket if I worked by that philosophy!"[10]

The truth is that even with my adult clients I don't want money to

---

[10] Steve has a great program for coaches that is available online here: https://www.coachingprosperityschool.info/ I highly recommend checking it out! As a new or even a seasoned coach, there is SO much value in his program. He interviews several successful coaches as well, which adds a depth of value to the whole experience. I even have an interview in there about my work with teens. At the very least, get connected to his mailing list and tap into the incredible source of wisdom, support and humor that Steve shares.

be where they find their primary motivation. Money can symbolize their commitment to the process, but what's far more important is their takeaway from the experience of coaching—that they have been impacted, they've been helped in some important way by the initial conversations we've had, and they see the value in continuing on.

This is especially true for teens—who aren't paying for their coaching.

One thing I *won't* do when working with teens is try to sell them on the idea of coaching as something they need in order to change their lives. In fact, I'll often tell them just the opposite: they don't need coaching or therapy or any other kind of intervention to be okay. They are *already* okay, already lovable and perfect, and my work is about helping them discover this truth within themselves, helping them feel the fact of this and begin making choices that reflect this understanding.

One of the ways I do this is by helping them feel supported and listened to. More than that, I help them learn to listen to themselves, to their own inner guidance and wisdom. For teens and for all of us, this is almost a foreign concept—the idea that you can rely on your own inner knowing to discover answers. We are trained, whether intentionally or not, to look outside ourselves for the answers. Understanding that we can rely on what's inside of us can come as a revelation.

As teens begin to experience this for themselves, they relax. They start to expand into the wholeness and completeness of themselves right in the moment. The idea that they need something else in order to be "enough" starts to fall away, and so does the pain that thinking this way has brought into their lives.

From here they move on to see how this understanding can impact their lives. It gives them a new perspective on the issues that brought them into coaching in the first place. Grades, friendships, romantic relationships, family dynamics, life choices—so much is happening outside of them that they can easily forget they have an inner guidance that can help navigate it all. But when they remember that they do, they gain a sense of clarity and calm that helps them move forward and make decisions with confidence and a deeper sense of trust in themselves.

If I can help create this experience within a teen—or any other human being, for that matter—the desire to have another conversation, and another and another becomes natural. Commitment to our work together becomes an effortless outgrowth of that process.

65

Where do I get my teenage clients from?

For everything you ever need to know about creating clients, see Steve Chandler's full collection of written material. He has so many wonderful books I read and give out all the time to my clients who are also coaches. Top of the list when it comes to creating clients are: *How to Get Clients*, *37 Ways to Boost Your Coaching Practice* and *The Prosperous Coach* (with Rich Litvin). If you haven't read all three of those, do it today. It will help you serve people really well, make a difference and make money immediately. I also have a series of videos hosted on my YouTube channel that have helped coaches with this called, Foundational Practices for Creating a Living as a Professional Coach.[11]

Creating teen clients is really no different than creating adult clients with one huge exception—you can't "market" to them or connect with them directly, or at least I wouldn't and don't recommend it. As I explained when discussing enrollment, it's vital that I connect with parents to make sure they are in alignment with

---

[11] www.youtube.com/playlist?list=PLZMIZqc5zL5RF_L4iH0AvnAAjdpXDZRUL

my coaching approach and process before ever working directly with a teen. This is both practically and ethically appropriate. With that said, I tend to connect with parents of teens in the same ways I would with my adult prospects. I get out into the world and talk freely about who I am and what I do. When I first started coaching I wasn't using social media at all and still don't as a way of intentionally creating clients. Occasionally I will post something I am up to on there but in truth I don't expect to get clients on there. I don't use a website to create clients either. I only created a website well after my practice was full with a waiting list. I use it more as a landing page for people who are already enrolled in a program I might be running, so that they can have easy access to dates and payment options. I do not ever hand it out; the same goes for business cards which I don't have. If someone asks me for my website in person or in e-mail, or when someone is referring another person to me, I will say, "Why don't we set up a time to talk. I am way more interesting than my website, and I can actually answer your questions in real time. I have time next week at 3:00 p.m. on Friday. Does that work for you?"

So how do I create clients? When I first started focusing on work with teens, I made a list of all my family, friends, colleagues and people in my business network, and I asked each one of them if I could talk to them. I let them know I had a question I wanted to ask them and wanted to do it over the phone or by video call.

Once there, I would be a normal human being and connect with them. I would ask about them and listen. I would care. I would enjoy connecting. Then I would share that I was looking to add more teenagers to my coaching practice. I wanted to help teens feel more relaxed and free in their ability to follow their inner guidance and experience greater happiness in their lives. It brings me joy to support young ones and I have space to add in a couple clients. Did they know anyone with teens who could benefit from something like that?

Of course they did.

Within a very short time, because of the effort I put in to connect with people in my world on a regular basis, week in and week out, people started referring teens in their world to work with me. In each one of these conversations I slowed down. I talked at length about why I was working with teens and the outcomes I was seeing. When they would say something like, "My nephew may be into coaching," I would say, "WHY?" I dug in there. I asked them to tell me everything about him. I'd get curious. I'd share how I might help the nephew.

I saw it as an act of service to slow it down, to share more, serve more. And I asked if connecting me to the nephew's mom or dad would be supportive—only after a long and thoughtful conversation, and if it seemed right. Nothing was done too fast. I actually wanted to hear more and also share things that might be helpful for the nephew so that this person I was talking to would actually see the value in connecting me. If this person didn't, it was very unlikely a connection would happen.

After connecting one-on-one with people in my life, daily, weekly, non-stop, at a gentle yet consistent pace, until I had possible clients on the calendar, I started putting on workshops for teens around mental skills and heart-centered leadership. And I continued telling everyone I knew about the work I was doing and putting myself out there in each conversation I had. For example, my husband coached youth volleyball, and I would go to the games with the intention of talking to parents. It wasn't a "hard sell" by any means—I wouldn't push the workshops or individual coaching. I would simply talk with them about their kids. In a way these interactions were for my benefit as well, because they helped me deepen my understanding of how parents perceive their kids and the things that are important in their family lives. We all have family experiences we can draw upon, of course, but getting out there and interacting with so many families helped me gain a more nuanced and rich understanding of the different challenges teens of today are navigating.

I found that when talking with parents, the more curious I got about how their teens were doing, the more openings I saw to share about what I did and how I might be somebody who could be helpful. It often became very natural to share that I had a workshop coming up that might be helpful for them. Or to ask, "Would you like to talk about your son's anxiety next week? I have a couple thoughts that might be helpful. Here are some available times." This is literally what I did. Again, there wasn't any hard sell, just natural, curious conversation. It helped that I *was* genuinely curious and interested in what they and their teen were experiencing.

I also sent emails and called the athletic directors at private schools, colleges and junior colleges within twenty miles of where I lived. I shared a little about who I was and then quickly segued into asking them if they had any mental skills training for their athletes. I explained how I worked in this area and could perhaps be of help to them. This resulted in a variety of work with several of these organizations. In these instances I went in through the "athletic" door because that's my history. I played basketball in college for a little while and spent years of my life invested in sports training and all that goes along with that—namely lots of upset, pain, disappointment and joy. As a coach, what I quickly came to understand is that athletes are just teenagers. Imagine that. My background was a natural fit for supporting teens from this angle.

In the same way, it could be worth looking at your own background in relation to where teens are at in their lives. What's your own academic experience and interest, for example? Did you play sports? Are you an artist or musician? Whether it's art or music or writing or computer programming or whatever, you will find teens there. It is not essential to have these kinds of specific elements in mind in order to be a supportive and successful teen coach, but exploring these questions can provide ideas for how to create clients in your practice.

So the short and specific answer to the question of how I get teen clients is this: through adults who love and care for them, and who want them to have meaningful support.

Beyond this it's as my coach Steve Chandler has said a million times: "There literally are clients wherever you are." It's just about having your head up and being willing to be curious and helpful right then and there, in the moment. It might be at the dog park, Trader Joe's, the gym, a church or a school function. Wherever there are people living their lives.[12]

---

[12] Steve Chandler has an audio called "The How-To versus the Want-To" that I highly recommend for clarifying the "how-to" create a coaching practice in this area.

The Heart of
the Matter

66

What we focus on expands, right?

I am sure you are all familiar with that age-old expression, "What you focus on expands." If I could only say one thing to coaches (and everyone else) about what I see to be most effective in terms of supporting teenagers and their families, it would be this:

Focus on the wisdom, the health, the natural knowing, the intuition, the resiliency, the lovability that is the very nature of who each person really is—including overwhelmed parents and out of control teenagers. Point it out, **amplify** it for them, magnify it, pull it out of the closet, bring it to the forefront.

In my mind, trying to fix behavior is like putting a bucket under a leaky roof. You're not solving the problem. You might be momentarily reducing the effect of it, but you're not actually addressing the cause. And what I believe to be true is that behavior that is reckless, destructive, extreme—it's simply a reaction to a human being feeling out of touch with the nature of who they are in the moment. They are swept up in an illusion of thought which, by the way, is the most human thing in the world.

As coaches we can have a profound impact by supporting teens and parents in reconnecting with their own nature, with the truth of

319

who they are. We can help them learn to distinguish between what is reality and what is their thinking, to connect with their wisdom, their trust that they are not alone, their understanding that there's a solution to every conundrum, that they are never stuck and they are not fundamentally flawed in who they are. When we help a parent or a teenager glimpse the fullness of who they are at their core, that essence can come more alive for them. It gets amplified, comes to the forefront, becomes a living reality rather than a nice idea. It helps them relax, breathe a little easier and feel a sense of optimism.

I think it's wonderful and helpful at times to do physical-world, behavior-changing support with teenagers and parents. Sometimes it is about them connecting to a fresh idea and a new way of doing something. But if we're not looking a little deeper, looking at the possibility that the behavior is stemming from some underlying misunderstanding about who they are, and what they are really up against, then we're missing a big opportunity to make a much more meaningful impact.

I don't do this by preaching to them about their soul and the spiritual nature of everything. That wouldn't go very far. Not for some people. I ask them what their intuition says about choices they are trying to make. I point them back to their own wisdom and common sense. I comment on the love and compassion I see them sharing in their life. I amplify the wellspring of brilliance that is within them already. I don't add anything to them; at best I act as a fan blowing away the smoke that's clouding their perception of themselves and their lives.

67

We came here with everything

"What we are is Peace, Love and Wisdom, and the power to create the illusion that we are not."

Jack Pransky

When I was twenty years old I started going to a spiritual community called Agape International. Up to that point my spiritual life had been very private. I kept it between myself, my meditation cushion and my community at the University of Santa Monica. So being in public at Agape in such an overt way was really uncomfortable for me at the time. I was openly looking for and honoring the Divine within a public space—and it was scary. In fact, I wanted to leave after my first fifteen minutes.

Just as I was gathering up my stuff and looking for the closest exit, the Reverend Dr. Michael Beckwith uttered words that awakened something inside me: "As human beings we can experience a peace that surpasses human understanding."

For some reason these words immediately brought me to tears, and I felt an incredible sense of freedom.

At that time I was struggling in every aspect of my life, especially financially. Taking care of myself and my dog was a daily struggle. There were many times during that year when I had to choose which one of us would eat that day—and it would always be my dog. I went on a lot of "spiritual fasts" simply because I didn't have money for food and was often too proud to ask for help from those around me, even though I am sure it would have been offered.

So hearing the words about experiencing a peace that surpasses understanding lifted a weight off my shoulders. It released me from the idea that I needed to be in some sort of pain or disturbance *because* of what was going on in my life. It gave me permission to feel the peace that exists within me no matter what's going on in my world. When I heard these words, they rang true for me. I had already understood the concept of feeling peaceful in spite of whatever challenging things were happening, but I didn't always give myself permission to let that peace be present, to really feel it within myself. To trust that I wasn't checking out of life, denying reality, but rather tapping into a much deeper truth about our nature and about life—that we are only ever experiencing a glimpse of the fullness of who we are, and that even in a moment of pain or fear, the depth of Love and Source energy that is the very nature of who we are is intact. It is undamaged. We are never broken, all is ***never*** lost, no matter the fearful and dismal thoughts moving through my consciousness.

For me, this was a pivotal moment in my own understanding of what we are all equipped with as human beings. We all have this capacity to have fresh insights and intuitive hits. We can have feelings of peace and calm, even in the worst-feeling times of life. We can tap into a wellspring of love, peace and wisdom while being in the face of physical world challenges and internal struggles.

This is touched on in the following excerpt from a great article by a mentor of mine, Rohini Ross:

> My misunderstanding was that my emotional suffering needed to be healed in order to get to wellbeing. I thought that I needed to eliminate the emotional suffering from my human experience to be okay. It wasn't until I had a session with Linda Pransky, one of the early students of Sydney Banks, that I realized the deeper truth that my feelings don't get in the way of my wellbeing. Wellbeing is there no matter what my emotional experience.
>
> Knowing I am okay no matter how I feel in the moment was revolutionary for me. It was a realization from within that I had not felt or seen before. In that moment, I deeply understood that I was not broken. I realized that I did not need to try to "fix" myself. I knew that I was good enough. Finally, I could relax and just be.
>
> This is as true for you as much as it is for me. I don't care what reasons you may [have] that you are an exception to this. I assure you, there are no exceptions. You are this wellbeing, love, and peace. None of us can ever be separate from it even though we have experiences that feel like separation. Just like a coin has both a head and a tail side, the sides of our nature may look very different, but they are part of one unified whole.
>
> Experiences of separation and oneness are part of the same complete package...[13]

---

[13] https://www.rohiniross.com/love/being-okay-with-your-feelings-is-the-best-thing-you-can-do-for-your-relationship/

The wisdom inside us is always working. It's always there. It's just that I'm not always aware of it. So I see my spiritual path as one of remembering and reconnecting with this wisdom as often as I can.

My professional path revolves around encouraging others to do the same thing with their own wisdom. I want to help others experience what they've come into this life equipped with. Because we didn't come here with nothing. **We came here with** *everything.*

Sure, sometimes it feels like we don't have a GPS system or a "how-to" guide on how to do this life, but in a very real way we do. That guide is our gut feeling that tells us not to get into a car with somebody we don't trust. It's the hunch we have to take a left instead of a right that helps us find a lost dog. It's that feeling of peace and inspiration we get when we think about a job we might apply for or an internship we might take. It's also the feeling of contraction or resistance that comes over us when we think about taking a certain step forward. Sometimes it's fear, but sometimes it's true guidance. We can learn to discern the difference, and this is another thing I help my clients do.

The more that I help them access their own wisdom, the more confident they feel. And the more space I give them to answer questions, the more easily they're able to hear the answers.

I might ask things like,

"What does your gut tell you about taking this job?"

"What would you do if you could truly go for what you want?"

"Are you moving forward out of fear or love and inspiration?"

In exploring how they find the answers to these questions—

paying attention to the feelings and ideas and thoughts that bubble up in response—they learn to understand their own inner voice, to differentiate between fear and the voice of wisdom.

Whenever I'm enmeshed in a dilemma or at a crossroads, I allow myself to get still. I remind myself that **there's no right or wrong— only that which feels most in alignment.** Next I ask myself questions like, "What would I do if I could do anything" or "What does my heart really want?" I always get answers. I might sometimes feel afraid to follow them, but I always get them.

I have absolute faith that this ability—to ask meaningful questions and get reliable, helpful responses—is within each of us. We are all, each and every one of us, extraordinary, but I also believe that our ability to access our inner wisdom is an ordinary mechanism built into all of us. I am not special by any means (no matter what my mom might tell you). I don't have unique abilities or capacities. We're all built with the same equipment.

It's a practice to learn to reach out to it, to embrace it, to invite it in, to welcome it. My intention—not only as a coach but as a human being—is to share with my clients and the people in my world that they can do the same thing, consciously and constantly, and in doing so it will help them move their lives in a meaningful and satisfying direction, even if they don't have the support or encouragement of their peers or parents, their teachers or mentors. They can learn to trust themselves and the path that is unfolding before them. This to me is true wellness. An appreciation that we are sourced by love and wisdom, that we come into this life with a resiliency that is unrelenting. That our minds return to neutral just as our bodies have a pull toward health. We get cut, our bodies begin to heal. We go into emotional turmoil, our mind naturally relaxes and returns to calm. If we trust the wisdom built into each of us, we can begin to consciously work with our systems, rather than flailing away in fear, worrying that we are broken or that our lives are broken.

To sit with teenagers in the middle of their messy lives and not be afraid of their experience, to see the fullness of who they are and what they came with—well, that is a blessing beyond measure for everyone. That is the stuff magic is made of. That is what is on offer as you begin the sacred and wild work of coaching teens.

Pure magic. Pure love.

68

A final thought: BREAK FREE

"The essential lesson I've learned in life is to just be yourself.
Treasure the magnificent being that you are and recognize
first and foremost you're not here as a human being only.
You're a spiritual being having a human experience."

Wayne Dyer

As I learn more about what is occurring on earth not only these last few years, but over the last several thousand, I see that perhaps more than ever we're closer to being collectively ready to live in an awakened, peaceful way, not only with others but within ourselves. Perhaps the first cannot happen without the second. And what I am feeling into is a peace that is found when we are inspired and encouraged to look within for our sense of well-being, our connection to something bigger than ourselves, to awaken into a peace, a joy, a love that, as Dr. Michael says, passes human understanding and transcends the daily minutiae of this world.

As I have shared, I was encouraged and invited to tune into my inner world at a very young age. I was invited into the mystery. Into a space within that I cannot see with my human eyes but can feel with my being, with the nature of who I am, and with the senses that come alive in a non-physical, intangible way. Practicing day in and day out connecting to this invisible self has given me access to a calm within that is unrelated to circumstance. An optimism that is connected to the understanding that the feeling of goodness, the feeling of love and gratitude arise from within—and can arise *without* condition.

I hope I have made it clear throughout this book that, as a coach, my intention is to play a small part in encouraging humans to begin and to continue the mysterious journey of tuning into their true nature, understanding who and what they are in a deeper way and that their well-being, their happiness, their sense of purpose and joy are independent of the physical world systems to which we have innocently acquiesced our sense of okay-ness to. I see that at times we have innocently let the school system, the workforce, the medical systems, the governments, determine our state of wellness and collective self-esteem. None of these systems is inherently wrong, but the way I see it, we have given away too much of our power and our sovereignty to things outside of ourselves.

We cannot be defined by anything from the physical world. **What we are is freedom itself.** We are living embodiments of energy in action. Even within a constricted physical world, we can turn within and feel into the majestic beings that we are, infinite and resilient creatures of light, and experience a moment of gratitude or a moment of peace that truly transcends the world. Transcends our own personal struggles. For teens it's a beautiful thing to see them feel a sense of goodness within, even when they don't get the grades school tells them to get, when they feel optimistic and hopeful even when they are let go from a job they love because they took time off to be with a sick loved one. Tapping into the truth that we are free, not only to create what we want from here, but also to experience a light heart and a quiet mind even if the world is yelling at us to feel chaotic or rushed or crushed.

No one can take that freedom away from us.

No one has that power over us, and if we have mistakenly given it away, we can take it back. Right now. We can reclaim what has always been ours. Our right to stand as a human being on the earth, free, peaceful, and living unimpeded, in kindness and in a way that is aligned with our heart and soul. No human or institution has power over you. Take that power back if you have given it away.

My encouragement to myself and my clients is to find a way to live a life where you are an expression of freedom, freedom to live a life that is true to your heart and your soul. The way is out there.

Say no to hours and pay that don't serve you. Say yes to a life that your heart and imagination has conjured. It's here for you.

Say no to constriction and yes to expansion. Let your life be an expression of freedom. It is inconvenient at times, and I believe it just might have been designed that way. To break free means to slowly but surely do more things each day that are truly for your heart, in alignment with your being—and fewer things that comply with someone else's system for what your life should be.

On a daily basis it's choice after choice of not complying with outer or inner world pressure that wants you to cooperate with maintaining the status quo. It's not for the sake of being a pain in the butt or a rebel, but it's saying no when everything in your being says no. Or saying yes when everything in you says yes. Doing so from a place of inner strength and integrity. Doing so with an attunement to who and what we really are, as we continue to wake up to the freedom that is ours—not only within ourselves but also as we live our lives on this beautiful, sacred planet of ours.

The vastness of who and what each one of us is truly unimaginable. A lovely person recently shared a visual with me, an image of our divine nature, that if we could see the fullness of who we are we would see a light being who is so enormous, so powerful that, standing tall, one foot would be on the Earth and the other foot would be on Jupiter.

The absolute magnitude of who we are in our non-physical, non-visible selves, the wisdom, the beauty, the love . . . it absolutely surpasses any human-level issue that may arise, any physical world conundrum that may pop up. It can handle it in an instant. A new idea comes in, a new pathway, clarity, peace of mind. A simple knowing.

We only need to remember that it is there for us. It seems to me that for centuries we have been encouraged to look outside ourselves for strength, for wisdom, for guidance, when all the treasures, all the answers, all the connection, all the intimacy, the love, the joy . . . all the gratitude that we could ever want is right here within, right now. Nothing else required.

The kingdom of heaven is at hand. I'm not one to quote anything religious, because I am not religious, but this expression has some relevance for me. Something that I consider on a daily basis. That *felt* sense of peace and love and understanding . . . it's just waiting for us, waiting with bated breath, with open arms. And all it takes is a moment of stillness. A moment of . . . not even closing your eyes—although you can—but a moment of turning your awareness within.

Considering the possibility that whatever quandary or difficulty or decision is on your mind, that by simply relaxing, allowing your mind to settle, you can and will tap into a wellspring of wisdom and guidance, and it will likely be cloaked in an envelope of unconditional love that guides you, with ease and common sense, to your next simple step.

Additional Resources

Q & A

The section that follows is a question and answer segment I did with several coaches who attended a webinar I led a few years ago. I couldn't get to everyone's questions on the live call so I asked them to email me their remaining ones and once all the questions were in, I compiled them and sent this back to them. I hope it is helpful to you in some way.

How do you discuss and talk about questions with parents regarding the difference between your coaching and therapy?

If I am asked if a kid should do therapy or coaching, I would say that both are great. But it really depends on the person coaching or the person counseling. Many coaches and counselors work within similar structures—as in, committed programs over time or one-off sessions. I know coaches and counselors who do both. So if the parents have a preference, I would encourage them to look for something that suits them. Often coaches don't take insurance; that's another thing to consider. But in terms of the actual work within the session, it really depends on the person. I always recommend that a parent try out a few coaches and a few counselors or therapists to see who is a fit. Sometimes they know right away, after talking to one person, but if for any reason there isn't resonance between their kid and the coach/therapist, I always say to keep looking.

A lot of people will say that therapy focuses on the past while coaching focuses on creating the future, but I haven't seen that to be 100% predictable. Many coaches are trained in deep healing modalities, while some therapists are trained in behavioral modifications in the here and now.

So again, I am a fan of both and I think it's about supporting the parent and teen in getting real-life experience with specific people in those roles to see who resonates.

How do you handle situations with high levels of responsibility, such as depression, suicidal ideation, and so on.

I don't work with teens who are actively suicidal or self-harming. Not that I don't think I could help, it's just that that kind of situation requires a lot of attention, and I'm not up for it at the moment. I used to be, but not so much now.

I do work with teens who have suicidal ideation and move through experiences of depression/anxiety. If I'm about to start a coaching agreement with someone who is dealing with a lot of depression/anxiety/eating disorders/self-harming, etc., I also recommend that they start seeing a therapist. I recommend building a support system. And then I become a part of that support system. I make it very clear that I am not an on-call coach; I have an agreement with clients that I have a forty-eight to seventy-two hour window before I need to respond to calls or emails. This is really important to talk about upfront. The coaching sessions can help create new thought patterns, new ways of being with pain, a new and healthier relationship with themselves—and that process takes time. It's not something that is typically a quick fix, although a lot can happen, and tends to over the course of several months.

I heard you say you include two parent sessions in the six-month programs you do with teens. How do you determine when to use the two parental sessions?

I tell them that we will set them up at the midway point and then near the end. I usually do it after the sixth or seventh session with the teen, and then either before my last session with a teen or after the last session. But I also let them know that they can reach out to me any time they like for a spot coaching call. Most don't take me up on this. If I have a sense during the enrollment process that the parents will want much more involvement, I might include sessions for them worked into the program and increase my fee a bit.

I have my teen clients fill out a reflection form midway through our program and near the end, and I send those to the parents before I have set up sessions with them.

Is that with one parent or both? And if one, have you found one gender to be more interested?

Many of my clients have divorced or separated parents. So I offer those sessions in whatever way makes sense. Sometimes it's together, sometimes it separate. This does make for more time on my end, but I'm happy to do it. And it's been a complete mixed bag in terms of who has more interest. In some families I only ever talk to the dad, and other families, just the mom.

What do you do if you clearly see that one or both parents are the issue and they are not interested in being coached?

I move on.

It does not work if the parents are a big part of the "problem" but not willing to explore it. Sometimes I might make an exception to this if it seems like working with the kid alone will make a profound difference; then I might be willing to explore that and have the two sessions with the parents be more of a sharing time rather than any kind of deep coaching or reflecting.

But in general, I only work with families who are really open to the transformational process.

Of course, there can be hesitancy and trepidation, but if they have a general sense of being open and willing to engage, I'm in.

If I sense there are closed doors all around I refer them on. The truth is there might be a better fit for them in terms of a coach or therapist or healer with whom they may, for whatever reason, be more open.

Are your sessions twice a month, and how many minutes long are they, and why do you choose that instead of three times a month?

Yes, two times a month for forty-five to sixty minutes with the teens and parents. I work through video calls with teens and over the phone with parents. I like to see my teenagers faces. I started out with a three-month format and found that my clients all tended to renew. So over the course of six months I noticed that things went so much deeper, and a gelling occurred in terms of the transformation in what we were working with. So I decided I just wanted to see if it would work out for us to move into that six-month format, and now it's all that I do. People do ask for shorter-term at times and I simply say, "I don't do that, and here's why . . ." It's never been an issue, and only once in all these years did I have someone stop early. (And even then, her remaining sessions we just moved over to another family member I was working with and it all worked out great.)

Everything I am doing now has come through trial and error. I used to offer more sessions a month, and it didn't seem to be as helpful as every other week. My sessions with teens used to be ninety to a hundred and twenty minutes. Poor kids! I thought the more time the better for everyone until I started doing the reflections midway and at the end. Without fail, they'd say they love the work but the sessions feel too long. I totally agreed and saw I was trying to over-deliver, but not in a good way.

It's all through trial and error, so just jump in with what makes sense to you and you can adjust once you get some real-time feedback, either from your own experience or from your clients.

What if they want homework? Maybe a resource to watch, read or listen to?

Occasionally I will ask them if there's something that they'd like to do or explore or read that would help them integrate whatever we talked about. I'll let them decide if they want to do it or not. When I first started coaching it felt like there was so much conversation around, "Did you do the thing that you talked about?" This tended to come with processing a lot of guilt and hesitation. So I took that out of the process and put it all on them. As in, "If you want to do X or Y, do it for yourself! Don't do it for me. And if you do it, tell me how it was! And if you don't do it, who cares!? But if you wanted to do it and you didn't do it, let's talk about that . . . Why are you withholding joyful, meaningful experiences from yourself? Don't you know you're worthy of having a life you love! Do you know that you can go for what you want? Do you know that you are capable of making healthy choices for yourself even when your brain is telling you to stay up all night eating chocolate?!"

Do you have forms for parents to fill out, before or after working with their teen in the six-month program? If so, what types of questions do you ask or have them reflect on?

I don't have anything for the parents, only for the teens. But that sounds like a fun idea if you're wanting some feedback from them. I like to reflect in real time with them all along the way, and if something feels off we look at it then and there and have a conversation.

Are the two sessions with the parents included in the six-month program?

My six-month programs typically look like fourteen sessions for the teen and two for parents as part of the fee. I also offer spot coaching to both and email support. Only if it seems like they are actually needing way more support do I consider adding in an additional program with a parent. I certainly err on the side of generosity in terms of supporting the families I work with. And I also know that in my mind my fees are substantial, so I don't feel like there's an imbalance in there at all. (I went through years of the imbalance and know that feeling well!)

Do you do a session every other week in the six-month program (so twice a month for six months, and you add in one to two

sessions if needed)?

Yes, and you can look at my attached coaching outline. For me when I go every other week it tends to be more like thirteen or fourteen sessions, so I rounded up to fourteen. With some clients I do twice a month and then that's what I'll put in the agreement. I change it up based on what I want to do in the moment and what works within my practice—and what I see could serve the family.

Just curious how you came up with your price structure? Or what was your thought process? As a new coach, not certified yet, I do not want to sell myself short from the get-go. So how did you eventually have the confidence and courage to figure out, "This is what me and my services are worth?

(I'm not certified, just FYI—not by any official standards! As I have heard Steve Chandler say about himself…"I am not certified or qualified!")

I started out at $35 an hour. I went through years and years of feeling grossly underpaid for what I was putting into the work but it's where I was comfortable getting started. And then at some point I simply did some math. I sat down with my coach and I looked at how many clients I could actually work with, how many I wanted to work with and how much time in the day I had to work. I also factored in that my enrollment process tends to take a couple weeks—and while many people become clients in the future, not everyone does so in the moment. Given all this, I saw that I could truly believe I could create at least one client a month. And if one client a month were paying me, what would my fees need to be for me to become a full-time coach??

So I started out at $3,800 for three months and I did that for a long time. And then I started seeing that most of my clients were renewing, so I made a shift to $5,000 for six months. Not long after that, because of a waitlist and my own increasing financial needs (a new baby and a husband who stopped working to full-time dad) I bumped up to $7500 for six months. I'd been at $7500 for six months for about 5 years and it felt like a great fee. Recently I bumped up to $10,000 for six months, and that's working out great too. Many of my clients now, when we renew, are on year-long programs with me. But I don't tend to offer that out of the gate simply because I truly don't know how those first six months will feel.

With all of the coaches that I work with who are getting started, I think it's wonderful to look at what you actually need to create in terms of income. Not a stretch goal, not a dream goal, but a real, logistical look.

And then look at how many hours in a day you have to devote to coaching—knowing that a good portion of those hours will be spent in conversation with people who might not become clients right now. Some will, of course! Your conversion rate will grow over time as you're connecting with people who resonate with you more and you get better and better at serving people. But in the beginning I think it's all about making it easy for people to work with you while staying on track, moving toward sufficiency in your income. In 2020 I hosted two webinars called: Creating Sufficiency as a Professional Coach and they can be found here:

https://youtube.com/playlist?list=PLZMIZqc5zL5RF_L4iH0Avn
AAjdpXDZRUL

https://drive.google.com/file/d/1vwFNVz9JoUjd2aKFgBloxg26bu1
7WTgw/view?usp=sharing

What I recommend is starting with a fee that you feel really good saying, and putting that inside of a program (meaning a series of sessions over a set period of time). I can't say enough about the value of programs versus one-offs. It's an absolute game changer—not only for coaches but also for clients.

And whatever that fee is, know that it will change over time. I would be doing short-term agreements, as in six weeks or three months, or something like that where you can actually dig your teeth in with a client and really serve them, but where you're also not committed in a long-term way. And then let your experience be your guide. You will feel in your heart that you were underpaid, or you will feel in your heart that you have landed on the perfect fee, or you will feel in your heart that for whatever reason your fee was too high. You can trust your instincts and let your heart tell you, but it's hard to figure this out ahead of time. You just need to dive in with something to get going. And try to take your eye off of what everyone else is doing and simply focus on what you need to create in your life in terms of income, given the time that you have.

You may have all of the thoughts and feelings: you're underpaid, overpaid, greedy, not worth it, totally worth it . . . your mind will go everywhere, and I think what's helpful is staying in practical-feeling reality and simply asking yourself: does this meet my needs? Does this make sense to me on an intuitive level? Does this feel right, right now? And remember, you can change it with each and every new client. You get to decide what to do as you stay in alignment with yourself.

Do you have, or have you done, coaching sessions with multiple teens at one time? Like a safe space for them to vent, ask questions? Such as, "Okay, what would you all like to discuss today?" I feel like they might be more open amongst their peers? Maybe not? Maybe this is more like a workshop for teens?

I have done dozens and dozens of workshops/clinics/in-person group sessions with teens, and they are wonderful! I highly recommend them. For a few years there I did a bunch of workshops called something like "Heart-centered leadership for teens," and then also, "Mental skills for athletes." I would charge $150 for a three-hour session and would have anywhere from 10 to 20 teens per workshop. I would also be talking to the parents before or after—often before to really connect with them and to hear any concerns they have about their children. Often I would do follow ups with parents, and this was a way to serve them and their teen in deeper ways and, of course, to create private clients as well. Groups are great.

You mentioned Nancy Kline. What would you recommend by her? I see she has a book; *Time To Think* is this something you would recommend? Or are there other products, books, that would be good for me to immerse about her?

Her books are great- she has two that I like: *Time to Think* and *More Time to Think*. Look her up. She has great programs, as well as a new book I haven't read yet, *The Promise that Changes Everything: I Won't Interrupt You*.

I am interested in the reflection forms you have; what types of questions or ideas should I use?

I've included a sample reflection form in this book, a few pages from here.

You mentioned you find that in 95 percent of conversations with parents, they want to trust their teens more. Is this correct? Or was it that most teens want their parents to trust them more?

It was that *teens* want their parents to trust them more. Not just with logistical stuff, but when the teen is in a bad mood to not freak out about it—trust the teen's resilience. And trust the teen to be able to do it on their own, whatever "it" is, knowing the teen may fail or make a mess of it, but they want to feel trusted and supported in having the experience, knowing they will be okay, and even better off for it.

What are the most common themes with teens in what they want out of coaching? What do you see as their biggest challenges, hang-ups or common language they use?

Just like adults, it seems to be across the board. But one thing I do talk a lot about is the nature of reality: that they are loved and supported, that they have wisdom in them, that even if they fail a test or at some sport, they are not a failure. They can ask for what they want in life. They can do hard things and have hope that life can get better and better. Many grapple with the reality that they are told what to do 99 percent of the time, so they crave freedom, and I assure them that there is of course inner freedom to experience. We talk about that, but in reality the older they get the more freedom they will have. I talk a lot about flexibility, that just because X happens doesn't mean Y is going to happen. That they have choice. That if they go to a college they don't love they can course-correct. That if they are in a relationship that doesn't feel good they can find a way to leave it. Many are afraid that they will make the wrong decisions, and I tend to relax them by saying, "Yes, you will, but that's not a problem. We all do. And we can course-correct. We are not wrong for changing directions or changing our minds. In fact, it's very liberating to allow yourself to do so."

What about parents? What are the common threads you have seen when working with them? Their concerns about their kid(s)?

The biggest thing I work with parents around is learning to trust their kids' wisdom and life path. To start to see that challenges are not an indicator that something is wrong, but that in fact something very important might be unfolding. To try to be flexible when it comes to their own desires for their teens, knowing that a happy life can take many shapes no matter how unique the path is. A lot of other stuff comes up too but this is a big one.

If I enroll in your school can you help me put together a one-off workshop for teens or parents? Or a program over time, like, say, a three-month program where teens and parents are both involved? Like, can I really pick your brain and use material you've tried out or already created?

Yes. All my clients know this: most anything I have created or done, I can share it all. It's pages and pages of curriculum and processes and handouts, so a lot to go through, but I'm happy to share. AND I also know that what you share with clients and their parents from *your* heart and soul is *way* more relevant than anything I've put together. And I love helping my clients/group attendees create their own material.

The school is bespoke; it can be used for you to create anything you want, and you will get the support to do it. There are a few topics we'll discuss deliberately along the way—setting fees, getting great at the enrollment process, where to get clients, etc.—but the majority of the time it's about meeting you in real time about your questions. It could be feeling stuck with a parent or teen, wanting to work on content development, or putting a program or workshop on the calendar and filling it. Whatever matters to you matters to me.

What's been the hardest things about working with teens?

Learning to trust my instincts! As in, saying no and referring people on faster, sticking to my fees earlier on in my practice instead of getting into negotiation land *every* time, and just going for it instead of trying to map it all out. We all have amazing instincts that we can trust. It all would've been easier had I been tuning into that from the get-go. Getting a lot of support along the way certainly helped as well. Once I was clear I was going to make a living doing this I invested heavily in working with people who would help me learn to trust myself (and get out of my own way!).

What does full-time coaching mean to you, and what does it take to make six figures?

I always joke that I'm a full-time coach but my kids think I'm a stay-at-home mom. I work on average twenty to twenty-five hours a week. I typically am running one or two three- to five-month-long groups a year and have fourteen to sixteen one-on-one clients at a time, not including parents. I try to have fewer, but that's just the truth. All my hours are spent with my clients, e-mailing my clients, or talking to potential clients. About 5 percent of my time is spent doing anything other than that. I don't market, aside from the occasional post on Facebook or email to my newly created and very small mailing list. Everything I do is through private connections and conversations.

In terms of what it takes to make a six-figure living, there is a practical aspect and an energetic aspect. Right now, my fees range from $7,500 to $35,000, depending on what I offer a client, and whether it's a teen, an adult or a coach/business owner. My group programs have a slightly lower fee in general than my one-on-one work.

I feel like I worked way harder when I was making $35,000 per year and charging $35 to $125 an hour. And on top of that there was the emotional stress of not making a solid living.

What I focus on now is higher quality—less volume. It was a very small tweak I made; or, I should say, several small tweaks the year I went from $35,000 to $135,000. And I did do that in just one year. The difference was that when I started doing programs instead of one-offs, I had fees that actually sustained me in an abundant way. I stopped doing anything that wasn't in direct correlation to serving real people in the moment. I stopped working on my website, writing blogs, writing books, writing content . . . I stopped doing anything that wasn't directly related to creating and serving clients. It's not that the other stuff wasn't important, but for me I needed to get very clear on what the activities *actually are* that create money and clients—and those activities are having conversations with real people and doing my best to help them. And because those conversations are so meaningful and so much fun, it was not painful to make this shift; it was very empowering and immediately more satisfying.

Once I started making way more than I needed, then I started putting other things back into my calendar, like writing and creative projects. But as a mom (not that that distinction matters although it does feel relevant when it comes to breast-feeding!) and the sole breadwinner, deliberate, intentional action has been very important to my happiness.

I do want my kids to think that I am essentially a stay-at-home mom.

I love my husband dearly and want to spend so much time with him, and I do love my work with all my heart.

But finding the balance has not meant sacrificing financial stability. In fact, just the opposite.

The time I spend away from my family needs to be time well-invested and well-compensated, and it is. And again, I feel like I work way, way less than I did when I was seeing thirty clients a week with no commitment.

Now with having my eight to ten clients a week along with two or three new client conversations, my life is very simplified. In fact, when I came back from my maternity leave in September, 2020, because I was exclusively breast-feeding my baby, I was only able to do one to three client sessions a day, three or four days a week and had at that time, my very best financial quarter of my career. And I do work. I do care. I do pour myself into my clients and want to give them everything I can that will be helpful. So I'm not saying I don't work hard. But the work has gotten deeper, and for me much more fun!

In the event that you're coaching a teen and you've bonded and the teen really loves it, what happens if the family can't afford to renew? Or maybe there have been two really great, non-paid experiences, and the family just can't afford to continue in a paid relationship? That can feel a little different than an adult 1:1 client because, I mean . . . it's a kid! How do you handle that?

I've recently had this experience. I can understand and empathize with the money situation. However, that's still just a "money story," right? At the end of the day, I still need to protect the integrity of my fee, my business, and the coaching profession, while understanding that the highest form of service is a paid coaching relationship.

Yes, this can be tricky. As I've mentioned, I don't have that first session with a teen if my fees are nowhere in reach for the parents. But if I've gone through a whole program and it comes time to renew and everybody wants to but the fees are an issue, I will ask about that a bit more. I'll get in there with the parents and find out if it's truly a cash-flow issue and if there's some way to make it more workable, as in breaking up the payments, spreading them out a bit, or even asking something like, "You know what my fee is; how close can you get to it?" There's a time and a place for things like this, for flexibility and making it work, especially if you have space in your practice. And then there are times when you simply can't afford to. You need to make a living, and you need to have those spots in your practice filled with people who are paying you. What I will say is that with every teen that I've ever worked with, they know that they can reach out to me if they need me.

And they do, well beyond our coaching agreements, but never in a way that feels invasive or overwhelming. I am there for them. I have children all over the world! It's a very sweet relationship, and they are the ones whom I invite to anything I'm doing that is complimentary, or to a group for a lesser fee. Occasionally they will circle back to me and dive in at my full fee, and other times it just becomes a very sweet relationship. I wouldn't get too hung up on worrying about this. With all the coaches I know who work with teens, this kind of thing tends to work itself out if you can remain open-hearted and present in the moment to see what makes sense in each case.

My biggest message here is to not connect with a teen prior to talking through fees with their parents. And again, in reality, this does not typically come up. I see that most parents who invest in one program, are up for and able to continue investing if it's serving their teen.

Questions to ask during sessions with teens

This is by no means a comprehensive or rigid list of questions you SHOULD ask teens during your sessions. I've just found that it can be handy to have questions like these at the ready, because they can invite teens (and clients of all ages) to open themselves to their wisdom and what they're feeling. There is obviously overlap here, but that's because these questions are always pointing teens inwards to explore what they really want.

What advice would you give your best friend?

If fear wasn't a factor what would you do?

If you knew that the outcome had nothing to do with how respected and loved you are, what would you do and how would you go about doing it?

If you really knew that you could choose anything and you'd still be loved, what would you choose?

If you knew that eventually your parents would support you, what you let yourself do/give yourself permission to do?

If you knew your success was guaranteed what would you chose?

What does your gut tell you?

If you were running this as an experiment without consequences, what would you try?

If you were to let yourself play around with this and have fun, what would you decide?

What's your soul trying to teach or show you through this situation? (This can be a good one for spiritually minded teens going through intense challenges; it's a USM-inspired question.)

If you drop out of you what you know and into that place that doesn't know, what occurs to you?

If you knew you wouldn't lose any friends, what would you decide to do?

If you didn't care what your friends thought, what would your heart tell you to do?

If you were on vacation, how would you interact with this person you have a crush on?

What questions do you want me to ask you? (Especially good with really quiet kids.)

What do you wish we were talking about now?

What are you afraid of telling me?

What are you nervous about telling me?

Reflection form

Following is a sample of a Mid-Program Reflection form. I make up new questions each time based on what feels appropriate but here is a sample of one I used a year or so ago. The Post-Program reflection is essentially the same.

Mid Program Reflection

1. Has the coaching relationship been supportive to you, and if so, how or why?

2. How do you feel in the sessions?

. . . and after the sessions?

3. As a direct result from coaching, has your relationship with yourself changed or improved—and if so, in what ways?

4. Has your relationship with others changed or improved—and if so, in what ways?

5. What have you enjoyed the most about coaching?

6. What do you feel would increase the value of the work—either from a shift or change on your end or on my end . . . or both?

7. Are you experiencing the changes in your life that you want to with

our coaching work?

8. What are you learning about Thought?

9. What are you learning about your inner guidance or your wisdom?

10. For yourself personally, what areas do you want to focus on going forward, and what outcomes would you like to experience?

Coaching outline / agreement

Below is an example of a coaching outline or as some coaches call it, a coaching agreement. The one below is from several years ago. I adjust the details to fit with whatever we decide to do together.

Six-Month Coaching Outline with Aila Coats

TEEN PORTION

This agreement between Aila Coats and X outlines our coaching work together. (Launch date: _____)

Structure

- We will meet every other week for 6 months. (14 sessions)
- Occasionally we will adjust our schedule to honor and support you. However we will do no less than 14 sessions.
- Our sessions will last approximately 45-60 minutes.
- Ongoing email and check-in session support will be available to you throughout the 6 months.

Client (x) Agrees to:

- Commit to yourself. Make your coaching goals a significant part of your life and follow through on agreed action steps. Enlist the help of friends and family whenever possible.

- Take care of yourself throughout our work together physically, mentally, emotionally and spiritually/creatively.
- Be truthful and forthcoming so I may assist you. Use me as a sounding board for any challenges that arise.
- Be on time for our sessions. Support yourself in keeping your word with yourself.
- Inform me at least 48 hours in advance if you need to reschedule. For any cancellations within 48 hours it will count as a missed session.
- Fill out the client reflection form mid-way and near the end of our contract, and share with me and your parents.
- Come prepared to each session—fully fed and in a space where you will not be interrupted.
- Reach out to me for support between sessions via email or phone if you feel it would be helpful. I AM HERE FOR YOU and COMMITTED TO YOUR SUCCESS AND HAPPINESS.

I Agree to:

- My role will be to serve as a partner and supporter of your success in all aspects of your life.
- My communication will be honest and straightforward, including asking questions and suggesting action steps.
- I will notify you 48 hours in advance if an unavoidable scheduling conflict arises and I need to reschedule.

Client and Coach Agree to:

- Create clear agreements about how we work together.
- Each session we will set the date for the next session. Come to the session prepared to do this.
- Regularly acknowledge, prize and appreciate the progress you make towards your goals and intentions.

PARENT PORTION

Six-Month Coaching Outline with Aila Coats

This agreement between Aila Coats and X, is intended to support the coaching work between myself and X.

I Agree to:

- Provide you a coaching reflection that your teen will fill out midway through our work together and near the completion of our contract.
- Honor, respect and empower your teen.

Parents Agree to:

- Attend 2 coaching sessions with me regarding X and the work she and I are doing in her coaching. It will be a time to ask questions and get support on anything going on in your world. (We will set this up around months 3 and 6).
- Communicate concerns regarding anything having to do with coaching to me. I AM HERE FOR YOU TOO!

- Remember that x is going through a transformational process that may bring about new behaviors and ways of being with herself and others.
- Acknowledge and appreciate yourself, for the opportunity you are creating for X to receive powerful and meaningful support.

Fee

The fee for 6 months of coaching is $7,500.

Recommended media

I wanted to include some videos I often share with my teen and parent clients and some of my favorite books to send.

Sometimes I will watch the video with them or I will send the book and we will read a section together. With my older teens I will occasionally send it and let them look at it when they are ready.

Videos

Dove Real Beauty Sketches: https://www.youtube.com/watch?v=dRKn1b8UCnM

Dove Choose Beautiful Campaign Reveals Beauty vs. Average Perceptions: https://www.youtube.com/watch?v=UjJALzZ24H0

Why Aren't We Awesomer? | Michael Neill | TEDxBend: https://www.youtube.com/watch?v=xr6VawX2nr4

5 Mental Debugs for Success & Global Prosperity by Inventor & Google Genius, Tom Chi: https://www.youtube.com/watch?v=25fUDjMtkuI

Videos from Innate Evolution:

The Missing Link Animation   https://youtu.be/LZhju2o7pm0
The Thought Filter Animation: https://youtu.be/UmVskJhBEXA

The Psychological Immune System Animation
https://youtu.be/indy0EIPm18
The Weather of our Minds Animation https://youtu.be/La-RqURQZjE

Websites

Insight Seminars: https://www.insightseminars.org
University of Santa Monica: https://www.universityofsantamonica.edu

Books

The Missing Link by Sydney Banks
The Go Giver by Bob Burg and John David Mann
Reinventing Yourself by Steve Chandler
The Story of You by Steve Chandler
The Alchemist by Paulo Coelho
Big Book of Unschooling by Sandra Dodd
The Prophet by Kahlil Gibran
Big Magic by Elizabeth Gilbert
How Children Learn by John Holt
How Children Fail by John Holt
The Relationship Handbook by George and Linda Pransky
Parenting From the Heart by Jack Pransky
Playing Big by Tara Mohr
The Surrender Experiment by Michael Alan Singer
Outrageous Openness by Tosha Silver
My Stroke of Insight by Jill Bolte Taylor

Appreciations

I want to thank Dhiraj. For every single thing. You are a dream to share a life with and an example to me every day of what it looks like to have a beginner's mind, to live with childlike enthusiasm, with joy, with playfulness, dedication to our family and endless love and creativity. The way you care for our family and our children is otherworldly. I love you.

Thank you, Steve Chandler, for being a source of incredible support and inspiration. Your humor, light-heartedness and belief in the human spirit has impacted me, my family and my work in such a huge way. My life is forever better for having been coached and mentored by you.

Thank you, Chris Nelson, for making my jumbled thoughts a readable book. And more than that, thank you for your depth of consciousness, your humor, wit and expansive insights and perspective on all things. You made this book a reality by being who you are and sharing the incredible gifts you have.

Thank you, Caity, for helping me move through the early stages of this book and thank you, Chase, for helping me move through the final stages. You are both magnificent human beings and I am honored and grateful to call you friends.

Thank you, Josephine for the beautiful cover design that so perfectly reflects who I am and what this book is all about. You are an amazing young woman and it's such a joy watching you blossom and share your incredible gifts with the world.

Thank you, Drs. Ron and Mary Hulnick, George and Linda Pransky, Michelle Bauman, Carolyn Freyer-Jones, Dicken Bettinger, Barb Patterson, Rohini Ross and Aaron Turner for sharing your insights and love with me, and in doing so, supporting me in accessing my own wisdom in even deeper ways.

Thank you, Dr. Wayne Dyer, Eckart Tolle, Carolyn Myss, Sonia Choquette and Sydney Banks for bringing amazing insight, humor and love to my life through your work. I have lived an inspired life, lit up from the inside out, listening, often daily, to your incredible words of wisdom for the last twenty-five years.

Thank you, Mike Kelly for the enriching conversations we had throughout my teenage life. Downieville Jr/Sr School was lucky to have you as a custodian. I was lucky to have you as a mentor and friend. You were a breath of fresh air for me during some very difficult, tumultuous years. Your support and encouragement around my athletic dreams and my spiritual interest made a lasting difference in my world.

And finally, a special thank you to Bernadett, for being a way-shower in my life, demonstrating to me what it truly looks like to live from your heart and to listen deeply to the inspiration and wisdom that flow from there.

About the author

It's been a true joy to support teens and their parents through my work as a professional coach. I remember very well, sitting in my 10th grade Algebra II class, daydreaming and writing in my journal, which had the words, Dream Big, boldly written on the front, that I wanted to spend my time on the earth helping teens have a more supportive, expansive and joyful experience of life. I often had my most important and meaningful thoughts at the most inappropriate times. It was this insight, this inner knowing, that propelled me on to receiving a B.A. in Human Behavior with a minor in Early Childhood Development, an M.A. in Spiritual Psychology with an emphasis in Consciousness, Health and Healing, and a dozen other certificates from programs all geared at helping me understand the human mind and soul.

I currently live with my husband, two sons, a baby girl on the way, and a dog named Oliver in the mountains in Northern California. You can find my work at www.ailacoats.com and several videos on my YouTube channel by searching for Aila Coats, M.A. You can also take a look at an online program I created for coaches who would like to work with teens, at https://coaching-teens-well.teachable.com/ You can also reach me directly by emailing: ailahale@yahoo.com

Also available

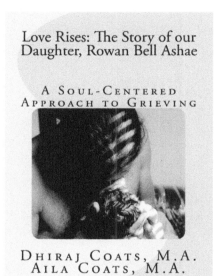

Love Rises: The Story of our
Daughter, Rowan Bell Ashae

A SOUL-CENTERED
APPROACH TO GRIEVING

DHIRAJ COATS, M.A.
AILA COATS, M.A.

*Love Rises: The Story of our
Daughter, Rowan Bell Ashae*

This is the story of our journey,
birthing our beautiful daughter at
home, a few hours after she had
passed away in the womb. We
share our experience in an intimate
conversation between the two of us
and tips for what has made the
experience one of upliftment,
healing and inspiration rather than
a journey of simply loss,
desperation and despair.

Available at Amazon.com

*An Online, Self-Paced Program for Coaches
who want to work with Teens*

- Have you always dreamed of working with teens but don't think you can create a thriving coaching practice around that goal?

- Does working with teens and dealing with their parents seem complicated?

- Do you already serve teens but would like to explore ways to have more impact and expand your practice?

The Coaching Teens Well online program is designed to support you in creating a coaching practice serving teens, their families—and yourself. It shares not just the nuts and bolts of a successful coaching business but also explores a mindset and state of consciousness that can transform your practice and your life.

If you have questions like these . . .

- How do I actually make a living serving teens and young adults when they are the poorest demographic in the world!?
- What does the intake process look like and how much are parents involved?
- What do I actually DO with a teen once we're working together? Do I give advice? (I'll share some of the actual processes and exercises I use at different times).
- What do I charge and what do my programs look like?
- Where do I get clients?
- What do I do in the workshops I facilitate and how do I fill them?

. . . this program will answer them in ways that can help you support teens—and make a living doing it. Learn more here:

https://www.ailacoats.com/coaching-teens-well-copy

"Aila Coats is one of those rare coaches who teaches this business of coaching with power and compassion. If you want a program that gets you real-world results, jump on hers ASAP!"

~ Steve Chandler, Author of Time Warrior

Made in the USA
Monee, IL
03 April 2023